DEAR MERCI

I HOPE YOU WILL LIKE
THIS BOOK. I AM
GETTING A LOT OUT OF
IT.
THANKS FOR OUR TIME.

TOR

*Translated from the Dutch by Arnold J. Pomerans*

*Foreword by Eva Hoffman*

*Introduction and notes by Jan G. Gaarlandt*

# Etty Hillesum

## An Interrupted Life

THE DIARIES, 1941–1943

*and*

## Letters from Westerbork

A HOLT PAPERBACK

HENRY HOLT AND COMPANY　　　NEW YORK

Holt Paperbacks
Henry Holt and Company, LLC
*Publishers since 1866*
175 Fifth Avenue
New York, New York 10010
www.henryholt.com

Library of Congress Cataloging-in-Publication Data
Hillesum , Etty, 1914–1943.
[Verstoorde leven. English]
An interrupted life: the diaries, 1941–1943; and , Letters from Westerbork / Etty Hillesum;
translated from the Dutch by Arnold J. Pomerans; foreword by Eva Hoffman; introduction
and notes by Jan G. Gaarlandt.
p.   cm.
Previously published (1st work): 1st American ed. New York: Pantheon Books, 1984.
Previously published (2nd work): 1st English language ed. New York: Pantheon Books, 1986
ISBN-13: 978-0-8050-5087-5
ISBN-10: 0-8050-5087-6
1. Hillesum, Etty, 1914–1943. 2. Holocaust, Jewish (1939–1945)—Netherlands—Personal
narratives. 3. Jews—Netherlands—Biography. 4. Netherlands—Ethnic relations.
I. Gaarlandt, J. G. II. Hillesum, Etty, 1914–1943. Denkende hart van de barak. English.
III. Title. IV. Title: Letters from Westerbork.
DS135.N6H54813   1996                                             96-2960
940.53'18'09492—dc20
CIP

First Holt Paperbacks edition 1996

DESIGNED BY KATE NICHOLS

Printed in the United States of America
30  29  28  27  26  25  24  23

# Contents

# Foreword

When we pick up Etty Hillesum's diaries and letters today, we know from the outset what will come at their tragic end. And yet, to start reading them is to be jolted into fresh surprise. All the writings she left behind were composed in the shadow of the Holocaust, but they resist being read primarily in its dark light. Rather, their abiding interest lies in the light-filled mind that pervades them and in the astonishing internal journey they chart. The trajectory of that journey echoes classical accounts of spiritual transformation; but Etty's pilgrimage grew out of the intimate experience of an intellectual young woman—it was idiosyncratic, individual, and recognizably modern.

Aside from a few fundamental facts about her family—she came from an assimilated Jewish background—we know little about her early history, her childhood temperament, or the formative episodes of her youth. She comes to us unmediated. But an encounter with her is instantly and compellingly direct. Etty wanted, aspired to be a writer, and she has a writer's knack for conveying herself onto the page with fluent immediacy, for drawing us right into her personal world. From the first entries she comes across as a wonderfully vivid personality: charming, unaffected, with funds of warmth and an eager appetite for pleasure. She enjoyed the quotidian details of her life and describes them with relish: the motley household in which she lived, the Russian lessons she gave, the walks she took through her beloved Amsterdam. On one level, then, a young woman of her time: emancipated, educated, urbane, with professional ambitions and a penchant for bohemian lifestyles. She had a variety of lovers, intimates, and a circle of interesting friends. She was a percipient observer, aware of the issues and movements of her time: socialism, fascism, anti-Semitism. Even her passing remarks about such things show penetrating and distilled insight.

But capable though she was of extroversion and engagement, her most intense need, and gift, was for the inner life. Her essential existence, she often reminded herself, took place in the privacy of self-reflection, at a desk covered with pinecones, vases of flowers, and books.

The private Etty Hillesum who revealed herself in her diary was impassioned, erotically volatile, restless, and often tormented. In the early entries, she repeatedly records swings from elation to brooding melancholy, from embracing excitement to depressed withdrawal, from expansive flights of fantasy to besetting self-doubt. She could easily be seen as one of the scores of over-sensitive, slightly neurasthenic young women from a cultivated and coddling milieu.

Such categories are not inappropriate; Etty herself thought in psychological terms. But they are also insufficient, for Etty had the kind of genius for introspection that converts symptoms into significance and joins self-examination to philosophical investigation. The diary is a continuous, animated dialogue with herself, a constant drive toward her own truth. She knew how to follow subtle movements of her feelings and how to question and criticize herself. Even in states of extreme distress, she retained an unerring sense of emotional proportion, a kind of perfect inward pitch. She recognized her own tendencies to false exaltation and self-denigration, her attraction to grandiose ideas, and her possessive greed; she upbraided herself for them, and countered them with insistence on moderation, and on the precise, modest word. "My protracted headaches: so much masochism; my abundant compassion: so much self-gratification," she wrote severely. Etty knew she had to master her own excesses and conflicts, and to "give some form to the chaos" inside her.

Her chosen guide in this endeavor was Julius Spier, a Jungian psychoanalyst cum palm reader and general guru. What can we make of the curious, ambiguous relationship between them? By today's standards, aspects of it seem questionable. As part of his therapeutic method, Spier engaged in eroticized tousles with his patients, which were not, apparently, supposed to lead to sexual intercourse. Etty's descriptions of his tantalizing touches and kisses, of the casual liberties he took with admiring female patients, strike us as highly incorrect, to say the least. Yet, in putting her trust in this strange mentor, Etty was acting in tune with her time. The interwar decades were a period of eclectic psychoanalytic experiments, of eccentric adventures in self-exploration. As is so often true with charismatic figures, Spier's virtues may have been discernible only through personal contact. Etty was sometimes perplexed by him; but even after their relationsip was consummated, she never doubted his integrity or his capacity to heal. She thought of him as gentle, good, spiritually complex; and she threw herself into her "work" with him unreservedly.

Perhaps Etty's relationship with Spier belonged less in the category of psychotherapy than in a much older tradition of active philosophical teaching. Because she believed in him, Spier became her "task," the person against whom she tested and questioned herself, the occasion of her struggle and growth. Her most arduous battle was with the problem of sexuality in its modern, feminine variant. Etty was both seduced and riven by her desires, torn between romantic yearnings for submergence and the need for independence. Through her real and metaphorical wrestlings with Spier, she trained herself to check her impulses and restrain the impetuousness of her needs. She discovered that she could exist on her own without losing herself in another, and feel affection without making proprietorial claims. In other words, she learned the kind of love that is closer to selfless agape than to urgent eros and that combines deep sympathy with calm detachment.

The process of change is always mysterious, but in the middle stages of Etty's diary, it becomes almost palpable. Her writing becomes suffused with simpler, more serious tones. As both her tenderness and detachment deepened, she reported a new serenity, a sense of identity that remained steadily itself. Increasingly, her writing points toward that border where attentiveness to subjectivity meets contemplation, where emotional intuition converges with moral thought.

In all of this, Etty had the courage to follow the thread of her own experience—and that thread took her further still, in more unexpected and radical directions. Etty never lost her mercurial responsiveness, even as she began to describe states we are accustomed to identify as religious: gratitude for all that was given to her, a profound self-acceptance and acceptance of others, and a conviction, not of any specific set of meanings, but of meaningfulness itself—of the inward beauty and rightness of life. By winding her way through her own psyche to the point of self-reconciliation, she had come to a place where she could feel the hidden harmony of the world.

Of course Etty was making her later journal entries as the world was being torn apart by war, as the atmosphere for Dutch Jews turned daily more dangerous, as her friends were being deported and killed. Was it escapist of her to keep looking inward at such a time? She asked the question herself and answered in the negative. "I feel like a small battlefield, in which the problems . . . of our time are being fought out," she wrote early in the diary, and she continued to be convinced that it was her vocation and everyone's duty to look first unto themselves and solve the war within. Certainly, her hard-won strength met the severest of tests. She faced the inexorable progress toward destruction without evasion. She confronted dangers to herself and her family with an almost stoical fearlessness, a balance that was no longer undermined by external assaults.

In the last stages of her amazing and moving journey, Etty seemed to attain that peace which passeth understanding. Even in her powerful and unflinching letters, written from the hellish transit camp of Westerbork, Etty talks about the sustenance she draws from reading and musing, and about savoring moments of beauty and quiet: the glorious blue sky, the field of purple lupins, the moonlight made of silver and eternity. She was perfectly capable of writing about Westerbork in presciently astute terms. She was lucid about the politics of the Jewish Council for which she worked, about the situation of the Dutch Jews, and about the peculiarly fascinating society of the transit camp. But what she found within herself seemed to her more capacious and important. At one point, she says she wants to write like Dostoyevsky; and there is indeed in her something of the Russian feeling—the sense of a majestic stream of life, which includes within itself pain and suffering as well as happiness and joy, and which has to be accepted in all its encompassing depths. Etty came to see herself and her fellow human beings as part of that stream, and their human condition—their ability to love and hate, to maintain or give up their dignity—as always and everywhere the same. She remained vitally engaged with the people around her, but she had "let go" of any grasping attachments. Her ideas and her compassion had become so completely incarnated in herself that she needed almost nothing else for a sense of fulfillment.

Finally, however, the violence and brutality she saw all around her overwhelmed even her capacity to understand. In her last letters, she spoke of what was happening at Westerbork as incomprehensible, mad, warped in a grotesque way. Perhaps herein lies a clue to her decision not to save herself. For the reader who comes to love Etty through her writing, as for the friends who tried to rescue her, it is not easy to come to terms with that often reaffirmed choice. But perhaps it was a consistent result of her development. She had become exquisitely attuned to the currents of moral beauty, and she could not bear the ugliness that was flooding the world. She did not suppose that she was entirely immune from that ugliness. Because she had looked at herself so closely, she refused to engage in projection or collective hatred—to declare that all evil existed within the enemy, and all goodness inside "us." For a heroically long time, she resisted the temptation to hate all Germans because of what many Germans were doing. But, finally, it became appropriate to hate. She found the guards at Westerbork bestial. She also felt that the position into which she and her fellow Jews were forced was horribly, hopelessly "twisted." Her descriptions of Westerbork inmates helping to load families, old people, and infants onto the doomed transport trains are ruthlessly candid and unbearably wrenching. She knew all too well that her survival would mean someone else's death, and the whole calculation seemed to her bitterly wrong. The meaning of staying alive had become utterly perverted, and perhaps the only way for her to save meaning was by accepting death.

Etty Hillesum lived at a time when the macrocosm of historical events almost completely crushed the microcosm of individual lives. It was her enormous act of resistance to reverse this order of importance, to assert that the microcosm of the soul can encompass the external world and, in addition, hold infinite space. By starting always with the origin of herself, she had forged an original and richly humane vision. Ultimately, no act of personal resistance or perception could withstand the impersonal forces unleashed in the Holocaust. But by knowing and feeling so deeply and fully, an unknown young woman became one of the most exceptional and truest witnesses of the devastation through which she lived and of the suffering humankind whose fate she chose to join.

—Eva Hoffman

# Introduction

Eight exercise books closely written in a small, hard-to-decipher hand—ever since I first read them, I have been preoccupied by what they reveal: the life of Etty Hillesum. These exercise books set out the story of a twenty-seven-year-old woman from Amsterdam. They cover the years 1941 and 1942, years of war and oppression for Holland, but for Etty a time of personal growth and, paradoxically enough, of personal liberation. Those were the very years when the scenario of extermination was being played out all over Europe. Etty Hillesum was Jewish and she wrote a counterscenario.

Between her entry for Thursday, 10 November 1941—"Mortal fear in every fiber. Complete collapse. Lack of self-confidence. Aversion. Panic"—and that for Friday, 3 July 1942—"Very well then, this new certainty that what they are after is our total destruction, I accept it. I know it now and I shall not burden others with my fears. I shall not be bitter if others fail to grasp what is happening to us Jews. I work and continue to live with the same conviction and I find life meaningful, yes, meaningful"—between these two entries, Etty's whole existence is bracketed. Her relationships with lovers and friends, family and colleagues, her moods and feelings, her thoughts about Judaism, women, passion, the growing evidence of disruption in the world around her—she examined everything and recorded it all frankly, clearly, and intensely. Lest she lose her grip on a "tempestuous, havoc-ridden world," she searched for the sources of her existence, finally discovering an attitude to life that is best described as radical altruism. The last words in her diary are: "We should be willing to act as a balm for all wounds."

The diary begins on Sunday, 9 March 1941. In late January or early February of that year, Etty had met a man who was to become the focus of her thoughts and emotions. That man was Julius Spier, the founder of "psychochirology," the study and classification of palm prints. Spier—whom Etty refers to as S.— was a Jewish emigrant from Berlin, born in Frankfurt on 25 April 1887. He had once been a bank manager, and over the years he had discovered a talent for reading hands and palms. He also founded a publishing house, took singing lessons, and then moved to Zürich for analysis training under Carl Gustav Jung. It was Jung who persuaded him to turn his psychochirology practice into a full-time profession.

Wherever Spier went, he attracted disciples. In 1939 he joined his sister in the Netherlands. His children, Ruth and Wolfgang, stayed on in Germany with his non-Jewish wife, from whom he had been divorced in 1935. A highly unusual man, Spier has been called a "magical personality" by many of his admirers, especially women. And indeed he seems to have had a most unusual gift for reading people's lives from their palms, and for interpreting the results with rare psychological insight.

For Etty, at least, he became a catalyst, setting her on a search for the essential, the truly human, in dramatic opposition to the inhumanity around her.

In the process, Etty developed a religious sensibility that gives her writings a profound spiritual dimension. The word "God" occurs in even her earliest entries, although there she uses it—as we often do in daily speech—almost unconsciously. Gradually, however, she moves toward an ever more intense dialogue with the divine. Etty's entries completely change style whenever she addresses God, and she addresses Him regularly, without the least embarrassment. Her religiosity is totally unconventional. In Holland today, Christians and Jews are claiming Etty as typically Christian or typically Jewish—an unprofitable discussion, because Etty chooses her own way. She has her own religious rhythm, not inspired by church or synagogue, or by dogmas, theology, liturgy, or tradition; all these were completely alien to her. She addresses God as she does herself. "When I pray," she writes, "I hold a silly, naive, or deadly serious dialogue *with what is deepest inside me, which for the sake of convenience I call God.*" And later: "I repose in myself. And that part of myself, that deepest and richest part in which I repose, is what I call 'God.' "

The way she is sometimes absorbed in her conversation with God seems to be pure mysticism. Was she a mystic? Perhaps, but she insisted that "mysticism must rest on crystal-clear honesty, and can only come after things have been stripped down to their naked reality." Her mysticism led her not into solitary contemplation but squarely back into the world of action. Her vision had nothing to do with escape or self-deception, and everything to do with a hard-won, steady, and whole perception of reality. Her God, in a sense, resided in her own capacity to see the truth, to bear it and find consolation in it.

We know little about Etty's life before the war. Esther—her official first name—was born on 15 January 1914 in Middelburg, where her father, Dr. Louis Hillesum, taught classical languages. After moves to Tiel and Winschoten, he and his family settled down in 1924 in Deventer, a medium-size city in the east of Holland, beautifully situated by the IJssel River. There he became assistant headmaster and four years later headmaster of the town gymnasium.

Etty's father was an excellent and disciplined scholar—books and intellectual pursuits filled his life. Etty's mother, Rebecca Bernstein, was Russian by birth and had fled to the Netherlands after yet another pogrom. She was passionate, chaotic, and in almost everything quite the opposite of her husband. That led to a tempestuous marriage in the stately house at 9 Geert Grootestraat. It is difficult to say how much that affected the three children.

What is certain is that Etty and her brothers, Mischa and Jaap, were all intelligent and gifted. Although Etty's own direction in those days in Deventer was not yet fixed, she was witty, vivid, eager to read books and to study philosophy, and in these ways she was far ahead of her school friends. Mischa was a brilliant musician who played Beethoven in public at the age of six. He was considered by many to be one of the most promising pianists in Europe. His talent as a musician dominated the daily course of the household. And her other brother, Jaap, discovered several new vitamins when he was seventeen, for which he won admission to the academic laboratories, an unusual honor for a medical student. He later became a doctor.

Etty left her father's school in 1932, went on to take her first degree in law at the University of Amsterdam, then enrolled in the Faculty of Slavonic Languages. By the time she turned to the study of psychology, the Second World War had broken out and her life had begun to assume the character we discern in these diaries.

Etty's life in Amsterdam is not easy to reconstruct. In her diaries she talks most of the time about two specific groups of people: one, the so-called Spier group; the other, the "family" of five with whom she lived.

Just before the war Etty had moved to a large house at 6 Gabriël Metsustraat, in South Amsterdam. Her room on the third floor overlooked the Museumplein, the main square in

Amsterdam, with the Concert-hall at one end, the Rijksmuseum at the other, and a skating rink in the middle.

The owner of the house, Han Wegerif, a widower of sixty-two, had asked Etty to live there as a sort of housekeeper. Besides Han (Etty usually refers to him as Father Han or Papa Han, although she soon developed an intimate relationship with him) and his twenty-one-year-old son Hans, who was studying economics, there was a German cook called Käthe, a reasonable "social-democrat" called Bernard, and Maria Tuinzing, a nurse who became one of Etty's best friends. These last two rented their rooms.

The other main circle that Etty describes is the group around Julius Spier, the psychochirologist. She had met him at a music evening at the home of Mien Kuyper, where her brother and another pianist, Evaristos Glassner, played and where Spier used to sing. Adri Holm, Henny ("Tide") Tideman, Dicky de Jonge, Liesl Levie, and Etty frequently gathered at 27 Courbetstraat in South Amsterdam where Spier rented a room in the house of the Nethe family. (Etty was separated from him, she writes, "by three streets, a canal, and a little bridge.") Spier talked with them about palm prints and psychology, and he also became a therapist to each one. After three or four therapy sessions Etty became his assistant ("my Russian secretary") and, after a while, his lover and intellectual partner.

Etty spent another part of her life in the academic world of students and professors of Russian language, such as Professors Van Wijk and Becker, and through them she made connections with the leftist student resistance. Becker recommended her as a Russian teacher and sent her pupils, which enabled her to earn some money. In her diary Etty mentions a number of friends and acquaintances, using just their first names. It is not essential to an understanding of the diary for us to know anything more about them, and indeed, in most cases I have not been able to find more information about them. Wherever I have thought it important I have added a note.

Etty was twenty-seven years old when she began her diary. At her desk in the small room on Gabriël Metsustraat Etty produced one of the most remarkable texts of our time—a testimony of faith and love written in the darkest hours of modern history. At the time she started writing Holland was increasingly under the sway of Germany's reign of terror. After Holland's capitulation in May 1940 the Germans began to isolate the Dutch Jews. When in February 1941 the first anti-pogrom strike in European history broke out in Amsterdam, the Nazis intensified their pressure on the Jews and on any form of Dutch resistance. Jews were thrown out of their jobs, forbidden to buy in stores frequented by non-Jews, and otherwise maltreated; ghettoes were created and "work camps" set up. In April 1942, the Germans launched their first major roundups of the Jews, required them to wear the yellow star, and, after moving all the Jews they could find to Amsterdam, declared the provinces *"judenrein."*

Through the influence of friends, Etty was given a job as a typist in one of the departments of the Jewish Council. As in other occupied countries, the Council was formed at the instigation of the Germans to mediate between the Nazis and the mass of Jews. The Nazis gave orders to the Council and then let it decide how to implement them. The Council was under the illusion that by negotiation it could save the Jews from the worst. Its declared purpose was to decide who was fit to be sent away for "labor service" and who was indispensable at home; its real purpose was to calm the fears of the panic-stricken Jews. In this way the Council became a subtle weapon in the hands of the Nazis.

A discussion of the role of the Jewish Council falls outside the scope of this introduction, nor is this the place to pass judgment on it. What is relevant is that Etty began work on 15 July 1942, at about the same time a girl named Anne Frank, hidden in a house a few miles away, began writing her diary. In the same month the first big street roundup took place in Amsterdam. The Nazis wanted to concentrate all the Jews in Westerbork, a transit camp (*Durchgangslager*) in the east of the Netherlands, not far from the German border. Though not itself an extermination camp, Westerbork would be the last stop before Auschwitz for more than 100,000 Dutch Jews. Etty volunteered to accompany the Jews arrested in the roundups to Westerbork, where she worked in the camp hospital. Thanks to a special permit from the Jewish Council she was able to travel to Amsterdam a dozen times. She brought letters and messages from Westerbork to Amsterdam and even to resistance groups, and picked up medicines to bring back. Etty's health was often very poor and in September 1942 she stayed in Amsterdam for almost three months. Finally, early in June 1943, she took leave of her close friends and departed Amsterdam for Westerbork, this time never to return.

Built at the end of 1939 by the Dutch government, Westerbork was originally intended to house some fifteen hundred German Jews who had fled to the Netherlands before the war. Etty arrived there just as the human landslide began, when room suddenly had to be found on the small site for thirty or forty thousand people, including the Jews of Amsterdam, who had been crowded into a ghetto during the previous months. Some reported voluntarily; the rest had been picked up in the streets or dragged out of their houses. From other prison and labor camps—for instance, the notorious camp in Vught and the ones in Amsterdam, Ommen, and Ellecom—Jews were packed off to Westerbork. (The exceptions were a small number of "cultural Jews"—intellectuals, artists, even bankers—who, at the intercession of a few high Dutch officials, could be assigned to a castle in the small town of Barneveld. Etty's brother Mischa was eligible for Barneveld, but he refused to go without his parents. Later all the Jews in this refuge were sent to Theresienstadt via Westerbork, and most survived.)

The camp was a community living in fear, doomed by the threat of the weekly transport train leaving for Poland. Every Monday a train pulled into the camp; every Tuesday the long line of freight cars pulled out again, packed with more than a thousand men, women, boys, girls, and infants. From 15 July 1942 until 3 September 1944, week in and week out, the trains left, ninety-three in all.

The aim of those dispatched to Westerbork, each clutching the "stamps" the Jewish Council had issued, was to remain there as long as possible. The stamps entitled them to stay a little longer in the camp—a week, two weeks, occasionally a few months. But in the long run, time ran out for all stampholders, including the members of the Jewish Council, most of whom were deported in June 1943.

As Etty wrote in one of her many letters during 1942 and 1943, mud and misery were the essence of Westerbork—as were sickness and overcrowding—a universe of noise and fear crammed into a patch of heath half a kilometer square. It was in this hell that she spent the last months of her life, continuing to keep her diary, to write her letters, and, with great devotion, to nurse the sick in the hospital barracks. And it was in this hell that she wrote again and again, "Despite everything, life is full of beauty and meaning."

Most of Etty's letters were addressed to the friends already familiar to readers of her diary: Han Wegerif, his son Hans, the housekeeper Käthe, Maria Tuinzing, and Tide. Then there were Klaas Smelik, his daughter Johanna ("Jopie") Smelik, Milli Ortmann, and Christine van Nooten, a colleague of Etty's father.

Milli Ortmann and Christine van Nooten kept sending food parcels to the Hillesums through the Red Cross, which did much to sustain them in Westerbork. Often the letters were simply addressed in the most general terms ("My dear people"), or not at all, meant to be passed around among the larger group of friends.

Etty's letters vividly describe the crowded wooden barracks, the muddy heath, the labyrinths of barbed wire, and the field of wildflowers at the edge of the camp. She captures the human atmosphere of Westerbork, from the hierarchy of camp leaders and guards to the daily struggle to stay alive, from the poignant reunions with friends and family to the wrenching departures on the weekly transport. As she put it in one of the last entries in her diary, she wanted to be the "thinking heart of the barracks." And she was. She fired the imagination of many camp inmates; survivors still speak of her "shining personality." Wherever she was, she attracted a community of human fellowship. So it is not surprising that her letters reveal the growth of a whole new circle of close Westerbork friends: Osias Kormann, who became her intimate companion, and to whom she wrote a number of letters from Amsterdam during her leave from Westerbork, Hedwig and Jupp Mahler, Jopie Vleeschhouwer, whom she called her "comrade-in-arms," Philip Mechanicus, author of *In Depôt,* a diary that became famous after the war, and, of course, Werner and Liesl Levie, old friends from Amsterdam. In time, they were joined by Etty's parents and her brother Mischa. Etty's older brother, Jaap, was allowed to remain in Amsterdam for a while to carry out his medical duties.

It was in this circle that Etty Hillesum displayed her courage and humanity to the fullest. In Westerbork her soul found its deepest expression: she placed herself unreservedly at the service of her people. During the time she was still permitted to travel, she spurned all attempts by her Amsterdam friends to take her to a safe house (on one occasion, by force). Later, when she was no longer allowed to leave the camp, she rejected all offers to help her escape. She was determined to share the fate of her fellow Jews, without bravado, but also without despair. "Poland" to her was synonymous with destruction; she did not delude herself on that score. She knew that she would not survive, although she tried to calm her friends by predicting her return. How death would come to her she did not know. No one in Westerbork had heard about the gas chambers, but many suspected that their fate was sealed.

On 7 September 1943, after a deportation order had been issued for Mischa, Etty, and her parents, Etty stepped onto the platform beside a waiting train bound for Poland. Jopie Vleeschhouwer described her departure in a letter to the friends in Amsterdam: "Talking gaily, smiling, a kind word for everyone she met on the way, full of sparkling humor, perhaps just a touch of sadness, but every inch the Etty you all know so well. . . . I saw Mother, Father H., and Mischa board car No. 1. Etty finished up in No. 12, having first stopped to look for a friend in car No. 14, who was pulled out again at the last minute. Then a shrill whistle and the 1,000 'transport cases' were moving out. Another flourish from Mischa, who waved through a crack in No. 1, a cheerful 'Bye' from Etty in No. 12, and they were gone."

The journey was to last three days. Before they finally left the Netherlands, Etty threw a postcard addressed to Christine van Nooten out of the train. It was found and sent by farmers: "We left the camp singing," it read. They reached Auschwitz on 10 September 1943. That very day, her mother and father were gassed.

On 30 November 1943, the Red Cross reported the death of Etty Hillesum. Her brother Mischa died on 31 March 1944. Jaap was sent to Bergen-Belsen at the beginning of 1944. He survived the camp but died on the way back to Holland.

Etty's diaries were finally published almost forty years after her death. Etty knew instinctively that she would not return from the camps and asked her friend Maria Tuinzing to give her diaries to Klaas Smelik and his daughter Johanna after the war. Klaas Smelik was the only writer she knew, and she hoped he could find a publisher. She wanted to leave some trace of her life behind and share her insights with future generations. But despite the Smelik family's best efforts, the diaries remained unpublished. After a number of years the Smeliks gave up the attempt, until 1980, when Klaas Smelik, Jr., asked me to look at the eight tattered notebooks. The very first sentences I read fascinated and shocked me, and they have remained with me ever since.

The letters came into my possession at the same time as the diaries. Most of them had circulated among Etty's friends during the war and had eventually ended up in Maria Tuinzing's hands. Two long letters from the camp—those of 18 December 1942 and 24 August 1943—had been clandestinely published at the end of 1943 in book form by the Dutch Resistance. As a result of the new and widespread interest in Etty's life, a number of new letters have come to light, and it is certainly possible that still more will be unearthed; during the last months of her life, Etty probably wrote over a hundred. But there will be no more diaries; Etty took her last notebook with her on the train to Auschwitz.

As of this writing, Etty Hillesum's diaries have been published in fourteen countries and translated into twelve languages. And now, the diaries and letters finally appear in one volume, which is appropriate, because they represent one integral narrative. Etty made no essential distinction between her journal and her correspondence. Her letters, in fact, are a kind of epistolary journal in which she shares with her friends her intimate thoughts, her passions, her insights. But having the two texts side by side does allow us to glimpse the fullest possible portrait of this extraordinary figure, whose very existence was, as Terrence Des Pres so movingly put it, "a marvelous gift."

Jan G. Gaarlandt
Haarlem, Holland
May 1996

# An Interrupted Life

THE DIARIES, 1941–1943

*Sunday, 9 March [1941].* Here goes, then. This is a painful and well-nigh insuperable step for me: yielding up so much that has been suppressed to a blank sheet of lined paper. The thoughts in my head are sometimes so clear and so sharp and my feelings so deep, but writing about them comes hard. The main difficulty, I think, is a sense of shame. So many inhibitions, so much fear of letting go, of allowing things to pour out of me, and yet that is what I must do if I am ever to give my life a reasonable and satisfactory purpose. It is like the final, liberating scream that always sticks bashfully in your throat when you make love. I am accomplished in bed, just about seasoned enough I should think to be counted among the better lovers, and love does indeed suit me to perfection, and yet it remains a mere trifle, set apart from what is truly essential, and deep inside me something is still locked away. The rest of me is like that, too. I am blessed enough intellectually to be able to fathom most subjects, to express myself clearly on most things; I seem to be a match for most of life's problems, and yet deep down something like a tightly wound ball of twine binds me relentlessly, and at times I am nothing more or less than a miserable, frightened creature, despite the clarity with which I can express myself.

Let me fix that moment earlier this morning, although it has nearly slipped from my grasp again. Through sheer brainwork I got the better of S. for an instant.[1] His penetrating, clear gaze, his full, sensual mouth; his bull-like, burly figure and his feather-light, easy movements. A fifty-four-year-old in whom the struggle between the spirit and the flesh is still in full cry. And it seemed as if I were being crushed under the weight of that struggle. I lay buried under his personality and could not get away; my own problems, which seemed to be much of the same kind, made me flounder. I can't really put it into words; in any case I am not yet as honest with myself as I should be, and it is always hard to get to the bottom of things with words.

First impression after a few minutes: a face that was not sensual, un-Dutch, a not unfamiliar type, not altogether sympathetic.

Second impression: intelligent, incredibly wise, age-old gray eyes, which drew one's attention from the full mouth, but not for long or altogether. I was awed by his skill, his ability to read my deepest conflicts from my second face: my hands. There was an oddly disagreeable moment, when my attention slipped and I thought he was referring to my parents when, in fact, he meant me: "Philosophically and intuitively gifted," he said, and more in the same vein. He spoke as one might when giving sweets to a small child. "Happy now? Look, here you are, you've got all these marvelous qualities, so why aren't you happy now?" I felt an instant dislike, a sense of humiliation, though it was probably only my aesthetic feelings that were hurt. Anyway, I thought he was pretty odious just then. But later those marvelously human eyes, sizing me up from out of gray depths, rested again on my own. I would dearly have liked to kiss those eyes.

Now that I think about it, there was another time, that Monday morning some weeks ago now, when he disgusted me. A year before, a pupil of his, Miss Holm,[2] had come to see him, covered from head to toe with eczema. Became his patient. Was cured. Now worships him, in a manner of speaking, although I'm not quite sure what manner that is exactly. My arrogance took over at one point, and I said I'd prefer to solve my own problems. Meaningfully Miss Holm said, "No man is an island." That had a nice, convincing ring to it. And then she spoke about the eczema that had afflicted her, including her face, so badly. And S. turned toward her with a gesture I can't recall accurately any longer but which I found very unpleasant: "And what's your complexion like now, then, eh?" He could have been talking about a cow at market. I don't know, but I thought he was vile at that moment, sensual, a bit cynical, and yet there was something else about him, too.

Then, at the end of the session: "Now we must ask ourselves, what can we do to help this person?" Or maybe it was, "This person needs help." By that point I had been won over by the demonstration of his skill and I felt in need of his help.

And then there was his lecture. I only went to it so that I could watch him from a distance, examine him from afar before yielding myself unreservedly to him. The impression was good. First-rate lecture.

A charming man. Charming smile, despite the false teeth. I fell under the spell of the inner freedom that seemed to emanate from him, of the suppleness, ease, and singular grace of his heavy body. His face looked quite different again—it seems different every time I see it; back home, by myself, I cannot conjure it up in my mind. I try to assemble all the pieces I know as one might a jigsaw puzzle, but they refuse to fit together, remain in dimly seen conflict. Sometimes I get a quick, clear glimpse of the face before me, but then it falls apart again into disparate pieces. Most annoying.

There were many attractive women and girls at his lecture. I was touched by the almost palpable love he was shown by several "Aryan" girls—he, the Jew who had fled from Berlin, who had to come all the way from Germany to help them to inner peace. In the corridor stood a slender young girl, with a peaky, delicate, not altogether healthy-looking face.³ As he passed—it was the interval—S. exchanged a few words with her, and she gave a smile so charged with devotion, so obviously from the very depths of her soul, and so intense, that it almost hurt me. I was suddenly filled with a vague sense of unease, wondered whether all was really as it seemed, had the feeling: that man is stealing this young girl's smile, and all the tenderness this child bears him is stolen from someone else, from the man who will later be her own. What he did was pretty mean and unfair. He was clearly a dangerous man.

Next visit. "I can only afford twenty guilders." "That's all right, you can come for two months, and I shan't turn you away after that either, if you still need me, that is."

I had done it now, me with my "spiritual constipation." He would bring order to my inner chaos, harness the forces now at loggerheads within me. He took me metaphorically by the hand and said, look, that's how you should live. All my life I had had the feeling that, for all my apparent self-reliance, if someone came along, took me by the hand, and bothered about me, I would be only too willing and eager to deliver myself up to his care. And there he was now, this complete stranger, this S. with his complicated face. And in just one week he worked wonders with me, almost in spite of myself. Gymnastics, breathing exercises, and illuminating, liberating words about my depression, my attitude to others, and the like. Suddenly I was living differently, more freely, more *flowingly;* the costive feeling vanished, a little calm and order came into my life, at first entirely under the influence of his magical personality, but gradually with the assent of my own psyche, of my own awareness.

But to go back. "Body and soul are one." That was no doubt why he began to test my physical strength in a sort of wrestling match. It was apparently more than adequate, for remarkably enough, I floored the man, big though he was. All my inner tensions, the bottled-up forces, broke free, and there he lay, physically and also mentally, as he told me later, thrown. No one had ever been able to do that to him before, and he could not conceive how I had managed it. His lip was bleeding. I was allowed to dab it clean with eau de cologne, an embarrassingly intimate thing to do. But then he was so "free," so guileless, so open, so unaffected in his movements, even as we tumbled about together on the ground. And even when I, held tightly in his arms and finally tamed, lay under him, he remained "objective," pure, while I surrendered to the physical spell he emanated. It all seemed so innocent, this wrestling, new and unexpected, and so liberating. It was not until later that it took hold of my fantasies.

*Sunday night in the bathroom.* Now I am immaculately clean from top to toe. Just the sound of his voice over the telephone tonight was enough to make my body betray me. But I swore like a navvy, telling myself that I was no longer a hysterical teenager. And I suddenly understood those monks who flagellate themselves to tame their sinful flesh. I fought a violent battle with myself. I raged, and then there was profound clarity and peace, and now I feel gloriously, immaculately clean inside and out. S. has been thrown again, for the umpteenth time. Will it go on like this for long? I am not in love with him, but sometimes I feel that his personality, not quite "rounded" yet, still at odds with itself, is weighing me down. At the moment it is not. I can view him with detachment now: a living, battling man endowed with primitive strength, and yet spiritual, with penetrating eyes and a sensual mouth.

The day began so well, with my head bright and clear, and I made up my mind to write it all down later. But later came a really bad fit of depression, an inescapable pressure in my skull and gloomy thoughts, much too gloomy to bear for long, and behind it all the emptiness of my quest; but that's something else I shall have to fight.

"Melodious rolls the world from God's right hand." This line by Verwey[4] was stuck in my head all day. I too wanted to roll melodiously out of God's hand. And now goodnight.

*Monday morning, 9 o'clock.* Come on, my girl, get down to work or God help you. And no more excuses either, no little headache here or a bit of nausea there, or I'm not feeling very well. That is absolutely out of the question. You've just got to work, and that's that. No fantasies, no grandiose ideas, and no earth-shattering insights. Choosing a subject and finding the right words are much more important. And that is something I have to learn and for which I must fight to the death: all fantasies and dreams shall be ejected by force from my brain, and I shall sweep myself clean from within, to make space for real studies, large and small. To tell the truth, I have never worked properly. It's the same with sex. If someone makes an impression on me, I can revel in erotic fantasies for days and nights on end. I don't think I ever realized how much energy that consumes, and how much it is bound to detract from any real contact. Reality does not chime with my imagination, because my imagination tends to run riot. That's how it was that time with S. as well. I had formed a fixed idea of my visit to him, and I went there in a kind of rapture, leotard under my woolen dress. But everything turned out quite differently. He was matter-of-fact again and remote, and I instantly turned rigid. And the physical exercises weren't any good, either. When I stood there in my leotard, both of us looked as embarrassed as Adam and Eve after they had eaten the apple. He drew the curtains and locked the door, and his usual freedom of movement had gone and I would have liked to run away and weep, it felt so horrible when we were rolling about on the floor, as I clung tightly to him, sensuously and yet revolted by it all. What he did was anything but exciting, and I was overwhelmed by disgust. Yet if I hadn't had those fantasies, everything would no doubt have been quite different. There was an immediate and mighty collision of my extravagant fantasy life with the sober reality: an embarrassed and sweating man tucking a crumpled shirt into his trousers when it was all over.

And it's exactly the same with my work. At times I can suddenly see a subject clearly and distinctly, think my way through it, great sweeping thoughts that I can scarcely grasp but which all at once give me an intense feeling of importance. Yet when I try to write them down they shrivel into nothing, and that's why I lack the courage to commit them to paper—in case I become too disillusioned with the fatuous little essay that emerges.

But let me impress just one thing upon you, sister. Wash your hands of all attempts to embody those great, sweeping thoughts. The smallest, most fatuous little essay is worth more than the flood of grandiose ideas in which you like to wallow. Of course you must hold on to your forebodings and your intuitions. They are the sources upon which you draw, but be careful not to drown in them. Just organize things a little, exercise some mental hygiene. Your imagination and your emotions are like a vast ocean from which you wrest small pieces of land that may well be flooded again. That ocean is wide and elemental, but what matter are the small pieces of land you reclaim from it. The subject right before you is more important than those prodigious thoughts on Tolstoy and Napoleon that occurred to you in the middle of last night, and the lesson you gave that keen young girl on Friday night is more important than all your vague philosophizings. Never forget that. Don't overestimate your own intensity; it may give you the impression that you are cut out for greater things than the so-called man in the street, whose inner life is a closed book to you. In fact, you are no more than a weakling and a nonentity adrift and tossed by the waves.

Keep your eye fixed on the mainland and don't flounder helplessly in the ocean. And now to the job in hand!

*Wednesday night.* [ . . . ] My protracted headaches: so much masochism; my abundant compassion: so much self-gratification.

Compassion can be creative, but it can also be greedy. Objectivity is better than swooning in great emotions. For example, clinging to one's parents: one has to see them as people with a destiny of their own. The desire to prolong ecstatic moments is misplaced. It's understandable, of course: you long for an hour's moving spiritual or "soulful" experience, even if it is followed by the inevitable jolt as you come down to earth again. Such jolts used to annoy me, I would be overcome with fatigue, and pine for more of those exalted moments. Call it by its proper name: ambition. What I put down on paper must be perfect right away; I don't like putting in the daily grind. And I'm not really sure of my own talent; it doesn't really feel like an organic part of me. In near-ecstatic moments I think myself capable of God knows what, only to sink back again into the deepest pit of uncertainty. That happens because I fail to work each day at what I believe is my real talent: writing.

Theoretically I have known that for a long time; a few years ago I scribbled on a scrap of paper, "Grace during its rare appearances must be welcomed with polished skill." But that was something that leaped out of my brain and still hasn't been translated into flesh and blood. Has a new phase of my life really begun? But the question mark is wrong. A new phase *shall* begin! Battle has been joined. "Battle" isn't right either, since at this moment I feel so good and harmonious, so utterly whole, or rather: my awareness is growing apace and everything that was locked up in my head until now in the shape of precisely worked-out formulae is about to flow into my heart. But my exaggerated self-consciousness will have to go first—I still enjoy this in-between state too much. Everything will have to become more straightforward, until in the end I shall, perhaps, finish up as an adult, capable of helping other souls who are in trouble, and of creating some sort of clarity through my work for others, for that's what it's really all about.

*15 March, 9:30 A.M.* [ . . . ] Yesterday afternoon we read over the notes he had given me. And when we came to the words, "If there were only one human being worthy of the name of 'man,' then we should be justified in believing in men and in humanity," I threw my arms round him on a sudden impulse. It is the problem of our age: hatred of Germans poisons everyone's mind. "Let the bastards drown, the lot of them"—such sentiments have become part and parcel of our daily speech and sometimes make one feel that life these days has grown impossible. Until suddenly, a few weeks ago, I had a liberating thought that surfaced in me like a hesitant, tender young blade of grass thrusting its way through a wilderness of weeds: if there were only one decent German, then he should be cherished despite that whole barbaric gang, and because of that one decent German it is wrong to pour hatred over an entire people.

That doesn't mean you have to be halfhearted; on the contrary, you must make a stand, wax indignant at times, try to get to the bottom of things. But indiscriminate hatred is the worst thing there is. It is a sickness of the soul. Hatred does not lie in my nature. If things were to come to such a pass that I began to hate people, then I would know that my soul was sick and I should have to look for a cure as quickly as possible. I used to believe that my inner conflicts were due to a particular cause, but that was much too superficial an explanation. I thought that they simply reflected a clash between my primitive instinct as a Jew threatened with destruction and my acquired, rationalist and socialist belief that no nation is an undifferentiated mob.

But it goes deeper than that. Socialism lets in hatred against everything that is not socialist through the back door. That is crudely put, but I know what I mean. I have recently made it my business to preserve harmony in this household of so many conflicting elements: a German woman, a Christian of peasant stock, who has been a second mother to me; a Jewish girl student from Amsterdam; an old, levelheaded social democrat; Bernard the Philistine, with his pure heart and his fair intellect, but limited by his background; and an upright young economics student, a good Christian, full of gentleness and sympathetic understanding but also with the kind of Christian militancy and rectitude we have become accustomed to in recent times.[5] Ours was and is a bustling little world, so threatened by politics from outside as to be disturbed within. But it seems a worthy task to keep this small community together as a refutation of all those desperate and false theories of race, nation, and so on. As proof that life cannot be forced into pre-set molds. But doing this causes a great deal of inner struggle and disappointment, and now and then means inflicting pain on others, and anger and remorse. Sometimes when I read the papers or hear reports of what is happening all round, I am suddenly beside myself with anger, cursing and swearing at the Germans. And I know that I do it deliberately in order to hurt Käthe, to work off my anger as best I can. Even if it is against a dear friend who I know is filled with love for her country of birth, which is only natural and understandable. But sometimes I can't bear the thought that she cannot share my hatred—I want to feel at one with my fellow beings even in that. And all this when I know perfectly well that she finds the new order as dreadful as I do, and is just as bowed down by the excesses of her people. But deep down she is of course one of her people, and while I understand, I some-times cannot bear it. The whole nation must be destroyed root and branch. And now and then I say nastily, "They're all scum," and at the same time I feel terribly ashamed and deeply unhappy but can't stop even though I know that it's all wrong. At other times, we all feel very close to Käthe and tell her encouragingly, "Yes, of course, there are still some good Germans, and anyway the soldiers can do nothing about it, and there are some quite nice ones even among them." But that is only in theory, of course; these few friendly words help us to tuck away what misgivings we have left. If we really felt like that, we should not have had to say it so emphatically since we should all be feeling the same way, the German peasant woman and the Jewish stu-dents, and then we could all talk about the nice weather or cabbage soup, instead of torturing ourselves with acrimonious discussions. For these discussions are hardly ever concerned with real politics, with any attempt to grasp major political trends or to fathom the underlying currents. On the contrary, everything looks so clear-cut and ugly, which is why it is so unpleasant to discuss politics in the present climate and why I felt that sudden urge to fling myself at S., an oasis in a desert. This is by no means my last word on the subject, but now I must think of my work, and take a breath of fresh air.

*Sunday morning, 11 o'clock.* [ . . . ] My life's priorities have been suddenly changed. In the past, I liked to start the day on an empty stomach with Dostoyevsky or Hegel, and during odd, jumpy moments I might also darn a stocking if I absolutely had to. Now I start the day, in the most literal sense, with the stocking and gradually work my way up through the other essential chores to higher planes, where I can meet poets and philosophers again. I shall have to sweat blood to rid my style of all that pathos if I am ever to make anything of it, but really it's all a matter of looking for the right words.

*Half-past twelve,* after my walk, which has by now become a cherished tradition. On Tuesday morning, while studying Lermontov, I jotted down that S.'s head keeps peering at me from behind Lermontov, that I want to speak to him and stroke his dear face, and that I can't do any work as a result. That seems quite a long time ago now. Everything has changed a little since. His head is still there when I work, but it no longer distracts me; it has become a familiar, beloved backdrop, his features have grown blurred, his face has dissolved into vapor, a wraith, call it what you will. And here I have hit upon something essential. Whenever I saw a beautiful flower, what I longed to do with it was press it to my heart, or eat it all up. It was more difficult with a piece of beautiful scenery, but the feeling was the same. I was too sensual, I might almost write too greedy. I yearned physically for all I thought was beautiful, wanted to own it. Hence that painful longing that could never be satisfied, the pining for something I thought unattainable, which I called my creative urge. I believe it was this powerful emotion that made me think that I was born to produce great works. It all suddenly changed, God alone knows by what inner process, but it is different now. I realised it only this morning, when I recalled my short walk round the Skating Club a few nights ago. It was dusk, soft hues in the sky, mysterious silhouettes of houses, trees alive with the light through the tracery of their branches, in short, enchanting. And then I knew precisely how I had felt in the past. Then all that beauty would have gone like a stab to my heart, and I would not have known what to do with the pain. Then I would have felt the need to write, to compose verses, but the words would still have refused to come. I would have felt utterly miserable, wallowed in the pain, and exhausted myself as a result. The experience would have sapped all my energy. Now, I know it for what it was: mental masturbation.

But that night, only just gone, I reacted quite differently. I felt that God's world was beautiful despite everything, but its beauty now filled me with joy. I was just as deeply moved by that mysterious, still landscape in the dusk as I might have been before, but somehow I no longer wanted to own it. I went home invigorated and got back to work. And the scenery stayed with me, in the background, as a cloak about my soul, to put it poetically for once, but it no longer held me back: I no longer "masturbated" with it.

And that's what it's like with S. as well, indeed with everyone nowadays. That critical afternoon, when I sat rigid, staring at him and unable to utter a word, was no doubt also a reflection of my "greed." That afternoon he told me a few things about his personal life. About his wife from whom he was divorced but to whom he still wrote, about the girlfriend in London whom he wanted to marry but who was so lonely and dejected now, about an old flame, a ravishingly beautiful singer, with whom he still corresponded as well.[6] Then we wrestled again, and I was deeply affected by his great, attractive body.

And when I sat facing him again and fell silent, I was moved perhaps just as I used to be by a walk through beautiful scenery. I wanted to "own" him. I wanted him to be part of me. True, I did not long for him as one longs for a man, he had not yet moved me sexually, and though I never felt quite relaxed with him he had touched me to the very depths of my being, and that was more important. And so I wanted to own him, and I hated all those women of whom he had spoken to me; I was jealous of them, and perhaps wondered, although not consciously, what part of him was left for me, and felt that I had no hold over him after all. These feelings were really petty, not on a high plane at all, but I did not realize that at the time. All I felt was wretchedly unhappy and lonely—I realize why now—and all I wanted was to get away from him and to write. I think I know what all the "writing" was about as well: it was just another way of "owning," of drawing things in more tightly to oneself with words and images. And I'm sure that that used to be the very essence of my urge to write: I wanted to creep silently away from everyone with all my carefully hoarded treasure, to write it all down, keep tight hold of it, and have it all to myself. And this grasping attitude, which is the best way I have of describing it, suddenly fell away from me. A thousand tyrannical chains were broken, and I breathed freely again and felt strong and looked about with shining eyes. And now that I don't want to own anything any more and am free, now I suddenly own everything, now my inner riches are immeasurable.

S. is completely mine now, even if he were to leave for China tomorrow. I feel him round me and I live in his aura; if I see him again on Wednesday that's fine, but I no longer sit about desperately counting the days as I did the week before. And I no longer ask Han, "Do you still love me?" "Do you still think I'm special?" or "Are you sure I'm still your favorite?" That, too, was a kind of clinging, a physical clinging to what can never be physical. And now I live and breathe through my "soul," if I may use that discredited word.

And now I know what S. meant after my first visit to him. "What's in here [and he pointed to his head] must get down there [and he pointed to his heart]." At the time it wasn't clear to me how his work could bring that about, but it did, I still cannot tell how. He assigned their proper places to all the things that went on inside me; it was like a jigsaw puzzle, all the pieces were mixed up, and he put them together properly. How he did it I can't tell, but it's his business after all, his profession, and people know what they're talking about when they speak of his "magical personality."

*Wednesday.* [ . . . ] I surprised myself with a need for music. I don't seem to be unmusical, am seized with interest whenever I hear a piece of music but have never had the patience to sit down specially to listen to it; my full attention has always been reserved for literature and the theater, areas that are within the province of my own thoughts. And now, quite suddenly, music is beginning to press its claims, and once again I find that I am open to an experience that makes me forget myself. And it is above all for the limpid, serene classics that I long, not for those mangled modern composers.

9:00 *P.M.* God help me and give me strength, for the struggle is bound to be difficult. His mouth and body were so close this afternoon that I cannot get them out of my mind. And I don't want to have an affair with him, though things are fast moving in that direction. But I *don't want it.* His future wife is in London, lonely and waiting for him. And my own ties are very precious to me as well. Now that I am gradually becoming more composed, I am able to acknowledge that I am really a very serious person who does not like to make light of love. What I really want is a man for life, and to build something together with him. And all the adventures and transient relationships I have had have made me utterly miserable, tearing me apart. But I always lacked the strength to resist, and my curiosity always got the better of me. Now that my inner forces have been concentrated, they have started to fight against my appetite for adventure and my far-ranging erotic curiosity. Really it is all just a game, and you don't need to have an affair with a man to have an intuitive understanding of him. But it's hard going this time all the same, God knows. His mouth looked so familiar and dear and close this afternoon, that I simply had to brush it softly with my lips. And our wrestling that began in such a matter-of-fact way ended with our resting in each other's arms. He did not kiss me, but gave my cheek a powerful nip, although the most unforgettable thing for me was that when he recovered his composure he asked shyly, almost painfully so, and with apprehension,

"What about my mouth—didn't it put you off?" That's where his weak spot is, then. The struggle against his own sensuality, localized in that heavy, wonderfully expressive mouth. And his fear of putting people off with it. A touching man. But my peace was shattered. And then he said again, "But one's mouth ought to be smaller." And he pointed to the right side of his lower lip, which protrudes in an odd way from the corner of his mouth, curving thickly, a piece of lip that seems to have got out of control. "Have you ever seen anything so willful, there's nothing like it . . ." I don't remember his precise words. And then I once again brushed my lips softly over that obstinate little piece of mouth. I haven't kissed him properly, there is no real passion in me yet, but he is infinitely dear to me and I would not want to spoil the fine, warm feeling I have for him with the complications of a sexual relationship.

*Friday, 21 March, 8:30 A.M.* Actually I don't want to write anything down now, for I feel so light and radiant and cheerful that all words seem leaden by comparison. Even so I had to pay for this morning's inner joy with a jittery and furiously beating heart. But then I washed all over in ice-cold water and lay down for a long time on the bathroom floor until I was completely calm again. I have become what he calls "combat ready" and even take an athlete's anticipatory pleasure in the "battle." [. . .]

This vague fear is something else I must conquer in myself. Life is difficult, it is true, a struggle from minute to minute (don't overdo it now, Etty!), but the struggle itself is thrilling. In the past I would live chaotically in the future, because I refused to live in the here and now. I wanted to be handed everything on a platter, like a badly spoiled child. Sometimes I had the certain if rather undefined feeling that I would "make it" one day, that I had the capacity to do something "extraordinary," and at other times the wild fear that I would "go to the dogs" after all. I now realize why. I simply refused to do what needed to be done, what lay right under my nose. I refused to climb into the future one step at a time. And now, now that every minute is so full, so chock-full of life and experience and struggle and victory and defeat, and more struggle and sometimes peace, now I no longer think of the future, that is, I no longer care whether or not I shall "make it," because I now have the inner certainty that everything will be taken care of. Before, I always lived in anticipation, I had the feeling that nothing I did was the "real" thing, that it was all a preparation for something else, something "greater," more "genuine." But that feeling has dropped away from me completely. I live here and now, this minute, this day, to the full, and life is worth living. And if I knew that I was going to die tomorrow, then I would say: it's a great shame, but it's been good while it lasted. I put that forward, in theory, before, one summer evening—I still remember it well—with Frans on the Reijnders' little terrace.[7] But what I felt then was resignation, not acceptance, something like, well if it's all up with me tomorrow, I shan't bother my head too much, that's life for you. And we know life, don't we? We have experienced everything, if only in the mind, and there's no need any longer to hang on for dear life. Something like that, I believe. We were very old then, very wise, and very weary. But now it is quite different. And so to work.

*Saturday, 8:00 P.M.* [ . . . ] I must make sure I keep up with my writing, that is, with myself, or else things will start to go wrong for me: I shall run the risk of losing my way. That's what it seems like to me at the moment, anyway, though it may all be due to tiredness, of course.

*Sunday, 23 March, 4 o'clock.* Everything has gone wrong again. I long for something and don't know what it is. Inside I am totally at a loss, restless, driven, and my head feels close to bursting again. I look back on the last two Sundays with some nostalgia: the days stretched before me then like broad, open plains that I could cross with great ease, that offered wide, unimpeded views. And now I am back in the midst of the scrubland again.

It started last night; then the turbulence began to swirl up inside me, as vapor swirls up from a swamp.

I half wanted to read some philosophy, or perhaps that essay on *War and Peace,* then felt that Alfred Adler suited my mood better, and ended up with a light novel. But all my efforts were just tilting against the natural lassitude to which I wisely yielded in the end. And this morning everything seemed fine again. But when I began cycling down Apollolaan, there it was back, all the questioning, the discontent, the feeling that everything was empty of meaning, the sense that life was unfulfilled, all that pointless brooding. And right now I am sunk in the mire. And even the certain knowledge that this too will pass has brought me no peace this time.

*Monday morning, 9:30* [ . . . ] It's silly, but he is still a stranger to me in a sense. Sometimes when he just strokes my face with his great, warm hand, or, with that inimitable gesture of his, runs his fingertips over my eyelashes, I begin to rebel. "Who told you that you could do this to me, who gave you the right to touch my body?" I think I know the explanation. When we wrestled the first time it was an enjoyable contest, and though it was a little unexpected I immediately "caught on": I realized it was all part of the treatment. And that's indeed what it was, for when it was all over he stated very matter-of-factly, "Body and soul are one." I was, of course, erotically aroused by then, but he was being so businesslike that I quickly recovered. And when we had sat down again and faced each other, he said, "Now look, I hope this doesn't excite you, because I keep touching you everywhere," and by way of demonstration he put his hands out and touched my breast, then my arms and shoulders. I thought something like, "Well, my friend, you ought to know just how 'excitable' I am, because I told you so myself, but all right, it's decent of you to discuss it so openly," and I recovered a little. Then he added that I mustn't fall in love with him, and that he always said this at the beginning. Well, it was fair enough, but I felt a bit uncomfortable about it.

But the second time we wrestled, things were quite different. Then he too showed passion. And when at one point he lay groaning on top of me, for just a brief moment, and made the oldest convulsive movement in the world, then the lowest of thoughts rose up in me like a miasma from a swamp, something like: "A funny way of treating patients you have, you get your pleasure out of it and you get paid for it as well even if it is just a pittance."

But the way his hands reached for me during the fight, the way he nipped my ear and held my face in his great hand, all that drove me completely mad. I could sense the skilled and fascinating lover behind all these gestures. Yet I also thought it exceedingly mean of him to abuse his position. In the end my rebelliousness died down and there was a sense of closeness between us, and more personal contact than we may ever have again. But while we were still lying on the floor, he said, "I don't want to have a relationship with you." And he added, "I must tell you honestly, I find you very attractive." And then he said something about similar temperaments. And a little later, "Now give me a friendly little kiss." But I was far from ready for that and turned my head away shyly. And he was quite himself again now that it was all over and said, as if musing to himself, "It's all quite logical, you know. As a boy I was something of a dreamer." And then he told me a bit about his life.

He talked and I listened, all surrender, and now and then he put his hand very tenderly on my face. And that's how I went home, with the most conflicting feelings, rebellious ones because I thought he was mean, and tender ones, overflowing with human kindness and warmth. And all the while I was overwhelmed by erotic fantasies brought on by the guileful movements of his hands. For a few days I could do nothing but think of him. Though you couldn't really call it thinking, it was more like a sort of physical endurance test he was subjecting me to. His great supple body threatened me from all sides, it was on top of me, under me, everywhere, it threatened to crush me, I was quite unable to work and thought in horror, my God, what have I let myself in for; I went to this man for psychological treatment to get some insight into myself and now this, it's worse than anything I've ever known. And I lived completely for our next meeting and had very erotic ideas about it, and that was the notorious occasion with the leotard under the woolen dress and the tremendous clash of my wild fantasies with his matter-of-fact realism. Afterward I understood it all perfectly. He had pulled himself together and deliberately adopted a matter-of-fact attitude; but he too had had quite a struggle. And he asked, "Did you think about me this week?" And when I made a few noncommittal remarks and lowered my head, he said, very honestly, "I must honestly tell you that I thought a lot about you the first few days of this week." All right, and then there was that wrestling match, but I have written quite enough about that, it was revolting and I had a sort of crisis. He doesn't know to this day why I went so stiff and strange, and still thinks it was because he aroused me sexually. But his own conflicts came out in the open as well that time. He said, "You are quite a challenge," and he told me that despite his temperament he had been faithful to his girlfriend for the past two years. But I felt that being a "challenge" was far too noncommittal. I wanted to be the only one for him; I was the spoiled child determined to "own" him, no matter that my heart was not in it, for my fantasies had declared that he was to be my man, that I had to know him as my lover, and that was that. I wasn't operating at a very high level, but I've written about that already.

And now I feel that I am a match for him, that my struggle is balanced against his, that in me, too, both impure and nobler impulses are fighting a mighty battle.

When he laid bare the man in him so suddenly, not waiting until I asked him to throw away his psychologist's mask, he lost some of his authority but has made me all the richer. He also gave me a little shock, inflicted a small wound, that hasn't completely healed and still makes me feel that he is a stranger: Who are you anyway, and who told you that you could meddle with me? Rilke has written a beautiful poem about this mood of mine, I hope I'll be able to find it again.

I did find the poem, the one of Rilke's that was on the tip of my tongue, after some searching. Years ago a friend read it to me. It was a summer evening on the Southern Walk, and at the time he felt it applied to me for some reason or other, probably because, despite our intimacy, I always thought of him as a stranger. That ambivalence in me is becoming clear to me now, thanks again to my clash with S. It is all in the last two lines:

> Strangely I heard a stranger say:
> I am with you.

*Tuesday, 25 March, 9:00 P.M.* [ . . . ] Because I am still so young and utterly resolved not to go under, and also because I feel that I am strong enough to pull myself together, I tend to forget how deprived we young people have become and how lonely. Or have I simply been anesthetized? Bonger is dead, Ter Braak, Du

Perron, Marsman, all are dead. Pos, and Van den Bergh, and many others are in concentration camps.[8] I shall never forget Bonger. (Odd how Van Wijk's death has suddenly brought it all back to me.) It was a few hours before the Dutch capitulation. And suddenly there was the heavy, cumbersome, unmistakable figure of Bonger shuffling along through the Skating Club, blue-tinted glasses, singular, heavy head tilted to one side and looking toward the clouds of smoke that came floating across the town from the faraway oil terminals. This image—the clumsy figure with neck craned and head tilted at the distant clouds of smoke—is something I shall never forget. On an impulse I ran, coatless, out through the doors behind him, caught up with him, and said, "Hello, Professor Bonger, I have thought a lot about you these last few days, may I walk a little way with you?" And he gave me a sidelong look through those blue glasses and obviously had no idea who I was, despite two exams and a year at his lectures. Still, those days people felt so close to one another that I just continued walking by his side. I can't remember the precise words we exchanged. It was that afternoon when people thought of nothing but getting away to England, and I asked, "Do you think it makes sense to escape?" And he said, "The young have to stay put." And I, "Do you think democracy can win?" And he, "It's bound to win, but it's going to cost us several generations." And he, fearless Bonger, was suddenly as defenseless as a child, almost gentle, and I felt an irresistible need to put my arms round him and to lead him like a child, and so, with my arm round him, we walked on across the Skating Club. He seemed a broken man and good through and through. All the passion and fire in him had been doused. My heart overflows when I think of how he was that afternoon—he, the college tyrant. And at Jan Willem Brouwers Square I took my leave of him. I stood in front of him, took one of his hands between mine, and he gently lowered his heavy head a little and looked at me through his blue glasses, which hid his eyes, and sounded almost like a stage comic as he said, "My pleasure."

And next evening at Becker's, the first thing I heard was, "Bonger is dead!" I said, "That's impossible, I spoke to him last night at seven o'clock." And Becker said, "Then you must have been one of the last people to speak to him. He put a bullet through his brain at eight o'clock."

And two of his last words had been addressed to an unknown student, one whom he had looked at kindly through a pair of blue glasses, "My pleasure!"

And Bonger is not the only one. A world is in the process of collapse. But the world will go on, and so for the present shall I, full of good heart and goodwill. Nevertheless, we who are left behind are just a little bit destitute, though inwardly I still feel so rich that the destitution is not fully brought home to me. However, one must keep in touch with the real world and know one's place in it; it is wrong to live only with the eternal truths, for then one is apt to end up behaving like an ostrich. To live fully, outwardly and inwardly, not to ignore external reality for the sake of the inner life, or the reverse—that's quite a task. And now I am going to read another silly little story in *Libelle*[9] and then to bed. And tomorrow back to work: studying, housekeeping, and working on myself, nothing must be neglected, and don't take yourself too seriously either; and now goodnight.

*Friday afternoon, 8 May [1941], three o'clock, in bed.* I must work on myself some more, there's nothing else for it. For a few months, I could do without this diary, life was so clear and bright inside me and so intense: good contact with the outer and inner worlds, life-enriching, broadening of the personality; student contacts in Leiden: Wil, Aimé, Jan; my studies; the Bible, Jung, and then S., and always S. again.

But now everything has ground to a halt, except for a bit of agitation, though it's not really agitation, I'm too depressed for that. Probably it is nothing but the physical fatigue everyone is feeling this chilly spring, and which has put me right out of tune with everything around me.

But I know perfectly well that the real trouble is my unstated, curious relationship with S. And I shall have to watch my every step.

*8:00 P.M.* We are always in search of the redeeming formula, the crystallizing thought. As I was cycling about in the cold, I suddenly thought: perhaps I am making everything much too complicated because I don't want to face the sober facts. I am not really in love with him. He captivates and sometimes fascinates me as a man, and I am learning an unbelievable amount from him. Ever since I met him, I have been experiencing a process of maturation, something I would never have thought possible at my age. There's really no more to it than that. But then we come to that confounded eroticism, with which he is bursting, as am I. As a result we are irresistibly driven toward each other physically, though neither of us wants it, as we both once said in so many words. But take that Sunday night, I believe it was 21 April, the first time I spent a whole evening with him. We spoke, that is he spoke, about the Bible, later he read me something from Thomas à Kempis, while I sat on his lap, it all felt so right, it was barely erotic, just a lot of human warmth and friendliness. But a moment later his body was suddenly on mine and I was in his arms, and then I suddenly felt sad and lonely. He kissed my thighs and I grew lonelier still. He said, "That was lovely," and I went home with a leaden, sad, abandoned feeling. And straightaway I began to devise wonderfully interesting theories about my loneliness. But couldn't it simply be due to the fact that I wasn't able to surrender to our physical contact with my deepest being? For I don't really love him, and I know that ideally he wants to be faithful to one woman, and that woman happens to be in London, but that's not really the point. If I were a woman of true worth and greatness I would break off all physical contact with him; it really does nothing but upset me deeply. But I can't bring myself to renounce all the possibilities that might then fall by the wayside. I think I am also afraid that I might bruise his manliness. Still, our friendship would no doubt rise to a much higher level, and he would presumably be grateful to me in the end if I helped him to stay faithful to one woman. But I happen to be a particularly petty and greedy person. Now and again I want to be back in his arms, but then I end up unhappy all over again. There is probably a bit of childish vanity about it all as well. Something like: here are all these girls and women who are mad about him, yet I, who have known him for the shortest time of all, am the only one with whom he is intimate. If that is truly what goes on inside me then it's absolutely sickening. Really I am running the risk of ruining our friendship for the sake of physical pleasure. [ . . . ]

*8 June [1941], Sunday morning, 9:30.* I think that I'll do it anyway: I'll "turn inward" for half an hour each morning before work, and listen to my inner voice. Lose myself. You could also call it meditation. I am still a bit wary of that word. But anyway, why not? A quiet half-hour within yourself. It's not enough just to move your arms and legs and all the other muscles about in the bathroom each morning. Man is body and spirit. And half an hour of exercises combined with half an hour of meditation can set the tone for the whole day.

But it's not so simple, that sort of "quiet hour." It has to be learned. A lot of unimportant inner litter and bits and pieces have to be swept out first. Even a small head can be piled high inside with irrelevant distractions. True, there may be edifying emotions and thoughts, too, but the clutter is ever present. So let this be the aim of the meditation: to turn one's innermost being into a vast empty plain, with none of that treacherous undergrowth to impede the view. So that something of "God" can enter you, and something of "Love," too. Not the kind of love-de-luxe that you revel in deliciously for half an hour, taking pride in how sublime you can feel, but the love you can apply to small, everyday things.

I might of course read the Bible each morning, but I don't think I'm ready for that. I still worry about the real meaning of the book, rather than lose myself in it.

I think I'll read a little bit of *De Hof der Wijsbegeerte* ("The Philosopher's Garden") each morning instead. I might of course confine myself to writing a few words on these blue-lined pages. To the patient examination of just one single thought, even if none of my thoughts is very important. In the past, ambition stopped me from committing such trivia to paper. Everything had to be marvelous, perfect, I simply could not allow myself to write down any old thing, even though I was sometimes bursting with the longing to do just that.

And, for goodness' sake, stop looking at yourself in the mirror, Etty, you fool. It must be awful to be very beautiful, for then one would not bother to look farther inside, one would be so dazzled by the blinding exterior. Others, too, would respond to the beautiful exterior alone, so that one might actually shrivel up inside altogether. The time I spend in front of the mirror, because I am suddenly caught by a funny or fascinating or interesting expression on this really not particularly pretty face of mine, could surely be spent on better things. It annoys me terribly, all this peering at myself. Sometimes I do find that I am looking pretty, but that's largely because of the dim lighting in the bathroom, and at such moments I can't tear myself away from my likeness and pull faces at myself in the glass, hold my head at all sorts of angles before my enraptured gaze, and then my favorite fantasy is that I'm seated in a large hall behind a table and facing a large company, all of whom keep looking at me and find me beautiful.

You keep saying that you want to forget yourself completely, my girl, but as long as you're so full of vanities and fantasies you have not made much progress in the art of forgetting yourself.

Even when I am working, I sometimes have a sudden urge to see my face; then I take my glasses off and look into the lenses. It can be quite compulsive. And I feel very unhappy about it all because I realize how much I still stand in my own way. And it doesn't help if I force myself not to take pleasure in my face. I must learn to feel genuinely indifferent to my appearance, not to care in the least how I look. I must lead a much more inward life. With other people, too, I pay much too much attention to appearances, dwelling on their looks. Yet what really matters is man's soul or his essence or whatever else you care to call what shines through from within.

*Saturday, 14 June, 7:00 P.M.* More arrests, more terror, concentration camps, the arbitrary dragging off of fathers, sisters, brothers.[10] We seek the meaning of life, wondering whether any meaning can be left. But that is something each one of us must settle with himself and with God. And perhaps life has its own meaning, even if it takes a lifetime to find it. I for one have ceased to cling to life and to things; I have the feeling that everything is accidental, that one must break one's inner bonds with people and stand aside for all else. Everything seems so menacing and ominous, and always that feeling of total impotence.

*Sunday, noon.* We are but hollow vessels, washed through by history.

Everything is chance, or nothing is chance. If I believed the first, I would be unable to live on, but I am not yet fully convinced of the second.

I have become just a little stronger again. I can fight things out within myself. Your first impulse is always to get help from others, to think you can't make it, but then suddenly you notice that you've fought your way through and that you've pulled it off all by yourself, and that makes you stronger. Last Sunday (was it only a week ago?) I had the desperate feeling that I was tied to him and that because of that I was in for an utterly miserable time. But I pulled myself out of it, although I don't quite know how. Not by arguing it out with myself, but by tugging with all my mental strength at some imaginary rope. I threw all my weight behind it and stood my ground, and suddenly I felt that I was free again. And then there were those brief meetings (in the evening at the bench on the Stadionkade, shopping in town) that were of an intensity that, for me at least, was greater than anything before. It was all thanks to that lack of attachment; all my love and sympathy and concern and happiness went out to him, but I made no more demands on him, I wanted nothing from him, I took him as he was and enjoyed him.

I'd just like to know how I did it, how I managed to break free. If I knew that, as I really should, then I might perhaps be able to help others with the same problems. Perhaps it is like a man tied to another with a rope and tugging until he breaks loose. He, too, probably won't be able to tell just how he did it; all he does know is that he managed to get away, that he had the *will* to do so, and that he struggled with all his might. That's what must have happened inside me. And the lesson I learned is this: thought doesn't help; what you need is not causal explanations but will and a great deal of mental energy.

For a moment yesterday I thought I couldn't go on living, that I needed help. Life and suffering had lost their meaning for me; I felt I was about to collapse under a tremendous weight. But once again I put up a fight and now I can face it all, stronger than before. I have tried to look that "suffering" of mankind fairly and squarely in the face. I have fought it out, or rather something inside me has fought it out, and suddenly there were answers to many desperate questions, and the sense of emptiness made way for the feeling that there was order and meaning after all and I could get on with my life. All was smooth going again after a short but violent battle from which I emerged just a fraction more mature.

I said that I confronted the "suffering of mankind" (I still shudder when it comes to big words), but that was not really what it was. Rather I feel like a small battlefield, in which the problems, or some of the problems, of our time are being fought out. All one can hope to do is to keep oneself humbly available, to allow oneself to be a battlefield. After all, the problems must be accommodated, have somewhere to struggle and come to rest, and we, poor little humans, must put our inner space at their service and not run away. In that respect, I am probably very hospitable; mine is often an exceedingly bloody battlefield, and dreadful fatigue and splitting headaches are the toll I have to pay. Still, now I am myself once again, Etty Hillesum, an industrious student in a friendly room with books and a vase full of oxeye daisies. I am flowing again in my own narrow riverbed, and my desperate involvement with "mankind," "world history," and "suffering" has subsided. And that's as it should be, otherwise one might go mad.

*Tuesday morning, 17 June.* [ . . . ] If you have an upset stomach you must start to eat sensibly instead of venting your fury like a spoiled child on all the delicious food you think is to blame for your condition. Much better to concentrate on your lack of self-control.

That is a piece of insight into myself I acquired today and with which I am most content. And the continuous sadness that has been gnawing at my insides these past few days is beginning to fade away as well.

*Wednesday morning, 18 June, 9:30.* Life itself must be our fountainhead, never something or someone else. Many people, especially women, draw their strength from others, instead of directly from life. A man is their source, instead of life. That attitude is as distorted and unnatural as it possibly can be.

*4 July. [1941].* I am full of unease, a strange, infernal agitation, which might be productive if only I knew what to do with it. A "creative" unease. Not of the body—not even a dozen passionate nights of love could assuage it. It is almost a "sacred" unease. "Oh God, take me into Your great hands and turn me into Your instrument, let me write." This all came about because of red-haired Leonie[11] and philosophical Joop. S. reached straight into their hearts with his analysis, but I still think people can't be reduced to psychological formulas, that only the artist can render human beings down to their last irrational elements.

I don't know how to settle down to my writing. Everything is still much too chaotic, and I lack self-confidence, or perhaps the urgent need to speak out. I am still waiting for things to come out and find a form of their own accord. But first I myself must find the right pattern, my own pattern.

In Deventer the days were like great sunny plains, each one a long, uninterrupted whole; there was contact with God and with every person I met, possibly because I met so few.[12] There were cornfields I shall never forget, whose beauty nearly brought me to my knees; there were the banks of the IJssel with the colorful parasols and the thatched roofs and the patient horses. And the sun, which I drank in through all my pores. And back here each day is a thousand fragments, the great plain is no more, and God, too, has departed. If this continues much longer then I'm bound to start asking myself about the meaning of life all over again, and that never means plumbing philosophical depths but is proof positive that things are going badly with me. And then there is that ridiculous unease that I still can't quite place, but that one day, I should think, might help me to write, if only I learn how to channel it properly.

You're not there by a long way yet, my girl, a lot of solid ground will have to be reclaimed from the raging waves, and chaos will have to make way for order. I can't help thinking of S.'s remark:

"You are not really as chaotic as all that, it's just that you refuse to turn your back on the time when you thought being chaotic was better than being disciplined."

*Monday, 4 August 1941, 2:30 P.M.* He said that love of mankind is greater than love of one man. For when you love one person you are merely loving yourself.

He is a mature fifty-five-year-old and has reached the stage where he can love all mankind, having loved many individuals in the past. I am an ordinary twenty-seven-year-old girl, and I too am filled with love for all mankind, but for all I know I shall always continue to be in search of my one man. And I wonder to what extent that is a handicap, a woman's handicap. Whether it is an ancient tradition from which she must liberate herself, or whether it is so much part of her very essence that she would be doing violence to herself if she bestowed her love on all mankind instead of on a single man. (I can't yet see how the two can be combined.) Perhaps that's why there are so few famous women scientists and artists: a woman always looks for the one man on whom she can bestow all her wisdom, warmth, love, and creative powers. She longs for a man, not for mankind.

It's not at all simple, the role of women. Sometimes, when I pass a woman in the street, a beautiful, well-groomed, wholly feminine, albeit dull woman, I completely lose my poise. Then I feel that my intellect, my struggle, my suffering, are oppressive, ugly, unwomanly; then I too want to be beautiful and dull, a desirable plaything for a man. It's typical that I always do end up wanting to be desired by a man, the ultimate confirmation of our worth and womanhood, but in fact it is only a primitive instinct. Feelings of friendship, respect, and love for us as human beings, these are all very well, but don't we ultimately want men to desire us as women? It is almost too difficult for me to write down all I feel; the subject is infinitely complex, but it is altogether too important not to be discussed.

Perhaps the true, the essential emancipation of women still has to come. We are not yet full human beings; we are the "weaker sex." We are still tied down and enmeshed in centuries-old traditions. We still have to be born as human beings; that is the great task that lies before us.

Where do we really stand, S. and myself? If I want to be clear about this relationship, then I must first clarify my relationship with all men and with all mankind, to use that sweeping word. Let me be full of pathos then, write down everything inside me, and when I have written all the unctiousness and exaggeration out of my system, perhaps I will then get down to myself.

Do I love S.? Yes, madly.

As a man? No, not as a man, but as a human being. Or perhaps it is more his warmth, his love, and his striving after goodness that I love. No, I can't work it out, try as I may. This writing is a sort of rough draft; I try things out, discard this and that, and hope all the pieces will fit together in the end. But I mustn't run away from myself, or from difficult problems, and I don't really—what I do run away from is the difficulty of writing it all down. It all comes out so clumsily. But then you don't put things down on paper to produce masterpieces, but to gain some clarity. I am still ashamed of myself, afraid to let myself go, to let things pour out of me; I am dreadfully inhibited, and that is because I have not yet learned to accept myself as I am.

It is difficult to be on equally good terms with God and your body. This thought kept haunting me at a musical soirée some time ago, when S. and Bach were both with me. There is something complicated about S. He just sits there full of warmth and human kindness, in which you can bask with no reservations. But at the same time there he is, this great big man sitting there, with his expressive head, large sensitive hands that reach out for you now and then, and eyes whose caress can be truly heart-rending. But the caress is impersonal, of course. He caresses the human being, not the woman. And the woman wants to be caressed as a woman, not as a human being. At least that's how I feel at times. But he presents you with a real task, makes you fight very hard for it. I am a task for him, he told me that one of the first times, but so is he for me. I must stop now, I keep feeling more and more miserable as I write this, a clear sign that I can't voice what is really going on inside me.

There is nothing else for it, I shall have to solve my own problems. I always get the feeling that when I solve them for myself I shall have also solved them for a thousand other women. For that very reason I must come to grips with myself.

All this devouring of books from early youth has been nothing but laziness on my part. I allow others to formulate what I ought to be formulating myself. I keep seeking outside confirmation of what is hidden deep inside me, when I know that I can only reach clarity by using my own words. I really must abandon all that laziness, and particularly my inhibitions and insecurity, if I am ever to find myself, and through myself, find others. I must have clarity, and I must learn to accept myself. Everything feels so heavy inside me, and I want so much to feel light. For years I have bottled everything up, it all goes into some great reservoir, but it will all have to come out again, or I shall know that I have lived in vain, that I have taken from mankind and given nothing back. I sometimes feel I am a parasite, and that depresses me and makes me wonder if I lead any kind of useful life. Perhaps my purpose in life is to come to grips with myself, properly to grips with myself, with everything that bothers and tortures me and clamors for inner solution and formulation. For these problems are not just mine alone. And if at the end of a long life I am able to give some form to the chaos inside me, I may well have fulfilled my own small purpose. Even while I write this down, my unconscious is protesting at such expressions as "purpose" and "mankind" and "solution of problems." I find them pretentious. But then I'm such an ingenuous and dull young woman, still so lacking in courage. No, my friend, you are not there yet by a long chalk, you ought really to be kept away from all the great philosophers until you have learned to take yourself a little more seriously.

I think I'd better buy that melon first, and take it to the Nethes tonight.[13] That's also part of living, isn't it?

Sometimes I long for a convent cell, with the sublime wisdom of centuries set out on bookshelves all along the wall and a view across the cornfields—there must be cornfields and they must wave in the breeze—and there I would immerse myself in the wisdom of the ages and in myself. Then I might perhaps find peace and clarity. But that would be no great feat. It is right here, in this very place, in the here and now, that I must find them. But it is all so terribly difficult, and I feel so heavyhearted.

Afternoon on the heath. His fine strong head staring into the distance, and I, "What are you thinking of?" and he, "Of the demons that plague mankind." (I had just told him how Klaas had beaten his daughter half to death because she had failed to bring him the poison he had asked for.) He was sitting under an overhanging tree, my head in his lap, and all of a sudden I said, or rather I didn't say it, it just burst out of me, "And now I would very much like an undemonic kiss." And he said, "You'll have to come and get it." And abruptly I got up, wishing I hadn't said anything, but then suddenly we were lying there in the heather, mouth upon mouth. And he said, "Do you call this undemonic?"

But what does a kiss really mean in our kind of relationship? It hangs, as it were, in the air. It makes me long for the whole man, and yet I don't want the whole man. I don't love him at all as a man, that's the maddening thing, so does it all come down to my confounded desire to be important, to want to own someone? To want to own his body, while I already have his spirit, which is much more important? Is it that confounded unhealthy tradition that insists that, when two people of the opposite sex are in close contact, they must necessarily want to have physical contact as well? That feeling is ingrained in me. My immediate reaction on meeting a man is invariably to gauge his sexual possibilities. I recognize this as a bad habit that must be stamped out. He is probably better at self-control than I am, though he, too, has to fight his erotic impulses. Sometimes it all seems so silly, just as if we were making life difficult on purpose, when everything should be so simple.

All the melons will probably have gone by now. I feel as if I were moldering inside, as if I were plugged up, and my body hurts. But don't delude yourself, Etty, it's not really your body, it's your ravaged little soul that afflicts you.

In a little while I shall no doubt be writing how beautiful life really is and how happy I am, but at the moment I can't even imagine what that feels like.

I still lack a basic tune; a steady undercurrent; the inner source that feeds me keeps drying up, and worse still, I think much too much.

My ideas hang on me like outsize clothes into which I still have to grow. My mind lags behind my intuition. This is not altogether a bad thing. But it means that my mind or my reason, or whatever you care to call it, must sometimes work overtime in order to seize the various premonitions by their coattails. A host of vague ideas keep clamoring for concrete formulation. I must stop and listen to myself, sound my own depths, eat well, and sleep properly if I am to keep my balance, or it will turn into something altogether too Dostoyevskian. But alas the emphasis these days is on speed, not on rest.

*Deventer, Friday morning, quarter past ten.* [ . . . ] Still no letter from S., the villain. Would just love to be with him there in Wageningen, in that cluttered household with the many pious daughters.

When I came downstairs, Mother's first words to me were, "I really do feel awful." It's so strange. Father has only to utter the smallest sigh and my heart just about breaks, but when Mother says with great pathos, "I really do feel awful, I couldn't sleep a wink again," and so on, I remain basically untouched.

I have no idea what I shall do today. I can't work in this house, I have no quiet spot I can call my own here, and I can't settle down to anything. I shall try to get as much rest as possible.

"Stop whining, for goodness' sake, you shrew, you nag, carrying on like that." Such are my inner reactions when my mother sits down to have a chat with me. My mother is someone who would try the patience of a saint. I do my best to look at her objectively, and I try to be fond of her, but then suddenly I'll find myself saying emphatically, "What a ridiculous and silly person you are." It's so wrong of me, I don't live here, after all, I just allow myself to vegetate, and I put off my life until I have gone again. I have no impetus here to do any real work, it is as if every bit of energy were being sucked out of me. It is now eleven o'clock, and all I have done is to hang about on this chilly window seat, looking at the uncleared breakfast table and listening to my mother's pathetic complaints about butter coupons and her poor health, etc. And yet she is not really a shallow woman. That's the real tragedy of it. She wears you out with all her unsolved problems and her quickly changing moods; she is in a chaotic and pitiful state, which is reflected all about her in the utterly disorganized household. And yet she is convinced that she is an excellent housewife, driving everyone crazy with her perpetual fussing over the housekeeping. As the days go by here, my head feels more and more leaden. Well, all one can do is just get on with it. Life in this house is bogged down in petty details. They smother you, and nothing important ever happens. I would degenerate into a real melancholic if I were to stay here for any length of time. There is nothing one can do either to help or to change things. The two of them are so capricious. One evening, when I gave them a glowing account of S. and his work, they did seem quite enthusiastic and responded with some imagination and humor. And I went to bed with such a warm feeling and thought to myself what nice people they really are. But next day it was all suspicion and feeble jokes again. It was as if they had lost confidence in their own enthusiasm, and I felt badly let down. Well, Etty, you're just going to have to pick yourself up again. Of course, my stomachache doesn't make me feel any brighter. I think I'll have a nap this afternoon and then go to the library to have a closer look at Pfister's writings. When all is said and done, I must be grateful to have all this time to myself, so let me use it well in God's name, silly girl that I am. And now enough of this scribbling.

*11:00 P.M.* I am beginning to think that it's going to develop into a very important friendship—"friendship" in its deepest and fullest sense. I feel very serious. It's not the kind of seriousness that floats above reality and later seems unnatural and overdone. At least I don't think so. When I received his letter at six this evening—I had just come back from Gorssel soaked to the skin—I had no inner contact with it at all. I was dead tired, physically as well as mentally, and did not really know what to make of the letter. And then I curled up on my bed and looked carefully at the familiar handwriting once more and was filled with such a staunch, strong feeling about our relationship. And I sensed how important he would be to my further spiritual growth, if only I could keep facing up honestly to myself, to him, and to the many problems that are bound to crop up now and then in our relationship. A momentous discovery. I will have to dare to live life with all the seriousness it demands and without thinking that I'm being pompous, sentimental, or affected. And I must not look at him as an end but as a means to growth and maturity. I must not want to possess him. It is true that women seek the concrete reality of the body, not the abstraction of the spirit. Woman's main interest is the ideal man; man's is the world at large. Can woman shift her focus without losing her own power, without doing violence to her real being? These and many other questions were prompted by his letter, which had a most fruitful effect on me.

Standing by another human being. Friendship, too, must have a direction.

Our house is a remarkable mixture of barbarism and culture. Spiritual riches lie within grasp, but they are left unused and unguarded, are carelessly scattered about. It is depressing, it is tragicomic, I don't know what kind of madhouse this really is, but I know that no human being can flourish here.

I don't seem to be putting everyday things down on paper. Clearly they are not uppermost in my mind.

*Wednesday.* [ . . . ] Cold-blooded, icy objectivity is something my nature prevents me from attaining. I am too full of emotion for that. But I no longer go to pieces under the strain of all my disparate feelings. Daan has fallen to his death from an airplane. So many of our most promising, vigorous young men are dying day and night. I don't know how to take it. With all the suffering there is, you begin to feel ashamed of taking yourself and your moods so seriously. But you must continue to take yourself seriously, you must remain your own witness, marking well everything that happens in this world, never shutting your eyes to reality. You must come to grips with these terrible times and try to find answers to the many questions they pose. And perhaps the answers will help not only yourself but also others. I sometimes feel like a post standing in a raging sea, lashed on all sides by the waves. But I am firmly moored, and the years have helped to weather me. I want to live to see the future, to become the chronicler of the things that are happening now (downstairs they are screaming blue murder, with Father yelling, "Go, then!" and slamming the door; that, too, must be absorbed, and now I am suddenly crying since I am not all that objective really and no one can breathe properly in this house; all right, make the best of it then); oh yes, a chronicler. I notice that, over and above all my subjective suffering, I have an irrepressible objective curiosity, a passionate interest in everything that touches this world and its people and my own motives. I have stopped crying. But my head still throbs. It is sheer hell in this house. I would have to be quite a writer to describe it properly. Anyhow, I sprang from this chaos, and it is my business to pull myself out of it. S. calls it "building with noble material"; he's a real treasure.

I am sometimes so distracted by all the appalling happenings round me that it's far from easy to find the way back to myself. And yet that's what I must do. I mustn't let myself be ground down by the misery outside.

A poem by Rilke is as real and as important as a young man falling out of an airplane. That's something I must engrave on my heart. All that happens happens in this world of ours, and you must not leave one thing out for the sake of another. Now go to sleep. Accept your inner conflicts, try to bridge them, to simplify them, for then your life will become simpler as well. Mull them all over, and perhaps they'll fall into place.

*11:00 P.M.* This is it, a moment of rest, a lull in the storm. I don't feel compelled to think any longer. It could of course be due to the four aspirins I took.

From a dialogue between Father and me on a walk along the Singel:

I: "I feel sorry for any woman who has anything to do with Mischa."[14]

Father: "The boy happens to be in circulation, what can you do about it?"

*23 August 1941, Saturday night.* Things are getting me down. I shall have to make a careful record of my moods again. It can't be just this stupid cold in my head alone that makes everything look so black. But what is the truth of the matter? On Thursday night in the train from Arnhem back here, everything was fine. Outside, night was falling, silent, all-embracing, and majestic. And inside, the cramped compartment was full of workers, noisy and lively. I sat withdrawn in my dark corner, my right eye looking at the peaceful scenery and my left eye at the expressive heads and graphic gestures of my fellow passengers. Yes, I loved it all, life and people. And then the long walk from Amstel station through the near pitch-darkness of the all but enchanted town. Quite suddenly I had the impression that I wasn't alone, that there were two of us. I felt as if I consisted of two people who were squashed tightly together and felt so good and so warm as a result. I was in such close touch with myself, full of inner warmth, and felt utterly self-sufficient. And then I had a long friendly chat with myself and walked happily down all the little Amstel side streets, completely immersed in myself. And I discovered with no small satisfaction that I got on very well with myself. And next day the feeling was still there. And yesterday afternoon when I went to buy S.'s cheese and walked through beautiful South Amsterdam, I felt like an old Jew, wrapped up in a cloud. No doubt that's recorded somewhere in our mythology: a Jew moving along, wrapped up in a cloud. It was a cloud of my own thoughts and feelings that enveloped and accompanied me, and I felt so warm and protected and safe. And now I have a cold in my head and I'm uneasy, uncomfortable, and cross. The incomprehensible thing is that I have taken against people I'm normally so fond of; I feel negative about everything, keep carping and complaining. And all this must be the direct result of a blocked nose! After all, it's not really me, this dislike of my fellow men. When I feel wretched physically, I ought really to put a stop to my thought machine, which, at times like this, begins to work extra hard, disparaging everything that can be disparaged. In any case, it would only be common sense to go to bed now, I really feel rather ill. It is probably as well that my actions just now do not reflect my thoughts. Hans was due to come back home tonight, and the very thought exasperated me. Whenever I feel antisocial he is always the one directly in line of my dislike, probably because we share the same house. And so I wasn't looking forward to his homecoming, especially as I thought him a deadly dull, slow-witted, plodding sort of fellow. And then in he came, wholesome and hearty from the sailing camp, and I suddenly realized that I was actually quite pleased and happy to sit down and have a talk with him, that his tanned face was fresh and interesting with its candid yet vague blue eyes. I leaped up, cooked him some soup, chatted some more, and found that I really like him, and for that matter every single one of God's creatures. I don't think there was anything forced in my attitude; no, it was rather that inner exasperation of mine that was out of character. It's not really part of me. So I really ought to keep it under control. Which means that when I can no longer work or read, as I can't tonight, I must go to sleep.

*26 August, Tuesday evening.* There is a really deep well inside me. And in it dwells God. Sometimes I am there, too. But more often stones and grit block the well, and God is buried beneath. Then He must be dug out again.

I imagine that there are people who pray with their eyes turned heavenward. They seek God outside themselves. And there are those who bow their head and bury it in their hands. I think that these seek God inside.

*4 September [1941], Thursday night, 10:30.* Life is composed of tales waiting to be retold by me. Oh, what nonsense—I don't really know anything. I am unhappy again. I can quite see why people get drunk or go to bed with a total stranger. But that isn't really my way. I must keep sober, keep a clear head. And do it alone. It is just as well that that villain wasn't in tonight. Otherwise I should have run to him again saying, "Please help me, I am so unhappy, I am bursting apart at the seams." And I expect others to straighten things out for themselves! "Listen to your inner voice." Yes, indeed. So I withdrew to the farthest corner of my little room, sat on the floor, squeezed myself in between two walls, my head bowed. Yes. And sat there. Absolutely still, contemplating my navel so to speak, in the pious hope that new sources of inspiration would bubble up inside me. My heart was once again frozen and would not melt; every outlet was blocked and my brain squeezed by a large vice. And what I am waiting for whenever I sit huddled up like that is for something to give, for something to start flowing inside me.

I really took on too heavy a burden when I read all those letters from his girlfriend. I wish I were completely uncomplicated, like that man tonight, or like a field of grass. I still take myself too seriously. On days like this I am sure that no one suffers as much as I do. Imagine somebody in pain all over his body, unable to bear anyone touching him even with the tip of a finger—that's the feeling in my soul, or whatever you want to call it. The smallest pressure causes pain. A soul without a skin, as Annie Romein once wrote about Carry van Bruggen.[15] I would like to travel to faraway places. And see other people, who need have no names. Sometimes I feel as if the people with whom I have really close contact rob me of my vision. My vision of what? Etty, you really are being a bit devious and not very conscientious. You should be able to trace the real reason for your melancholy, and for your awful headache. But alas, you're not really interested in doing so. You are just plain lazy. Lord, grant me a little humility.

Am I too busy? I want to get to know this century of ours inside and out. I feel it every day anew. I run my fingertips along the contours of our age. Or is that pure fiction?

But I always project myself back into reality. I make myself confront everything that crosses my path, which sometimes leaves me feeling battered. It is just as if I let myself crash violently into myself, leaving dents and scratches. But I imagine that it has to be like that. I sometimes feel I am in some blazing purgatory and that I am being forged into something else. But into what? I can only be passive, allow it to happen to me. But then I also have the feeling that all the problems of our age and of mankind in general have to be battled out inside my little head. And that means being active. Well, the worst of it is now past. I tore round the Skating Club like a drunken fool and addressed a few stupid remarks to the moon. The moon, too, wasn't born yesterday. No doubt he has looked down on plenty of characters like me, seen a thing or two. Well, well. A hard life is in store for me. Sometimes I don't feel like carrying on. At the moments when I feel I know exactly what is going to happen to me, what life will be like, I get so tired and feel no need to experience things as they come. But life always gains the upper hand, and then I find everything "interesting" and exciting again, and I am full of courage and full of ideas. One must give things a rest, but I wilt during the pauses, or so it seems to me. And now goodnight.

It just occurred to me. Maybe I take myself too seriously, and I also want others to do likewise? S. for instance. I want him to realize how much I suffer and at the same time try to hide it from him. Could this be due to the antagonism I so often feel toward him?

*Friday morning, nine o'clock.* Right now I feel like someone recovering from a serious illness. Light in the head and a bit shaky on the legs. It really was a bit much yesterday. The fact is I don't lead a simple enough inner life. I indulge in excesses, bacchanalia of the spirit. Perhaps I identify too much with everything I read and study. Someone like Dostoyevsky still shatters me. I really must become a bit simpler. Let myself live a bit more. Not always insist on the results straightaway. I know what the remedy is, though: just to crouch huddled up on the ground in a corner and listen to what is going on inside me. Thinking gets you nowhere. It may be a fine and noble aid in academic studies, but you can't think your way out of emotional difficulties. That takes something altogether different. You have to make yourself passive then, and just listen. Reestablish contact with a slice of eternity.

I really ought to be simpler and less grandiloquent in my work, as well. When I do a simple Russian translation, the whole of Russia spreads out before my mind's eye and I feel I must write another *Brothers Karamazov,* at the very least. I make very high demands on myself and in inspired moments consider myself quite capable of meeting them, but inspiration doesn't last forever, and in my more mundane moods I am filled with sudden fears that I might not fulfill the promise of those "exalted" moments. But why do I have to achieve things? All I need do is to "be," to live and to try being a little bit human. One can't control everything with the brain; must allow one's emotions and intuitions free play as well. Knowledge is power, and that's probably why I accumulate knowledge, out of a desire to be important. I don't really know. But Lord, give me wisdom, not knowledge. Or rather the knowledge that leads to wisdom and true happiness and not the kind that leads to power. A little peace, a lot of kindness, and a little wisdom—whenever I have these inside me I feel I am doing well. That's why I was so hurt when the sculptress, Fri Heil, said to S. that she found me a real Tartar and that all I needed was a wild horse to carry me through the steppes. Human beings don't know much about themselves, do they?

Hertha[16] said in one of her letters to S., "Yesterday you laid your hand on me."

Reality is not entirely real to me, and that is why I can't get down to doing things, fail to appreciate their true importance and significance. A single line of Rilke's seems more real to me than moving house or anything like that. I ought to spend all my life behind a desk. Yet I don't really think I am a foolish dreamer. Reality does fascinate me, although only from behind my desk, not in the living and the doing. To understand ideas and people you must go out into the real world, onto the ground on which everything lives and grows.

*Tuesday morning, 9 September.* S. is the moving force behind quite a few women. In one of her letters, Henny[17] calls him, "My Mercedes, my lovely, great big, darling Mercedes." On the floor above him lives the "little one." He says that when she wrestles with him she is like a huge cat treading warily for fear of inflicting pain. On Friday night he rang Riet, and his voice sang over the wires as he addressed that eighteen-year-old child, "Hello, Rieeet." And meanwhile his other hand kept stroking my face, and on the table lay the letter from the girl he wants to marry, with the words "My darling Jul" right across the top, I couldn't help staring at them.

I have been so sad, so very, very sad these last few days. Why, I wonder? I am not sad all the time, I manage to shake it off now and then, but later I drop back into it.

I have never met anybody who had as much love, strength, and unshakable self-confidence as S. That Friday he said something like, "If I were to devote all my life and strength to just one person I would destroy them." Perhaps that's why I sometimes feel I am being buried under his weight. I don't really know. I sometimes think I ought to be running to the ends of the earth to rid myself of him, but I also know I must get him out of my system without running away. And quite often he is no problem at all. Then everything seems so right. At other times—now, for instance—he makes me feel ill. Why should that be? After all, he is neither a mysterious nor a complicated character. Is it the enormous amount of love he bestows on such endless numbers of people and which I would far rather have all to myself? There are indeed moments when that is in fact exactly what I want—his concentrated, undivided love. But is that not being much too physical? And much too selfish?

I must just try to recapture something of that Friday evening. I had the feeling then that I had seen right into the heart of this mystery man, or rather of this non-mystery man. That was the evening when he handed me the key to the secret of his personality. And for a few days it was as if I had locked him into my own heart, carrying him with me never to lose him again. Why am I so out of touch with him, and why do I want nothing more to do with him? Has he become more than I feel I can handle? When he sits facing me, large, gentle, with a kind of sumptuous sensuality about him and yet so full of human kindness, then he sometimes brings to mind the private life of a Roman emperor, I don't know why. There is something so voluptuous and yet so infinitely warm and good that lies over his whole figure—much too much for one person so that it spreads out over a vast area. Why then does he remind me of a decadent Roman? I really do not know.

Stomachache and depression and that taut sensation inside me and the feeling of being crushed under a heavy weight are the price I have to pay for my grasping insistence on knowing everything about life, on being aware of everything. Sometimes it becomes too much. When I took that character test, it appeared that I was someone who demanded everything of life but also assimilated everything. I shall, no doubt, cope with my present troubles as well; my inner traffic jams are certainly part of it all, but they must be cut to a minimum, otherwise I really can't go on. When I cycled home yesterday, so unspeakably sad and as heavy as lead inside, and heard an airplane overhead, I was suddenly struck by the notion that a bomb might put an end to my life, and I felt liberated. It's been happening more often, that feeling that it's easier not to go on . . .

*Thursday morning, nine o'clock.* [ . . . ] Yes, we women, we foolish, idiotic, illogical women, we all seek Paradise and the Absolute. And yet my brain, my capable brain, tells me that there are no absolutes, that everything is relative, endlessly diverse, and in eternal motion, and that it is precisely for that reason that life is so exciting and fascinating, but also so very, very painful. We women want to perpetuate ourselves in a man. Yes, I want him to say, "Darling, you are the only one and I shall love you for evermore." I know, of course, that there is no such thing as eternal love, but unless he declares it for me, nothing has any meaning. And the stupid thing is that I don't really want him, don't want him forever or as the only one in my life, and yet I demand it of him. Do I demand absolute love from others because I'm unable to give it myself? And then I always expect the same level of intensity, when I know from my own experience that it cannot last. And I take flight just as soon as I notice the other becoming lukewarm. That's an inferiority complex of course, something like: if I can't inspire him enough to be on fire for me at all times, then I'd rather have nothing at all. And it's so damned illogical, I must rid myself of it. After all, I wouldn't know what to do if somebody really was on fire for me all day long. It would annoy me and bore me and make me feel tied down. Oh, Etty, Etty!

Last night he said, "I believe I am your stepping stone to a truly great love." Strange, isn't it, for I have been a stepping stone for so many others.

And while what he says may be true, somewhere it hurts terribly and his words trouble me greatly. I think I know why. I want him to be madly jealous at the thought that a great lover may enter my life one day. He must love me eternally and me alone. It's a kind of compulsion with me. During the last few days I have been feeling extremely sensual. Last night in particular. And when he rang at nine o'clock saying, "Would you still like to come over?" I went with joy and physical longing and surrender. But you are fooling yourself, my girl, if you think it was all to do with sensuality, for we did not fly directly into each other's arms. First we talked. And I hung on his words, delighting in the clear and pertinent way he expressed himself and feeling that I was learning an enormous amount. And truly this spiritual contact gives me much greater satisfaction than the physical one. Perhaps I tend to overrate the physical aspect, no doubt because of the fairy tale that it is so feminine.

Odd, isn't it? Right now I feel that all I want is to fling myself into his arms, and just be a woman, or perhaps even less, just a piece of cherished flesh. I dwell too much on my sensuality; after all it only lasts a few days at a time, this rising wave. And that little bit of sensuality is what I then try to project onto the whole of life, until it overshadows all the rest. Then I need words of dedication like "You alone for evermore." I'm sure I'm expressing myself badly, but the main thing is to get it down on paper. I dwell so much on the importance of sensuality because I tend to fan the little bit of warmth people now and then seek from each other with such exalted vows as "I love you forever." Yet one should accept things as they are and not try to lift them to impossible heights; only if you let them be will they reveal their true worth.

*11:00 P.M.* Some days seem very long, for so much happens in them. I am utterly content at the moment, sitting behind this desk. My head rests heavily on my left hand; I am filled with well-being and resolve. The chirology demonstration in Tide's room was fun. Before I'd have thought it rather weird. So many women. Yet it was really enjoyable, lively and stimulating. Swiep[18] supplied the pears, Gera[19] the cakes, and I the depth psychology. And when it was all over, Tide, indefatigable as ever, on her feet since five o'clock in the morning, went back to work.

I can't write anything of consequence right now, there is too much chitchat going on in the room for that. Hans, Bernard, and Han are doing a puzzle. In the past I could never have sat down in a corner writing or reading if there were several people in the room—I was much too nervous—but now I sit here so sure of myself that the others don't distract me in the least. It would be the same even at a mass meeting, I'm sure. If I acted my age, I would retire to my virginal bed in my little room, but my social instinct as well as habit, a friendly little habit, make me linger in this bed. Well, well. I've also swallowed three aspirins, that's probably why I feel so snug and drowsy. Tomorrow back to work properly again. Potential schizoid that I am with an "unholy father-complex," I shall keep my nose to the grindstone again tomorrow, writing that letter for S., then preparing the Russian lesson, and I really ought to ring up Aleida

Schot.[20] But first I must have a good sleep. Life is worth living. God, You are with me after all, if only a little bit.

*Saturday night.* [ . . . ] Suarès on Stendhal: "He has severe attacks of melancholy, betrays it to his friends, conceals it in his books. His spirit is a mask for his passions. He coins witticisms so as to be left alone with his exalted feelings—"

That is your disease: you want to capture life in formulas of your own. You want to embrace all aspects of life with your intellect instead of allowing yourself to be embraced by life. You want to create the world all over again each time, instead of enjoying it as it is. There is something compulsive about it all.

*6 October [1941], Monday morning, nine o'clock.* One sentence let drop at midday yesterday still lingers. I asked Henny, "Tide, have you never wanted to get married?" And she replied, "God has never sent me a man." Should I adopt the same criterion? It would have to run like this: if I live by my own lights I shall probably never marry. Anyway, it's not something to worry about. All I need do is listen honestly to my inner voice, and I should be able to tell at any given moment whether or not a man has been "sent to me by God." But I mustn't start brooding about it. Or temporize, or jump into marriage for all the wrong reasons. I must have confidence and hear my inner voice and not think, "Won't I be lonely later on in life if I don't take a husband now? Will I be able to earn my own living? Will I finish up an old maid? What will the world say, will they be sorry for me if I don't have a husband?"

Last night I asked Han in bed, "Do you think someone like me ought to get married? Am I a real woman?" Sex for me is not all that important, although sometimes I give the impression that it is. Isn't it cheating to allow men to be taken in by that impression and then be unable to give them what they want? I am not really an earthy woman, at least not sexually. I am no tigress, and that sometimes gives me a feeling of inferiority. My primitive physical passion has been diverted in many different ways and weakened by all sorts of intellectualizations, which I am sometimes ashamed of. What is primitive in me is my warmth; I have a sort of primitive love and primitive sympathy for people, for all people. I don't think I am cut out for one man. I even find the loving of one man a bit childish sometimes. Nor could I be faithful to one man. Not because of other men, but because I myself am made up of so many people. I am now twenty-seven, and it feels as if I have had my fill of loving and being loved by men. I feel very, very old. It is no accident that the man I have been living with these past five years is of an age that precludes any common future, and that my best friend plans to marry a young girl in London. I don't think my path will be: one man and one love. But I do have a strong erotic streak and a great need for caresses and tenderness. And I have never had to go short of these. I notice I'm not able to put what I felt last night and this morning into proper words.

"God has never sent me a man."

My intuition stops me from saying yes to a man for life, and my inner voice must be my sole guide in everything, but particularly in these matters. I must not not-marry just because one sees so few happy marriages. That would merely be out of a sort of contrariness and anxiety and lack of faith; no, if you do not marry it must be because you know that it is not for you. And do not take comfort in the spiteful remarks of spinsters, that marriage is not as good as people make out. I do believe in happy marriages, and perhaps I could have one myself, but just let it come, don't have any theories about it, don't ask yourself what's best for you, and don't be calculating. If "God sends you a man," so be it, and if not, then so be it as well. But don't be bitter afterward and don't ever say, "I really ought to have done this or that." You must never ever say that, which is precisely why you must heed your inner voice now and turn a deaf ear to people who tell you otherwise. And now to work.

*Monday morning, 20 October.* They ate themselves to a standstill and clung ever more firmly to solid earth. This following one tomato sandwich, one apple syrup sandwich, and three cups of tea with real sugar. I tend to toy with asceticism, to think I would love to brave hunger and thirst, cold and heat. But it's all romantic nonsense, for as soon as it gets the least bit cold what I like best is to crawl into bed and not get out again.

Last night I told S. that all those books are really bad for me, some of them, anyway. That they make me lazy and passive, and I want to do nothing but read. I only remember one word from his reply: "corruption."

Sometimes it takes so much effort to get through the daily round—getting up, washing, exercises, putting on stockings without holes, laying the table, in short getting through the basics—that little is left over for other things. Yet when, like any other decent citizen, I get up on time, I feel proudly that I have achieved something marvelous. That's what I need desperately: discipline from without as long as my inner discipline is still so imperfect. If I stay in bed an extra hour in the morning, it doesn't mean I need more sleep, but simply that I'm unable to cope.

There is a strange little melody inside me that sometimes cries out for words. But through inhibition, lack of self-confidence, laziness, and goodness knows what else, that tune remains stifled, haunting me from within. Sometimes it wears me out completely. And then again it fills me with gentle, melancholy music.

Sometimes I want to flee with everything I possess into a few words, seek refuge in them. But there are still no words to shelter me. That is the real problem. I am in search of a haven, yet I must first build it for myself, stone by stone. Everyone seeks a home, a refuge. And I am always in search of a few words.

Sometimes I feel that every word spoken and every gesture made merely serve to exacerbate misunderstandings. Then what I would really like is to escape into a great silence and impose that silence on everyone else.

Do whatever your hand finds to do and don't take thought for the morrow. Make your bed and carry your dirty cups to the kitchen and face the rest as it comes. Get Tide some sunflowers today, teach that teenage girl some Russian pronunciation, and work the schizoid tendencies that elude your psychological powers of understanding out of your system. Do whatever your hand and spirit find to do, live every hour to the full, and stop fussing about with your thoughts and fears. I shall have to take your education in hand once again, my girl.

*21 October, after dinner.* It is a slow and painful process, this striving after true inner freedom. Growing more and more certain that there is no help or assurance or refuge in others. That the others are just as uncertain and weak and helpless as you are. You are always thrown back on to your own resources. There is nothing else. The rest is make-believe. But that fact has to be recognized over and over again. Especially since you are a woman. For woman always longs to lose herself in another. But that too is a fiction, albeit a beautiful one. There is no matching of lives. At least not for me. Perhaps for a few moments. But do those moments justify a lifetime together? Can those few moments cement a shared existence? All they can do is give you a little strength. And perhaps a little happiness. God knows, being alone is hard. For the world is inhospitable. In the past I used to dream of giving it to one person. But it was not to be. And when you reach such painful truths at the age of twenty-seven, you sometimes feel quite desperate and lonely and *anxious,* although independent and proud at the same time. I have confidence in myself, and I shall manage by myself. The only measure you have is yourself. And the only responsibility you can shoulder in life is responsibility for yourself. But you must do it with all your strength. And now to ring up S.

*Wednesday morning, eight o'clock.* Oh, Lord, give me fewer thoughts first thing in the morning and a little more cold water and exercises.

Life cannot be captured in a few axioms. And that is just what I keep trying to do. But it won't work, for life is full of endless nuances and cannot be captured in just a few formulas. Not that you yourself cannot become simpler . . .

*Thursday morning.* Fool that you are. You try to draw yourself life-size in words, in colorful, sweeping words. But no words will ever be able to contain all of you. God's world and God's heaven are so wide.

Back into darkness, into your mother's womb, into *the collective.* Break free, find your own voice, vanquish the chaos within. I am pulled to and fro between these two poles.

*24 October.* The Levi girl is due for a lesson this morning. We must not infect each other with our bad moods. Tonight new measures against the Jews. I have allowed myself to be upset and depressed about it for half an hour. In the past I would have consoled myself by reading a novel and abandoning my work. Now I must finish working out Mischa's psychoanalysis. Wonderful that he is taking it so well. One must not be too optimistic, but he deserves help. As long as one can get through to him, if only through the smallest chink, one must continue to try. Perhaps it will have some effect in his life. Don't expect wonders, but keep hoping for small advances instead. For two days I have done nothing but work and ward off my moods.

How adult of me!

Yet I am so attached to this life of mine.

What do you mean by "this life"? The comfortable life you now lead? Whether you are truly attached to life in the raw, in whatever form it may come, is something the years alone will be able to tell. There is energy enough inside you. There is also this: "Whether you spend your life laughing or crying, it is still your life." But I am still attached to Western notions of the good life: being healthy, growing wiser and stronger, learning to stand on one's own two feet. But now to work.

*After a conversation with Jaap:*[21] We occasionally throw each other crumbs of information about ourselves, but I don't think we understand each other.

*Thursday morning [10 November 1941].* Mortal fear in every fiber. Complete collapse. Lack of self-confidence. Aversion. Panic.

*11 November, morning.* It feels as if weeks have gone by and as if I myself have gone through a great deal, and yet I keep finding myself back with the same problem: the urge—fiction or fantasy, whatever you want to call it—to possess one man for life. It's something I must eradicate. That hunger for the absolute must be crushed inside me. And the belief that without it we grow poorer. We grow richer, more complex, more diversified. To accept the ups and downs in human relationships and to see them as positive features, not as causes for sadness. Not wanting to possess another does not mean ignoring him. Granting another complete freedom, even inner freedom, does not mean washing your hands of him. I'm only just beginning to understand all that passion in my relationship with Max.[22] It was sheer desperation, because I knew he was unobtainable, and that very knowledge spurred me on, no doubt because I tried to reach him in the wrong way. Too absolute. And the absolute does not exist. Life and human relationships are full of subtleties. I know that there is nothing absolute or objectively valid, that knowledge must seep into your blood, into your self, not just into your head, that you must live it. And here I always come back to what one should strive after with all one's might: one must marry one's feelings to one's beliefs and ideas. That is probably the only way to achieve a measure of harmony in one's life.

*21 November.* It is odd that while I have been so full of creative impulses, busy covering sheets of paper with a novel—The girl who could not kneel, or something like that, and a piece about the Levi girl—and so many, many other things, I should suddenly write this: "I leap up from the divan's blue coverlet as if bitten by an adder, a burning question on my lips, *the* question . . ." And while I ostensibly ponder problems of ethics and truth and God Himself, I have developed an "eating problem." Something for analysis, no doubt. I ruin my digestion simply by eating too much. Through lack of self-control, in other words. I know I have to watch myself, but I am sometimes seized by a greed so powerful that it brooks no argument. I realize full well at the time that I am going to have to pay dearly for that extra little morsel or that one bite too many, and yet I can't stop myself. I am convinced that this eating problem can be rooted out. Ultimately it is purely symbolic. Greed probably figures in my intellectual life as well, as I attempt to absorb a massive amount of information with consequent mental indigestion.

First I shall have to get to the bottom of it all. And it will probably turn out to have some connection with my dear mama. Mother always talks about food as if nothing else mattered. "Come on, have a little more. You can't have had enough. How thin you've grown." I still remember watching my mother eating at some housewives' function years ago. I was sitting on the balcony of the little theater hall in Deventer. Mother was at a long table in the middle of a crowd of other domesticated ladies, wearing a blue lace dress. She sat down to eat. She was completely engrossed. She ate with utter abandon. As I watched her from the balcony I suddenly felt quite revolted.

Her gluttony gave her the air of being terrified of missing out on anything. There was something terribly pathetic about her as well as something bestially repulsive. That's how it seemed to me. In fact she was just an ordinary housewife in a blue lace dress eating her soup. If I could only fathom what I really felt deep down, why I observed her so closely, then I would understand a great deal about my mother. That fear of missing out on things makes you miss out on everything. Keeps you from reality.

Psychologically, you could put it like this, if you're interested in the musings of a layman, that is: I have an unresolved antipathy for my mother, and that is precisely why I do the things I abhor in her. At heart, I am not deeply concerned about food, although it has its pleasurable and social aspects. But that's not the problem. It is willingly and knowingly, or rather against one's better judgment, ruining one's digestion time and again. And the opposite as well: longing for the ascetic life—black bread, fresh water, and a little fruit.

What S. blames analysts for is their lack of real love, their materialism. "You cannot heal disturbed people without love." And yet I could imagine their problems being tackled in a purely objective manner. I agree with S., though, that an analysis that goes on for years is a bad thing. He thinks that as a result people are rendered unfit for society. I am putting it all very crudely of course. I really don't have the time to go into it all right now. The whole thing is so complex, and I am only a layman.

*Saturday morning.* I hope for, and at the same time I dread, the day that I shall be completely alone with myself and with a blank sheet of paper. Then I shall do nothing but write. I haven't dared do it yet. I don't know why. When I was at the concert with S. on Wednesday, indeed whenever I see a lot of people together, I want to write a novel. During the interval I felt compelled to get hold of a piece of paper and to jot something down. I didn't know what. To spin out a few ideas. Instead, S. dictated something about a patient. Interesting enough. And bizarre as well. But it meant that I had to ignore my own promptings, my desire to give an account of myself. I have this ever-present need to write but not yet the courage to get on with it. I think I tend to ignore my own inner needs. I sometimes get the feeling that my personality is growing stronger, but all I demonstrate to others is unwavering amiability and concern and benevolence even when it means effacing myself. The theory is that we should all put a good face on things, be sociable, and not bother others with our moods. In fact, when I suppress so much I become all the more antisocial: I don't want to see or speak to anyone for days.

There is a sort of lamentation and loving-kindness as well as a little wisdom somewhere inside me that cry to be let out. Sometimes several different dialogues run through me at the same time, images and figures, moods, a sudden flash of something that must be my very own truth. Love for human beings that must be hard fought for. Not through politics or a party, but in myself. Still a lot of false shame to get rid of. And there is God. The girl who could not kneel but learned to do so on the rough coconut matting in an untidy bathroom. Such things are often more intimate even than sex. The story of the girl who gradually learned to kneel is something I would love to write in the fullest possible way.

I protest too much. I have all the time in the world to write. More time than anyone else, probably. But there is that inner vacillation. Why, I wonder? Because I think I must come out with nothing but brilliant ideas? Because I haven't yet worked it all out? But that can only come with practice. "Above all be true to yourself." S. is quite right. I am so fond of him and at the same time have such antipathy for him. And this antipathy is related to deeper things, things that are beyond me.

*Sunday morning, ten o'clock.* Remarkable, this connection between certain moods and menstruation. Yesterday evening I was certainly flying high. And tonight it is suddenly as if my bloodstream has been transformed. Life feels altogether different. At first you don't know what is happening, and then suddenly it dawns on you: that premenstrual feeling. I used to think: I don't want any children, so why must I go through this senseless monthly performance, put up with all the inconvenience that goes along with it. And in a rash and pleasure-loving moment I thought of having my womb removed. But you have to accept yourself as you were created, and you simply can't say that it's nothing more than a nuisance. The interaction of body and soul is a most mysterious thing. The remarkable, dreamy and yet illuminating mood I was in last night and this morning was due to this very change in my body.

My sudden eating complex elicited a dream last night. It was very clear, at least I thought so, but now that I want to write it all down much of it has gone. A lot of people round a table with S. at the head. He said something like, "Why don't you go and visit other people?" And I, "Because of all that bother about eating." And then he gave me that famous look of his that I would need a whole lifetime to put on paper, a look he has when he is annoyed and which makes his face as expressive as it can possibly be. And I read in it something like, "So, that's what you're really like, eating is all that matters to you." And I suddenly got a feeling of, "He's seen right through me; now he knows exactly how materialistic I am." I haven't described this dream properly, it cannot be done. However, what can be described is the sudden realization: now he has seen through me, knows what I am really like. And the horror of it.

Something of last night's "illuminating" expansiveness lingers on. Peace and space again for everything. A little love and lots of affection for Han. And no more antipathy for S. Not even for the work. I shall go my own way in the end, and the detour has done me no harm. What is the hurry, after all? Life grows slowly toward fulfillment—that sort of feeling. If only it were true. This whole wide, spacious day lies spread out before me. I shall let myself slide very slowly into it, without hindrance, without haste. Gratitude, fully conscious deep gratitude suddenly for this bright, spacious room with the wide divan, the desk and the books, the peaceful old, and yet very young, man. And the friend with the fine, full mouth who has no secrets from me and who can nevertheless become so secretive, in the background. But above all, clarity and peace of mind and also confidence in myself. As if I had suddenly reached a clearing in a dense forest where I could lie down flat on my back and stare into the wide sky. In an hour's time it can all be quite different, I know. Particularly in this precarious state when my lower anatomy is in a ferment.

*Tuesday morning, half-past nine.* Something has happened to me, and I don't know if it's just a passing mood or something crucial. It is as if I had been pulled back abruptly to my roots, and had become a little more self-reliant and independent. Last night, cycling through cold, dark Lairessestraat—if only I could repeat everything I babbled out then! Something like this:

"God, take me by Your hand, I shall follow You dutifully, and not resist too much. I shall evade none of the tempests life has in store for me, I shall try to face it all as best I can. But now and then grant me a short respite. I shall never again assume, in my innocence, that any peace that comes my way will be eternal. I shall accept all the inevitable tumult and struggle. I delight in warmth and security, but I shall not rebel if I have to suffer cold, should You so decree. I shall follow wherever Your hand leads me and shall try not to be afraid. I shall try to spread some of my warmth, of my genuine love for others, wherever I go. But we shouldn't boast of our love for others. We cannot be sure that it really exists. I don't want to be anything special, I only want to try to be true to that in me which seeks to fulfill its promise. I sometimes imagine that I long for the seclusion of a nunnery. But I know that I must seek You among people, out in the world."

And that is what I shall do, despite the weariness and dislike that sometimes overcome me. I vow to live my life out there to the full. Sometimes I think that my life is only just beginning. That the real difficulties are still to come, although at times I feel that I have struggled through so many already. I shall study and try to comprehend, I shall allow myself to become thoroughly perplexed by whatever comes my way and apparently diverts me, yes, I shall allow myself to be perplexed time and again perhaps, in order to arrive at greater certainty. Until I am no longer perplexed and a state of balance has been achieved, but with all paths still open to me. I don't know if I am able to be a good friend to others. And if I cannot be, because it is not in my nature, then I must face that as well. In any case I must not try to fool myself. And I must keep within my own limitations. And remember that I alone can set these.

It is as if my relationship with S. had suddenly changed. As if I had finally wrenched myself clear of him, when I had imagined I was perfectly free all along. I felt it deep down inside me then: my life must be completely independent. A few weeks ago when there was talk of all Jews being sent to a concentration camp in Poland, he turned to me and said, "Then we shall get married, so that we can stay together and at least do some good still." And although I realized he meant for our work, his words filled me with happiness and warmth and a feeling of great closeness to him. But that feeling has gone now. I don't know what it is, a sudden sense of complete emancipation from him, of continuing all by myself. No doubt a great deal of my energy is still invested in him. Last night on the cold bicycle ride, in a sudden flash of insight, I understood the depth of the intensity, the commitment I have made to this man and his work and his life. He has become an inseparable part of me. And with this new part of me I must now go on, but alone. Outwardly nothing is changed, of course. I remain his secretary, continue to take an interest in his work, but inwardly I am much less bound.

*The relationship of literature to life.* I must work things out for myself.

*Friday morning, 8:45.* Last night I felt that I must ask his forgiveness for all the ugly and rebellious thoughts I have had about him these last few days. I have gradually come to realize that on those days when you are at odds with your neighbors you are really at odds with yourself. "Thou shalt love thy neighbor as thyself." I know that the fault is always mine, not his. Our two lives happen to have quite different rhythms; one must allow people the freedom to be what they are. Trying to coerce others, of course, is quite undemocratic, but only too human. It is psychology that will probably pave the way to true freedom. We tend to forget that not only must we gain inner freedom from one another, but we must also leave the other free and abandon any fixed concept we may have of him in our imagination. There is scope enough for the imagination as it is, without our having to use it to shackle the people we love. Yesterday afternoon I cycled off to see him. At the corner of Apollolaan and Michelangelo I was suddenly overcome by the compelling urge to write something in my notebook, and there I stood, writing in the cold, about the fact that literature is so full of dead bodies and how strange that is. So many frivolous deaths, too. Well, how ridiculous if every time you are convinced that God knows what magnificent ideas are taking shape in your head, all that emerges is some incoherent ramblings on a few blue lines, on a street corner in the freezing cold! I walked into S.'s place, into those small, familiar rooms that he almost overwhelms with his size. Gera was there; we chatted a bit, and that feeling of ease crept over me again. And then, since I was still feeling out of sorts, I began to throw my coat, my hat, my gloves, my bag, my notebook, everything, across the room, to the astonished amusement of S. and Gera, who asked what was the matter with me this time. Whereupon I said, "Look, I don't feel up to it, I feel like breaking something, so thank your lucky stars that the flowerpots on the windowsill aren't smashed to bits." My outburst plainly did Gera good.

That was because I had exploded just as she must often have wanted to do but hadn't dared in front of him. "Well done," she said; my raising the roof probably expressed the kind of feeling that keeps flaring up in her and in most other people when they come up against a much stronger personality. We should never say to ourselves beforehand, not even five minutes beforehand, "I'm going to do so-and-so, and say such-and-such." I had planned everything I was going to say to him. Matters of principle. Objections to chirology, etc. All urgent and so important. And just before I came in the mood had changed so much that I scarcely wanted to say anything at all.

And as soon as Gera had gone, I at once had a quick wrestle with him, threw him onto the divan, nearly killed him, and then we were ready to get down to hard work. But instead he sat down suddenly in the big armchair in the corner so beautifully covered by Adri, and I curled up as always round his feet and we were suddenly having an animated discussion about the Jewish problem. And his words made me feel once again that I was drinking from a powerful source of energy. And I was once again face to face with that life of his, undistorted this time by my own irritation. I have recently been picking odd sentences from the Bible and endowing them with what for me is a new, meaningful, and experiential significance. God created Man in His own image. Love thy neighbor as thyself. Etcetera.

My relationship with my father is something I shall at long last have to tackle as well—with determination and love.

Mischa announced that Father would be arriving on Saturday evening. First reaction: Oh, my God. My freedom threatened. A nuisance. What am I to do with him? Instead of: How nice that this lovable man has managed to get away for a few days from his excitable spouse and his dull provincial town. How can I make things as pleasant as possible for him with my limited resources and means? Wretched, good-for-nothing, indolent worm that I am. Oh yes, the cap fits. Always think of yourself first, of your precious time—time you only use to pump more book-learning into your addled brain. "What shall it profit a man if he has no love?" Fine theories to make you feel comfortable and noble, but in practice you shrink from even the smallest act of love. No, what is needed here is not a small act of love. It is something fundamental and important and difficult. To love your parents deep inside. To forgive them for all the trouble they have given you by their very existence: by tying you down, by adding the burden of their own complicated lives to your own. Well, no matter. Now I must make up Pa Han's bed, prepare the lesson for that girl Levi, etc. But the main item for this weekend's program: to love my father deeply and sincerely and to forgive him for disturbing my pleasure-seeking life. When all is said and done I think a great deal of him, but in a rather complicated way: my love for him is forced, spasmodic, and so mixed with compassion that my heart almost breaks. Masochistic compassion. A love that leads to outbursts of sadness and pity, but not to simple acts of tenderness. Instead there is much effusiveness and a desire to please so violent that each day of one of his visits once cost me a whole tube of aspirins. But that was a long time ago. The last time things were much better. But still, there is always that hunted feeling as well as the related wish that he wouldn't always bring his troubles to me. And for that I must learn to forgive him this time. And also learn to think and genuinely mean: How nice that you have managed to get away. Well, that's a prayer for this morning.

*Sunday morning, 10:30.* [ . . . ] There is still not enough room inside me for all my inner and outer conflicts. The moment I come to terms with any single one of them, I become disloyal to the rest. On Friday evening a discussion between S. and L. about Christ and the Jews. Two philosophies, sharply defined, brilliantly presented, rounded off, defended with passion and vigor. But I can't help feeling that every hotly championed philosophy hides a little lie. That it must fall short of "the truth." And yet I myself will have to find a philosophy to live by, a fenced-in space of my own, violently seized and passionately defended. But then wouldn't that be giving life short change? The alternative may well be floundering in uncertainty and chaos. Be that as it may, after that discussion I went home feeling deeply stirred, although I couldn't help wondering, isn't it all a lot of nonsense? Why do people work themselves into such a passion? Aren't they deluding themselves? That doubt always looms at the back of my mind.

And then my father arrived. With so much love, so much tried and tested love. The day before, after that fervent morning prayer, I had suddenly felt happy and lighthearted. But when he eventually turned up on my doorstep, my little Papa, with the umbrella he had picked up instead of his own, a new checked tie, and a lot of small packets of sandwiches, seemingly helpless, I felt terribly self-conscious again. All my strength vanished, and I felt inhibited and terribly sad. And because I was still under the influence of last night's discussion, I could not give him the warmth he deserved. And there was no love to help—it had dried up completely. I was again all chaos and confusion inside. A few critical hours and the kind of relapse I used to have during the worst times. It helps me, I suppose, to reexperience how bad things sometimes used to be. I crept into my bed in the middle of the day. Life out there had once more become a great tale of woe. And so on. Too much to put down on paper.

Then something dawned on me. At a fairly advanced age, my father had traded all his uncertainties, doubts, and probably also his physical inferiority complex, his insurmountable marriage problems, for philosophical ideas that though held in perfect sincerity and full of the milk of human kindness are totally vague. Those ideas help him to gloss over everything, to look just at the surface instead of plumbing the depths he knows full well are there, perhaps precisely because he knows it. And so he can never hope to attain clarity. Beneath the surface, his resigned philosophy simply means: Oh, well, which of us knows anything, all is chaos within and without. And it is that very chaos that also threatens me, that I must make it my life's task to shake off instead of reverting to it time and again. And no doubt my father's expressions of resignation, humor, and doubt appeal to something in me that I share with him, but which I must nevertheless outgrow.

About the razor-sharp debate last night: deep down I have an inkling that quite a lot of sense was spoken after all, and this tacit feeling was suddenly intensified by my father's intrusion into my world. Hence my resentment of his presence, my paralysis and impotence. It really has nothing to do with my father. That is, not with his person, his most lovable, pathetic, dear person, but with something in myself. The generation gap. From my parents' chaos, their failure to speak out, I must learn to take a definite standpoint, learn to come to grips with things, despite the recurrent feeling that it's all a waste of time. "Well, children, there it is, life's like that . . ." And so on, and so on.

When the realization dawned on me, my strength returned, and also my love, and the few hours of panic had vanished.


*Wednesday morning, eight o'clock, in the bathroom.* Woke up in the middle of the night. And suddenly remembered my important dream. A few minutes of intense effort to bring it back. Gluttonous. Greedy. Had the feeling that the dream was part of my personality, that I had the right to hang on to it, that I must not let it escape me, that I had to be certain of it if I am to be a rounded and whole person.


At five o'clock that choked feeling again. Queasy and a bit giddy. Or was I imagining it all? For five minutes I was swept by all the fears of all those young girls who suddenly, to their horror, realize that they are expecting a baby they do not want.

The mother instinct is something of which I am completely devoid. I explain it like this to myself: life is a vale of tears and all human beings are miserable creatures, so I cannot take the responsibility for bringing yet another unhappy creature into the world.


*Later:* I have earned *some* immortal deserts: I have never written a bad book, and I have not added another unhappy being to those peopling this sorrowful earth.

I kneel once more on the rough coconut matting, my hands over my eyes, and pray: "Oh, Lord, let me feel at one with myself. Let me perform a thousand daily tasks with love, but let every one spring from a greater central core of devotion and love." Then it won't really matter what I do and where I am. But I still have a very long way to go. I shall swallow twenty quinine pills today; I feel a bit peculiar down there, south of my midriff.

*Friday morning, nine o'clock.* Yesterday morning, running about in the mist, once again that feeling: I have truly reached my limits, everything has happened before, I have been through it all, so why do I go on? I know it all so well; I can go no farther than I have already gone, the frontiers are too close, and to cross them means making straight for a mental institution. Or for death? But I haven't yet thought that far. The best cure for it all: study a dry-as-dust piece of grammar or go to sleep. The only fulfillment for me now is to lose myself in a piece of prose or in a poem with each word of which I have to wrestle. I can do without a man. Is it because I have always had so many of them round me? Sometimes I feel totally replete with love, in a nice way. Life has really been very good to me, and still is. It's difficult to say things like that after the night I have had. And now my feet into water. Even this muddle about an unborn child is something I do so badly. No doubt it will all turn out all right.

*Shortly before 4:45 P.M.* What matters is not to allow my whole life to be dominated by what is going on inside me. That has to be kept subordinate one way or another. What I mean is: one must not let oneself be completely disabled by just one thing, however bad; don't let it impede the great stream of life that flows through you. I keep trying to take myself in hand, telling myself to get down now to preparing tomorrow's lesson, or to make a start on Dostoyevsky's *Idiot,* not just as a diversion, but seriously working my way through the book. Like a day laborer. And in between I shall keep running downstairs to perform those rites with the water. I have the feeling of something secret deep inside me that no one knows about. It means, after all, being part of life. That was an exhilarating short walk I had with S. at two o'clock. He was so cheerful and boyish again. He just radiates love in all directions, a little at me as well, and I radiate back. White chrysanthemums. "So bridal." I am really faithful to him, inwardly. And I am faithful to Han as well. I am faithful to everyone. I walk down the street next to a man, I carry white flowers that could be a bridal bouquet, and look up at him radiantly. Yet just twelve hours ago I lay in the arms of another man and loved him then and love him now. Is that sordid? Is it decadent? To me it feels perfectly all right. Perhaps because the physical thing is not so essential to me, no longer so essential. The love I now feel is different, wider. Or am I fooling myself? Am I too vague? Even in my relationships? I don't think so.

*Saturday morning, 9:30.* First I must make sure of keeping my chin up, muster a little courage for the day. When I woke up early this morning there was that leaden oppression again, that utter blackness of mood, that unrelieved gloom. No trifling matter, when all is said and done.

It feels to me as if I am occupied in saving a human life. How preposterous: to save a human life by doing my utmost to keep it from living! But all I want is to keep someone out of this miserable world. I shall leave you in a state of unbornness, rudimentary being that you are, and you ought to be grateful to me. I almost feel a little tenderness for you. I assault myself with hot water and blood-curdling instruments, I shall fight patiently and relentlessly until you are once again returned to nothingness, and then I shall have the knowledge that I have performed a good deed, that I have done the right thing. After all, I can't give you enough strength, and besides, my tainted family is riddled with hereditary disease. When Mischa got so confused and had to be carried off to an institution by force and I was witness to the whole horror of it, I swore to myself then that no such unhappy human being would ever spring from my womb.

Just so long as it doesn't all drag on too long. I get so terribly worked up. It's only just been a week, and already I am exhausted by the whole performance. But I shall bar your admission to life, and truly you should have no complaints.

*Friday morning, nine o'clock.* People complain about how dark it is in the mornings. But this is often the best time of my day, when the dawn peers gray and silent into my pale windows. Then my bright little table lamp becomes a blazing spotlight and floods over the big black shadow of my desk. Last week it really felt marvelous. I sat engrossed in *The Idiot,* solemnly translated a few lines, wrote them down in an exercise book, made notes, and suddenly it was ten o'clock. Then I felt: Yes, that's how you should always work, so deeply immersed that you forget the time. This morning I am wonderfully peaceful. Just like a storm that has spent itself. I have noticed that this always happens following days of intense inner striving after clarity, birth pangs with sentences and thoughts that refuse to be born and make tremendous demands on you. Then suddenly it drops away, all of it, and a benevolent tiredness enters the brain, then everything feels calm again, then I am filled with a sort of bountifulness, even toward myself, and a veil envelops me through which life seems more serene and often much friendlier as well. And a feeling of being at one with all existence. No longer: I want this or that, but: Life is great and good and fascinating and eternal, and if you dwell so much on yourself and flounder and fluff about, you miss the mighty, eternal current that is life. It is in these moments—and I am so grateful for them—that all personal ambition drops away from me, that my thirst for knowledge and understanding comes to rest, and that a small piece of eternity descends on me with a sweeping wingbeat. True, I realize that this mood will not last, that it will probably be gone within half an hour, but I have nevertheless been able to draw new strength from it. And whether today's bountifulness and expansiveness is due to my swallowing six aspirins or to Mischa's playing, or to Han's warm body last night, in which I almost completely buried myself, who can say, and what does it matter anyway? These five minutes have been mine. Behind me the clock ticks away. The sounds in the house and on the street are like distant surf. A bare electric bulb in a neighbor's house cuts through the drabness of this rainy morning. Here, beside this great black surface that is my desk, I feel as though I am on a desert island. The statue of the Moorish girl stares out into the gray morning with a serious dark look that is carnal and serene at the same time. And what does it matter whether I study one page more or less of a book? If only I listened to my own rhythm, and tried to live in accordance with it. Much of what I do is mere imitation, springs from a sense of duty or from preconceived notions of how people should behave. The only certainties about what is right and wrong are those that spring from sources deep inside oneself. And I say it humbly and gratefully, and I mean every word of it right now, though I know that I shall again grow rebellious and irritable. "Oh God, I thank You for having created me as I am. I thank You for the sense of fulfillment I sometimes have; that fulfillment is after all nothing but being filled with You. I promise You to strive my whole life long for beauty and harmony and also humility and true love, whispers of which I hear inside me during my best moments." And now to clear the breakfast table and make some preparation for the Levi girl's lesson and put a little paint on my face.

*Sunday morning*. Last night, shortly before going to bed, I suddenly went down on my knees in the middle of this large room, between the steel chairs and the matting. Almost automatically. Forced to the ground by something stronger than myself. Some time ago I said to myself, "I am a kneeler in training." I was still embarrassed by this act, as intimate as gestures of love that cannot be put into words either, except by a poet. A patient once said to S., "I sometimes have the feeling that God is right inside me, for instance when I hear the Saint Matthew Passion." And S. said something like, "At such moments you are completely at one with the creative and cosmic forces that are at work in every human being." And these creative forces are ultimately part of God, but you need courage to put that into words.

This phrase has been ringing in my ears for several weeks: you need courage to put that into words. The courage to speak God's name. S. once said to me that it took quite a long time before he dared to say "God," without feeling that there was something ridiculous about it. Even though he was a believer. And he said he prayed every night, prayed for others. And, shameless and brazen as always, wanting to know everything there is to know, I asked, "What exactly do you say when you pray?" And he was suddenly overcome with embarrassment, this man who always has clear, glass-bright answers to all my most searching and intimate questions, and he said shyly: "That I cannot tell you. Not yet. Later—I often wonder why this war and everything connected with it afflicts me so little. Perhaps because it is my second great war? I was in the thick of the first, and then relived it in all the postwar literature. So much rebelliousness, so much hatred, the passion, the arguments, the call for social justice, the class struggle, etc.—we have been through it all. To go through it a second time just won't do, it becomes like a cliché. It's happening all over again: every country praying for its own victory, the same old slogans, but now it's like a déjà vu and there is really no point in flying into a passion about it."

I said last night to twenty-one-year-old Hans, right in the middle of a conversation, "Look, politics really isn't everything in life, you know."

And he, "You don't have to talk about it all the time, but it's probably the most important thing all the same."

Between his twenty-one and my twenty-seven years lies a whole generation. It is now 9:30 A.M., Han lies snoring gently and familiarly, far behind me in the dim room. The gray, soundless Sunday morning is turning into a bright day, and I shall grow along with it. These last three days I seem to have grown years older. And now like a good, disciplined girl back again to translation and Russian grammar.

*2:00 P.M.* While cataloging S.'s books, I unexpectedly came across Rilke's *Book of Hours*. Paradoxical though it may sound: S. heals people by teaching them how to suffer and accept.

*Wednesday evening.* Ruth[23] is given presents by stage-door admirers in a small German provincial town, and Hertha gets kindness from prostitutes who visit her bookstall in a London park. The blond musical comedy star is twenty-two years old and the melancholy dark-haired girl is twenty-five, the second is to become the stepmother of the first. And the real mother is fifty and "engaged" to a man of twenty-five. And the ex-husband, the father and prospective groom, lives in two small rooms in Amsterdam, reads the Bible, shaves every day, and has only to stretch out his eager hands for the breasts of the many women round him, which are like so many fruits in a lush orchard. And I, his "Russian secretary," am trying to make sense of it all. The result is a friendship whose roots take an ever-firmer hold on my restless heart. I still use the formal *Sie,* perhaps to keep the right distance, to survey the scene. The foolish and passionate desire to "lose" myself in him has long ago vanished, has grown "sensible." All I have left of that feeling is the will to "yield" myself up to God, or to a poem.

The great cranium of mankind. The vast intellect and great heart of mankind. All ideas, however opposed, spring from a single brain: the brain of mankind, of all mankind. I feel it is indivisible, and perhaps that explains why I am sometimes filled with a deep sense of harmony and peace, despite the many clashes. One has to know all thoughts and let all emotions pass through one to judge what has been devised in that immense cranium and what has passed through that great heart.

And so life is a passage from one deliverance to the next. And I shall probably have to seek my deliverance in bad pieces of prose, just as a man in extremis may seek deliverance in what is aptly called a "tart," because he needs someone to still his deep hunger.

*Monday, 5:00 P.M.* I know the intimate gestures he uses with women, but I still want to know the gestures he uses with God. He prays every night. Does he kneel down in the middle of his small room? And does he bury his heavy head in his great, good hands? And what does he say? Does he kneel before he takes his dentures out or afterward? That time in Arnhem: "Let me show you how I look without my teeth. I look so old and so 'knowing.'"

"The girl who could not kneel." This morning, in the gray dawn, in a fit of nervous agitation, I suddenly found myself on the floor, between Han's stripped bed and his typewriter, huddled up, my head on the ground. As if I were trying to seize peace by force. And when Han came in and seemed a bit taken aback by the spectacle, I told him I was looking for a button. But that was a lie. And Tide, that strong thirty-five-year-old redhead, said quite frankly one evening, speaking in her bright, clear voice, "You see, I'm just like a child about this, when I am in trouble I kneel down in the middle of my room and ask God what to do." Her kisses are like a shy little girl's, S. once showed me, but her gestures to God are mature and certain.

Many people have fixed ideas, and so they bring their children up in rigid ways. The result is not enough freedom of action. With us it was precisely the other way round. I think my parents always felt out of their depth, and as life became more and more difficult they were gradually so overwhelmed that they became quite incapable of making up their minds about anything. They gave us children too much freedom of action, and offered us nothing to cling to. That was because they never established a foothold for themselves. And the reason why they did so little to guide our steps was that they themselves had lost the way.

And I see our own task more and more clearly: to allow their roving talents to mature and take more solid shape in us, their children.

*31 December 1941, Thursday morning, ten o'clock.* It was such an odd feeling waking up in Deventer: I was all sharp corners and edges as I advanced into the ice-cold morning.

Just a few words on the occasion of my being, for a short while, a guest in my childhood room with my faithful old lamp by the bedside. Simple things. I have noticed that it is best for me to get up early. And as always I have to brace myself like a hero to plunge into the cold water. I am really a very healthy person. The main thing for me is to keep my mental balance; the rest follows. My breakfast plate was graced with a chicken leg. Darling mamynka, who translates all her love into chicken legs and hard-boiled eggs.

The train to Deventer. The open skies, peaceful and also a little sad. I look out of the window, and it is as if I were riding through the landscape of my own soul. Soul-landscape. I feel like that often: that the outer landscape is the reflection of the inner. Thursday afternoon along the river IJssel. A radiant, sweeping, bright landscape.

Mother. Suddenly a wave of love and sympathy that washes away all the petty irritations. Five minutes later, of course, I am on edge once more. But later in the day again the feeling: perhaps there will come a time, when you are old, when I'll be spending a while with you, and then I'll be able to help you see what really goes on inside you and smooth away your anxieties, for I am gradually coming to realize what disturbs you.

*8:00 P.M.* The lung man more or less grinned his way over S.'s great big chest. No matter what he asked—did S. cough a lot, did he produce a lot of phlegm, or God knows what—S. had only the one reply, "I'm afraid the answer is no." And the first thing he said when he stepped out of the surgery was, "It's Davos for me right away, but I insisted that the entire harem must come along. Yes, Switzerland will be grateful to me." I was still chuckling out on the street. And he kept threatening me, "Just you wait until Friday, when the X rays will be ready." We managed with great difficulty to get three lemons from a barrow, by paying ten cents apiece instead of the usual seven. But we were determined to have some cake and whipped cream. And then we roamed the streets again, I hanging playfully onto his arm with my Cossack hat askew on my head and he with a silly-looking alpine cap above his gray mane, like two crazy lovers. And now it is almost 8:30. The last evening of a year that has been my richest and most fruitful and yes, the happiest of all. And if I had to put in a nutshell what this year has meant—from 3 February, when I shyly pulled the bell at 27 Courbet-straat and a weird-looking character wearing some sort of antenna on his head examined my palms—then I would say: greater awareness and hence easier access to my inner sources. In the past I, too, used to be one of those who occasionally exclaimed, "I really am religious, you know." Or something like that. But now I sometimes actually drop to my knees beside my bed, even on a cold winter night. And I listen in to myself, allow myself to be led, not by anything on the outside, but by what wells up from deep within. It's still no more than a beginning, I know. But it is no longer a shaky beginning, it has already taken root.

It is now 8:30. A gas fire, yellow and red tulips, an unexpected piece of chocolate from Aunt Hes,[24] the three fir cones from Laren Heath, and my Pushkin, of course. I feel so "normal," so terribly normal and nice, without any of those terribly profound and vexing thoughts and oppressive feelings—normal, full of life and depth, but a depth that also feels perfectly "normal." And I should also mention the salmon salad that is waiting for me tonight. Now I am making tea and Aunt Hes is knitting a cardigan and Pa Han is fiddling about with a camera, and why not after all; within these four walls or within four other ones, what does it matter? The essential is somewhere else. And I hope to make some progress with Jung this evening.

*7 January, 1942. Wednesday, 8:00 P.M.* Walked along the snow-covered canal tonight, after the unexpected encounter at the Jewish Council. Then he said, "I am much less sure of my technical skill than I am of my human warmth."

And later, each of us hanging on to a strap on the number 24 tram, "It was good of you to come along; you always stimulate me, because you feel things so strongly and I am really a 'sounding board,' you could say."

We reported to the Jewish Council at 4:30. His heart wasn't really in it. Questions, income, emigration certificate, Gestapo, and similarly edifying matters. A young man behind a table.

Sensitive, weak, intelligent face. Me, his "Russian secretary," tagging along brazenly as if I were indispensable, ostensibly because of his hearing, but really in order to be with him. And was amply rewarded again. After the peaceful chitchat between him and the meek, really a very nice young man, someone suddenly stepped eagerly up to S. "Good evening, Herr S." S. looked at the man, who had a marvelously sardonic Mephistophelian head on a small body, without recognizing him, and then said on the off-chance, "Oh, yes, you must have been on one of my courses." That happens to him all over Europe, I imagine. When I walk with him in the street someone is bound to come up every few yards or so wanting to shake hands, and S. invariably says, "Oh, you must have been to consult me." This man, with the sharp, sardonic features that contrasted so strongly with the weak face of the young man, had in fact never attended S.'s classes but had met him through the Nethes, and seemed extremely keen to become a client. And the sharp one said to the meek one, "Watch out for Mr. S., he can tell everything about you. From your hands." And the meek one immediately opened his right hand and put it out on the table. S. had time to spare, so he looked at it. And it really is very difficult to describe how he does it. It's like this: when S. says, "This is a table," and when someone else says, "This is a table," then the two tables are quite different. The things he says, even the simplest ones, sound more impressive, more important, I would almost say more highly "charged" than the same things said by anyone else. And not because he adopts a portentous air, but because he seems to draw on deeper, stronger, and more truly human sources than most others. And in his work he looks for human, not sensational, results, although he invariably causes a sensation just because he is able to look so deeply into people.

But back to the bare little office at the Jewish Council, to the sensitive young man who held out his hand, the eager Mephistopheles, and S., who after a few preliminary remarks established a very strong contact with the young man. And remember, we had gone there to answer questions about our financial position. I can't recall everything that S. told him, but one thing he did say was, "You do your work here most thoroughly, but it is alien to your nature." And then quite casually, "He is quite an introvert, this young man." It is very difficult for me to repeat all of it. Like a good pupil, I joined in myself, saying, "There is also something a little soft and sensitive about him." And that the young man seemed to have talents that were not being fulfilled because of his lack of self-confidence. S. took it up and said, "When you are given clear orders you always do your best, but if you are presented with alternatives you vacillate." And more of the same. As a result, in a very short time the young man was, as it were, bowled over, and said in utter astonishment: "But Herr S., everything you've said to me here in a couple of minutes is almost exactly word for word what came out in a test I had to take." He promptly made an appointment for a consultation and was immediately forthcoming with a hundred and one pieces of advice on how to fill in all the forms. I see that I have underplayed the humorous side of this strange meeting. Later we stood like exultant schoolchildren shouting with laughter on the snow-covered canal—at the unexpected and funny course of that official interview: an appointment for a consultation and an official who suddenly exuded benevolence and was willing to do anything he could to bend the law for us.

*11 January, 11:30 P.M.* I am so glad that there is all that washing-up waiting for me in the disorganized kitchen. A sort of penance. I have some sympathy for monks in rough habits kneeling on cold stone floors. I feel a bit sad again tonight, but then I myself wanted those embraces. The dear man had just made up his mind to lead a chaste life during these few weeks until he reports to the Gestapo. Or as he put it with such childlike simplicity: to radiate nothing but sweetness to harness the cosmic forces of goodness. No reason not to believe him. And then along comes this wild "Kirghiz" girl and confounds his dreams of chastity. And I asked whether he would have regrets. "No," he said, "I never regret anything, and anyway it was beautiful and has taught me that I can't escape my earthy nature. But for me," he added, "physical contact is always preceded by some kind of 'spiritual closeness,' and that is why it is so good."

And what do I come away with? With sadness. I realize I cannot fully express my feelings for a person in embraces. And I also feel that that person eludes me in my arms, precisely because he is in them. I think I would rather see his mouth from a distance and long for it than press it to my own. In very rare moments that brings me a kind of happiness, if I may use so big a word. And tonight I shall sleep next to Han, out of pure sadness. Everything has become chaotic again.

Now I know for certain: he prays *after* he has taken out his teeth. Really that's quite logical. You must first get all your mundane chores out of the way.

I seem to be blossoming right now, I radiate warmth all round, says S., and he enjoys it. A few years ago I was really a terribly sick person, what with my two-hour naps each afternoon, my monthly pound of aspirins—it was all quite horrifying when I look back on it. Today I was leafing through these scribblings again. They have become "ancient literature" for me; they all seem so remote now, all those problems I used to have. Now my inner world is all peace and quiet. It was a difficult road, though it all seems so simple and obvious now. One phrase has been haunting me for weeks: "You must also have the courage to say openly that you believe; to say God." Right now, a little spent and tired and sad and not altogether satisfied with myself, I don't feel it with the same intensity, but it still remains part of me. Tonight I shall probably say nothing to God, although I do yearn for cold stone floors and contemplation and seriousness. Seriousness about things of the body. My body still has its own way much of the time, is not yet at peace with my soul. Yet I firmly believe in that oneness. And I believe less and less that one man is enough to satisfy my body and my soul. I am now sad in quite a different way.

I no longer plumb the depths of despair. My sadness has become a springboard. In the past I used to think that I would always be sad, but now I know that those moments too are part of life's ebb and flow and that all is well. This is a sign of confidence, of very great confidence, even in myself. I have gradually come to realize that I am going to manage my life properly.

And yet: I don't want his body at all, although I sometimes have the sudden feeling that I am madly in love. Is this perhaps because I feel for him so deeply, so "cosmically," that the body simply cannot keep pace?

Tide and I are closest to him, and yet we are quite different. We must be very fond of each other. Today, when Tide saw the two of us out and kissed us both, there was such a wonderful intimacy between the three of us for a moment. And now will you for goodness' sake go to bed?

*19 February 1942. Thursday, 2:00 P.M.* If I had to tell what made the greatest impression on me today I would say: Jan Bool's[25] great big purple chilblained hands. Somebody else was martyred today. That gentle boy from "Cultura."[26] I still remember how he used to play the mandolin. He had a nice girlfriend at the time. She had since become his wife, and there was also a child. "He was one of the best," said Jan Bool, in the crowded university corridor. They have finished him off. And Jan Romein and Tielrooy and several more of the fragile old profs. They are now prisoners in a drafty barracks, in the same Veluwe where they used to spend their summer holidays in friendly guest houses.[27]

They are not even allowed their own pajamas, or anything else of their own, Aleida Schot said in the cafeteria. The idea is to demoralize them completely and to make them feel inferior. Morally they are all strong enough, but most of them are rather frail. Pos has retired to a monastery in Haren and is writing a book. Or so they say. It was very gloomy at this morning's lectures. And yet it wasn't altogether depressing. There was one bright spot. A short unexpected conversation with Jan Bool as we walked through the cold, narrow Langbrugsteeg and then waited at the tram stop. "What is it in human beings that makes them want to destroy others?" Jan asked bitterly. I said, "Human beings, you say, but remember that you're one yourself." And strangely enough he seemed to acquiesce, grumpy, gruff old Jan. "The rottenness of others is in us, too," I continued to preach at him. "I see no other solution, I really see no other solution than to turn inward and to root out all the rottenness there. I no longer believe that we can change anything in the world until we have first changed ourselves. And that seems to me the only lesson to be learned from this war. That we must look into ourselves and nowhere else." And Jan, who so unexpectedly agreed with everything I said, was approachable and interested and no longer proffered any of his hard-boiled social theories. Instead he said, "Yes, it's too easy to turn your hatred loose on the outside, to live for nothing but the moment of revenge. We must try to do without that." We stood there in the cold waiting for the tram, Jan with his great purple chilblained hands and his toothache. Our professors are in prison, another of Jan's friends has been killed, and there are so many other sorrows, but all we said to each other was, "It is too easy to feel vindictive." That really was the bright spot of today.

And now to have a nap and then to learn a little about Rilke's girlfriend. Life goes on, and why not! I should write more regularly. But there is much too little time.

*25 February, Wednesday.* It is now half-past seven in the morning. I have clipped my toenails, drunk a mug of genuine Van Houten's cocoa, and had some bread and honey, all with what you might call abandon. I opened the Bible at random, but it gave me no answers this morning. Just as well, because there were no questions, just enormous faith and gratitude that life should be so beautiful, and that makes this a historic moment, that and not the fact that S. and I are on our way to the Gestapo this morning.

*27 February, Friday morning, ten o'clock.* [ . . . ] How rash to assert that man shapes his own destiny. All he can do is determine his inner responses. You cannot know another's inner life from his circumstances. To know that you must know his dreams, his relationships, his moods, his disappointments, his sickness, and his death.

[ . . . ] Very early on Wednesday morning a large group of us were crowded into the Gestapo hall, and at that moment the circumstances of all our lives were the same. All of us occupied the same space, the men behind the desk no less than those about to be questioned. What distinguished each one of us was only our inner attitudes. I noticed a young man with a sullen expression, who paced up and down looking driven and harassed and making no attempt to hide his irritation. He kept looking for pretexts to shout at the helpless Jews: "Take your hands out of your pockets . . ." and so on. I thought him more pitiable than those he shouted at, and those he shouted at I thought pitiable for being afraid of him. When it was my turn to stand in front of his desk, he bawled at me, "What the hell's so funny?" I wanted to say, "Nothing's funny here except you," but refrained. "You're still smirking," he bawled again. And I, in all innocence, "I didn't mean to, it's my usual expression." And he, "Don't give me that, get the hell out of here," his face saying,

"I'll deal with you later." And that was presumably meant to scare me to death, but the device was too transparent.

I am not easily frightened. Not because I am brave, but because I know that I am dealing with human beings and that I must try as hard as I can to understand everything that anyone ever does. And that was the real import of this morning: not that a disgruntled young Gestapo officer yelled at me, but that I felt no indignation, rather a real compassion, and would have liked to ask, "Did you have a very unhappy childhood, has your girl-friend let you down?" Yes, he looked harassed and driven, sullen and weak. I should have liked to start treating him there and then, for I know that pitiful young men like that are dangerous as soon as they are let loose on mankind. But all the blame must be put on the system that uses such people. What needs eradicating is the evil in man, not man himself.

Something else about this morning: the perception, very strongly borne in, that despite all the suffering and injustice I cannot hate others. All the appalling things that happen are no mysterious threats from afar, but arise from fellow beings very close to us. That makes these happenings more familiar, then, and not so frightening. The terrifying thing is that systems grow too big for men and hold them in a satanic grip, the builders no less than the victims of the system, much as large edifices and spires, created by men's hands, tower high above us, dominate us, yet may collapse over our heads and bury us.

*12 March 1942, Thursday evening, 11:30.* How indescribably beautiful it all was, Max, our cup of coffee, the cheap cigarette, and that walk through the darkened city, arm in arm, and the fact that we two were together. Anyone who knew about our past would have found it strange and quite incredible, this meeting out of the blue—just because Max intends to get married and wants me of all people to give him advice. But that's what was so beautiful—to be able to come back to a friend of one's youth and see oneself reflected in the light of his own greater maturity. At the start of the evening he said, "I don't know what it is, but something in you has changed. I think you have turned into a real woman." And at the end, "The change is not for the worse, believe me, your features, your gestures, they're as lively and expressive as ever, but now there's so much more wisdom behind them, it's so nice to be with you," and he shone his flashlight briefly in my face, nodded in recognition, and said decidedly, "It's you all right." And then, half clumsily and half familiarly, our cheeks brushed and we moved on and drew apart. It really was beautiful. And paradoxical though it must sound, perhaps it was our first real meeting. As we walked on he said suddenly, "I think that perhaps over the years we can grow into real friends." And so nothing is ever lost. People do return to you, you live with them inside you until a few years later they are back with you again.

On 8 March I had written to S., "My passion used to be nothing but a desperate clinging to—to what, exactly? To something one cannot cling to with the body."

And it was the body of this man, who now walked beside me like a brother, to which I had once clung in terrible despair. That, somehow, was the most gladdening thing: something had survived, the pleasing and familiar exchange of ideas, the sharing of each other's presence, the revival of memories that no longer haunted us, who once had lived so destructively off each other. Although by the end, of course, we were both emotionally exhausted.

Still, it was the old Max who suddenly asked, "Have you had an affair with anyone else since then?" I held up two fingers. Later when I said I might marry a refugee so that I could be with him when they sent him to a camp, he pulled a face. As we took our leave, he said, "You won't do anything foolish, will you? I'm so afraid you'll come to grief." And I, "I won't come to grief, don't worry." And I wanted to add something, but by then we had moved too far away from each other. If you have a rich inner life, I would have said, there probably isn't all that much difference between the inside and outside of a camp. Would I myself be able to live up to such sentiments? There are few illusions left to us. Life is going to be very hard. We shall be torn apart, all who are dear to one another. I don't think the time is very far off now. We shall have to steel ourselves inwardly more and more.

I would love to read the letters I wrote to him when I was eighteen. He said, "I always had such ambitions for you, I expected great works from you." I said, "Max, they'll come. There's no hurry. Can't we be patient?" "Yes, I know you can write. Now and then I read over the letters you wrote to me; you can write."

Still, it's a comforting thought that things like that can still happen in this riven world of ours. Many more things perhaps than we are prepared to admit to ourselves. A youthful love suddenly rediscovering itself, smiling back at its own past. And reconciled to it. That's what had happened to me. I set the tone that evening, and Max went along with it, and that said a good deal.

So, everything is no longer pure chance, a bit of a game now and then, an exciting adventure. Instead I have the feeling that I have a destiny, in which the events are strung significantly together. When I think how we talked together through the dark city, older now, softened by the past, feeling that we still had so much to tell each other but vague about when we should meet again, I am filled with a profound and solemn gratitude that this could happen in my life. It is now close on midnight, and I'm going to bed. It's been a good day. At the end of each day I feel the need to say: Life is very good after all. I have my own philosophy now, one I'm prepared to speak up for, which is saying a lot for the self-conscious girl I've always been.

*Tuesday morning, 9:30.* Last night, when I bicycled over to see S., I was filled with a warm, intense longing for spring. And as I rode dreamily along, over the asphalt of Lairessestraat, looking forward to seeing him, I suddenly felt the caress of balmy spring air. Yes, I thought, that's how it should be. Why shouldn't one feel an immense, tender ecstasy of love for the spring, or for all humanity? And one can befriend the winter, too, or a town, or a country. I well remember a wine-red beech tree from my youth. I had a very special relationship with that tree. At night, filled with a sudden longing, I would bicycle for half an hour to reach it, then dance round it, captivated and bewitched by its blood-red look. So, why shouldn't one fall in love with spring? The caress of the spring air was so soft and so all-embracing that a man's hands, even his hands, seemed coarse to me by comparison.

And so I came to him. The small bedroom held a glimmer of light from his study, and when I walked in I saw that his bed had been turned down and above it a heavily-laden spray of orchids had been hung to spread its fragrance. On the little table beside his pillow stood daffodils—so yellow, so poignantly yellow and young. The turned-down bed, the orchids, the daffodils—there was no need to lie down in that bed; even as I stood in that dimly lit room it was as if I had had a whole night of loving. And there he was sitting at his small desk, and I thought again how much his head resembled some gray, weather-beaten, age-old landscape.

Yes, we need patience. Our desire must be like a slow and stately ship, sailing across endless oceans, never in search of safe anchorage. Then suddenly, unexpectedly, it will find a mooring for a moment. Last night it came across just such a one. Was it only fourteen days ago that I had been so wild and wanton, pulling him toward me, bringing him down on top of me and later feeling so unhappy that I could scarcely bear to go on living? And was it only a week ago that I slid into his arms and was still unhappy somehow because something about it seemed so forced?

No doubt those ports of call were necessary in order to reach these calm waters, this intimacy, this cherishing and valuing of each other. A night like this lingers as large as life in one's memory. And not many such nights may be needed for the feeling that life is rich and full of love.

9:00 P.M. The solemn Moorish girl looks out at the flower garden, with her dark glance, serene and sensual. The small crocuses, yellow and purple and white, droop spent and exhausted over the rim of the chocolate tin, all life gone since yesterday. And then the yellow bell-flowers in the translucent green crystal vase. What are they really called? S. bought them in a flush of spring fever. And last night he came back with that bunch of tulips. The small red buds and the tiny white ones, so tight, so inaccessible, so incredibly dear—I had them to look at all afternoon, while listening to Hugo Wolf.[28] The Rijksmuseum, too, was there outside the window, so invitingly fresh and new in its contours and at the same time so old and familiar.

We are not allowed to walk along the Promenade any longer, and every miserable little clump of two or three trees has been pronounced a wood with a board nailed up: No Admittance to Jews.[29] More and more of these boards are appearing all over the place. Nevertheless there is still enough room for one to move and live and be happy and play music and love each other. Glassner[30] brought a little sack of coal and Tide some wood, S. sugar and biscuits, I had some tea, and our small Swiss vegetarian artist suddenly arrived with a big cake. First S. read to us about Hugo Wolf. And when he came to some passages about Wolf's tragic life, his mouth quivered a little. That's another reason why I love him so much. He is so genuine. And lives every word he says or sings or reads. When he reads sad things, he is genuinely sad. And I am touched by the fact that at that moment he looks as if he is about to burst into tears. And I would gladly weep in unison with him.

Glassner gets better and better at the piano. This afternoon I whispered to him how happy his piano playing made us.

There are moments in which it is suddenly brought home to me why creative artists take to drink, become dissipated, lose their way, etc. The artist really needs a very strong character if he is not to go to pieces morally, not to lose his bearings. I don't quite know how to put it properly, but I feel it very strongly in myself at certain moments. All my tenderness, all my emotions, this whole swirling soul-lake, soul-sea, soul-ocean, or whatever you want to call it, wants to pour out then, to be allowed to flow forth into just one short poem, but I also feel, if only I could, like flinging myself headlong into an abyss, losing myself in drink. After each creative act one has to be sustained by one's strength of character, by a moral sense, by I don't know what, lest one tumble, God knows how far. And pushed by what dark impulse? I sense it inside me; even in my most fruitful and most creative inner moments, there are raging demons and self-destructive forces. Still, I feel that I am learning to control myself, even in those moments. That is when I suddenly have the urge to kneel down in some quiet corner, to rein myself in and to make sure that my energies are not wildly dissipated.

It's late evening now, and I have just been held by S.'s searching light-gray gaze, which drew me in, and by his dear, full mouth. For a moment I felt so sheltered and sustained by this gaze. I had been straying all day in endless space, and then suddenly I came up against a frontier—the frontier that turns back shiftlessness and boundless despair.

This morning I noticed the dark branches outside forming a lattice in the translucent spring light. I saw the treetops when I woke up, outside my window. And I saw the trunks this afternoon, from the wide windows of the floor below. And inside, the red and the white tulip buds, bending toward one another, the noble piano, black and mysterious and complex, a being in itself, and further away still the Rijksmuseum. And S., now so strange, now so familiar, very distant and yet very close, one moment an ugly, ancient goblin, the next a stout, good-natured, biscuit-loving uncle, then the chamber with the warm voice, always changing, so remote and yet so close.

*Saturday morning, ten o'clock.* Some mornings I wake up with a complete sentence in my head, a few words I must have said to myself softly in the middle of the night, half asleep. I don't know exactly where they spring from, but they come back to me in the morning. Today, after I had lain awake for a bit, this phrase from out of the night came to me: "A gradual change from the physical to the spiritual."

And that change is connected with my relationship to S.

Keeping a diary is an art I do not understand. Quite a lot has happened this morning. Our latest clerk turned up triumphantly with three clandestine turnips and bartered them with Käthe for sauerkraut. And I was on the telephone to S. first thing asking him to be sure he gave Liesl the eggs in time for dinner. But he had already seen to it, thoughtful and conscientious man that he is. Do I really have to write down things like these? Whole books would be filled, and although I can believe that one day they might make exciting reading, let others write them, not me.

And then, a week ago, I thought I would keep a record of everyone I spoke to each day. But that would be bound to use up an awful amount of paper. And what would be the point, anyway? Sometimes my day is crammed full of people and talk and yet I have the feeling of living in utter peace and quiet. And the tree outside my window, in the evenings, is a greater experience than all those people put together. I sometimes think so many things happen in my life, so many interesting people, so many books, so much talk, it's a pity I can't write it all down for the years to come. But then, my real life is something quite different: hanging about for three hours at Lippmann and Rosenthal's.[31] I know they are bullies and thieves. And yet? I have never been so close to S. and so at peace with him as I was in those three hours of waiting. All my pent-up energy and good humor came to my aid then, and it was as if, during those hours, we grew more inseparable still. Life may be brimming over with experiences, but somewhere, deep inside, all of us carry a vast and fruitful loneliness wherever we go. And sometimes the most important thing in a whole day is the rest we take between two deep breaths, or the turning inward in prayer for five short minutes.

Take that day, for instance, when I had to deliver his wedding ring to Lippmann and Rosenthal in the morning and that same day to Van Meerloo's with Liesl, and on to the Café de Paris with Herbert Nelson and Sylvia Gross and Dr. Levie, who became "Werner" for the first time (I was most gratified to see that my last bit of snobbery has gone: in the past I would have reveled in taking coffee with "celebrities" and saying "Du" to a stage director, but all that has completely gone now and what remains is human warmth stripped of any trappings, and I am grateful that it should be so), so, the Café de Paris, and in the evening spaghetti, and then the discussion, back here, about S.'s book, and my heart-to-heart talk with S. about that youthful correspondence of mine that had suddenly turned up, and then the walk through the bright night, a night in which the deep feelings between us were deepened further still, then on to the Levies', with Weil, the journalist from Frankfurt, who has intellectual water on the brain, an undernourished soul, and hungry eyes—a shivering little ape but one with the philosopher's swellings on his left palm. ("He comes from a materialistic background and has brought his materialism into his spiritual world," said S., who, so to speak, took the man in hand for five minutes and built up his character, adding, "Yes, seeing so many destinies pass through one's hands every day, as I do, one gradually comes to recognise how to build up each human being—one sees the finished building in one's mind's eye, but he himself has to supply the stones and the labor.")

And as he sat there with his expressive, gesticulating hands and said, "Yes, seeing so many destinies pass through one's hands"— at that moment once again he was a great man, and I was so irritated by Weil with his pigheaded, know-it-all attitude, but when we were alone again, S. merely said, "The poor fellow!" And it is with the help of such quiet comments that he helps me to grow.

Then the short walk to S.'s place, and back home by myself through the bright night, and then, though it was 12:30 A.M., a talk with Han, again about my correspondence with A., and how strange it was that something I myself had left behind me so long ago still bothered him. That was my day, then, a long day. And the most important thing about it all? That the branches of the tree outside my window have been lopped off.

The night before, the stars had still hung like glistening fruit in the heavy branches, and now they climbed, unsure of themselves, up the bare, ravaged trunk. Oh, yes, the stars: for a few nights, some of them, lost, deserted, grazed over the wide, forsaken, heavenly plain.

For a moment, when the branches were being cut, I became sentimental. And for that moment I was deeply sad. Then I suddenly knew: I should love the new landscape, too, love it in my own way. Now the two trees rise up outside my window like imposing, emaciated ascetics, thrusting into the bright sky like two daggers.

And on Thursday evening the war raged once again outside my window and I lay there watching it all from my bed. Bernard was playing a Bach record next door. It had sounded so powerful and glowing, but then, suddenly, there were planes, ack-ack fire, shooting, bombs—much noisier than they have been for a long time. It seemed to go on right beside the house. And it suddenly came to me again: there must be so many houses all over the world that are collapsing each day under just such bombs as these.

And Bach went gallantly on, now faint and small. And I lay there in my bed in a very strange mood. Filaments of light along the menacing bare trunk outside my window. A constant pounding. And I thought to myself: any minute now a piece of shrapnel could come through that window. It's quite possible. And it's equally possible that there would be a lot of pain. And yet I felt so deeply peaceful and grateful, there in my bed, and meekly resigned to all the disasters and pains that might be in store for me.

All disasters stem from us. Why is there a war? Perhaps because now and then I might be inclined to snap at my neighbor. Because I and my neighbor and everyone else do not have enough love. Yet we could fight war and all its excrescences by releasing, each day, the love that is shackled inside us, and giving it a chance to live. And I believe that I will never be able to hate any human being for his so-called wickedness, that I shall only hate the evil that is within me, though hate is perhaps putting it too strongly even then. In any case, we cannot be lax enough in what we demand of others and strict enough in what we demand of ourselves.

Yes, the trees, sometimes at night their branches would bow down under the weight of the fruit of the stars, and now they are menacing daggers piercing the bright spring air. Yet even in their new shape and setting they are unspeakably beautiful. I remember a walk along an Amsterdam canal, one dreamlike summer night, long, long ago. I had visions then of ruined cities. I saw old cities vanish and new cities arise, and I thought to myself, even if the whole of this world is bombed to bits, we shall build a new world, and that one too will pass, and still life will be beautiful, always beautiful.

Even ill-fated Rotterdam. What a bizarre new landscape, so full of eerie fascination, yet one we might also come to love again. We human beings cause monstrous conditions, but precisely because we cause them we soon learn to adapt ourselves to them. Only if we become such that we can no longer adapt ourselves, only if, deep inside, we rebel against every kind of evil, will we be able to put a stop to it. Airplanes, streaking down in flames, still have a weird fascination for us—even aesthetically—though we know, deep down, that human beings are being burned alive. As long as that happens, while everything within us does not yet scream out in protest, so long will we find ways of adapting ourselves, and the horrors will continue.

Does that mean I am never sad, that I never rebel, always acquiesce, and love life no matter what the circumstances? No, far from it. I believe that I know and share the many sorrows and sad circumstances that a human being can experience, but I do not cling to them, I do not prolong such moments of agony. They pass through me, like life itself, as a broad, eternal stream, they become part of that stream, and life continues. And as a result all my strength is preserved, does not become tagged on to futile sorrow or rebelliousness.

And finally: ought we not, from time to time, open ourselves up to cosmic sadness? One day I shall surely be able to say to Ilse Blumenthal, "Yes, life is beautiful, and I value it anew at the end of every day, even though I know that the sons of mothers, and you are one such mother, are being murdered in concentration camps. And you must be able to bear your sorrow; even if it seems to crush you, you will be able to stand up again, for human beings are so strong, and your sorrow must become an integral part of yourself, part of your body and your soul, you mustn't run away from it, but bear it like an adult. Do not relieve your feelings through hatred, do not seek to be avenged on all German mothers, for they, too, sorrow at this very moment for their slain and murdered sons. Give your sorrow all the space and shelter in yourself that is its due, for if everyone bears his grief honestly and courageously, the sorrow that now fills the world will abate. But if you do not clear a decent shelter for your sorrow, and instead reserve most of the space inside you for hatred and thoughts of revenge—from which new sorrows will be born for others—then sorrow will never cease in this world and will multiply. And if you have given sorrow the space its gentle origins demand, then you may truly say: life is beautiful and so rich. So beautiful and so rich that it makes you want to believe in God."

What with one thing and another—that cup of coffee (which must nowadays be drunk with reverence, for each day it may be our last) and chatting with Käthe and big and small Hans round the stove—it has turned 11:30 A.M. I must still type out that talk with Hetty, things like that are awfully difficult, and my program now includes *The Idiot,* which I have neglected for a long time, and Jung's *Symbols of Transformation,* of which I found a tattered copy in S.'s library. And at 6:30, I have to meet S., and then with him and Glassner to the L.s' (I am most curious about Liesl's cooking), and then Tide in the evening. And tomorrow afternoon music at my place. And so on.

*Sunday evening, 9:30.* I tell myself: keep calm, Etty, why get so worked up about a young lady with the sleek head of a boy, who wears trousers, has piercing blue eyes, and wants you to teach her Russian? Or about her provocative girlfriend, who so wants to get to know you because she finds you so "charming," which of course flatters your vanity. And then the bacon and eggs. Things like that are quite an adventure these days—any moment now I shall be writing about nothing but food. "A real week for guzzling," said S. this afternoon.

And she with the sleek boy's head said to S., "Hallo, friend. You're really something. All those Madonnas on your wall, and Christ, and that old tapestry. You're really something." And that telepathic young man who said last week, "There is something of the Early Christian about you. If you believed in reincarnation I would tell you that you lived at the time of the Apostles."

Then, last night's haute Sauternes and his growing lack of inhibitions. And my enormous respect for this man who, despite his strong sensuality, his overwhelming sensuality that I could feel bubbling under the wine—alas, just two glasses—lives a life that could almost be called austere. A wholesome life, literally.

There are other, quite different things to write about, but my impatience still stops me from writing them down. And this evening that unprecedented emotional response to that girl's unexpected blue eyes and strange face. And suddenly I was back behind my desk, and by chance my eyes fell on this passage of Rilke:

". . . I realized then that I must follow him, Rodin: not by reshaping my own creation, but in my inner articulation of the artistic process: I must learn, not his art, but his deep inner serenity for the sake of creation. I must learn to work, to work, Lou, I need to so much! *Il faut toujours travailler—toujours*—he said to me one day, when I spoke to him of the awful chasms that have opened up between my good days."

And suddenly, I knew it again, and all was peace and serenity, which never abandon me for as long as they used to, not even in my most emotional moments. I looked round my desk. There were the two volumes of Rilke's letters—I really must read them systematically, and in the near future, too. Then there was the book by Jung on which I had started. And Dostoyevsky's *Idiot* that has to be properly studied, for its language no less than its contents: my growing number of pupils forces me to perfect my knowledge of the language all the time. And then there is the work for S.; I must keep myself ready for him, must be open to him and learn to share his way of experiencing things. There is always something new to learn from him, always a little more— but, at the same time, I must not neglect my Russian studies.

And the people, the friends, my many friends! Nowadays there are hardly any accidental relationships left; you have a deep if subtly different relationship with each person, and must not be disloyal to one for the sake of the other. There are no wasted and boring minutes any longer, one has to keep learning how to take one's rest between two deep breaths or in a five-minute chat.

I was not worked up only because of those two women; there was also my vanity: that petite, dynamic Hagen, who said to me so pertly and yet so frankly, "I noticed you straightaway on that course—you were the only really 'notable' person, after all." And it wasn't even vanity but perhaps more exultation that all kinds of human beings should feel free to open themselves to me, that no human being is alien to me any longer, that I can find the way to people of every sort. And that, after all, isn't vanity but joyful love for all the many kinds of people, and happiness because I shall always be able to find my way to each one of them.

And back to me came the words I wrote down months ago in one of these notes to myself, words I shall keep writing down time and again, until they are part of me: Slowly, steadily, patiently.

And tonight I had to bring these words to mind once again. There is so much work, and I can't tell what will come of it.

*Wednesday morning, eleven o'clock.* What made the biggest impression on me last night? That small globe on top of the bookcase, so small that I could hold the entire earth with its oceans and continents in my two hands, smaller even than that silly little orange lamp that used to hang above the red-lacquered piano.

And my reaction to Mischa and his music? Suddenly, right in the middle of a Beethoven piece, a desperate compassion for— Little Brother, my little brother. What is the good of it all, what good is all your brilliant playing before your enthusiastic and often sensation-hungry public, when you have that line of suffering round your twisted little mouth? Poor boy! It is just as Leonie said, "It's impossible to enjoy the music because you can't stop wondering about what is going on inside the pianist." That's what all the drama is about.

And S.'s face looming up from far away after the interval, so pale with his penetrating, now almost light green eyes, with all that terrible pity in them. And just as important: something of that dear and gentle and "open" look was back in Werner's face.

It is a good thing from time to time to feel the emptiness and weariness in yourself for a moment or two, just to recall how things used to be and how they are now. Monday night, on going to bed, I said, "Dear God, today I cannot praise you, I honestly don't feel happy enough." The tree outside the house seemed a lifeless lump of timber stabbing a dull sky. But the feeling of deep unhappiness lasted for only a moment. The day seemed to start out so bleakly yesterday. But after an hour of calm and concentrated work everything was fine again. And then there was that man from Enkhuizen with his generous gift of coffee beans and his offer of hospitality, and after the lesson, so touchingly, a cheese sandwich made of bread he had baked himself. And he said, "Have a bite," probably thinking, This poor lamb is dying of hunger, and he lit a pipe and we had a little chat.

And after that Leonie: her emotional attachment to me is so terribly strong. I probably behave much too guilelessly and unconsciously toward others and take it for granted that everyone is just as free inside as I am. But I shall have to work on her "transference."

"You, my beloved, my dearly beloved, priceless, private, psychological university. I have so much to discuss with you again and so much to learn from you."

Last night, as I sat there under the autocratic head of that Knight of the Cross, watching the goldfish, which always seems to take things lightly and really is a model example of someone happily going his own way—it was just then that I had that strange feeling again: There sits Adri, I thought, and Tide over there, and there the Levies and S., and Leonie on my left, and my little brother behind the piano, all my good friends around me, and I felt a great bond with each one in a different way, a bond that was not a chain. And as a result so many inner forces were freed. So much inner freedom and independence, and finding myself so immersed and happy and strong. And now before coffee I shall treat myself to an hour with Rilke's letters.

*A little later.* I still have to learn to adjust to others. I tired Leonie with my description of the girl with the boy's head, the blue eyes, and the man's clothes. She merely got the feeling—as she told me afterward—that I had met some middle-class girl who was unable to get on with life.

And why did I have to tell Jaap that I shall be attending the night rehearsals at the Jewish theater? It can only upset him. Is it pure swank on my part, perhaps, or just showing off what an "interesting" life I lead, despite the fact that I've rid myself of my last bit of snobbery—or have I? When I still feel the need to blurt out things like that? True, you have to talk about something, and you can't tell every Tom, Dick, and Harry about your intimate relationship with a tree outside your window. But you should always ask yourself what another is able to cope with, certainly when that other is slightly unstable and a bit of a problem.

Not only "listening in to oneself" but also "listening in to others." And as long as there is still so much noise and hubbub inside, so long will it be hard for others to approach you, except for those who look deeper and feel the undertow, the life current that never stops flowing in the depths. But you should never make life difficult for others. And you must not be too ingenuous and too unaware in your intercourse with others, but try to be more in tune with them, to learn what each one of them can take in and cope with.

Slowly but surely I have been soaking Rilke up these last few months: the man, his work, and his life. And that is probably the only right way with literature, with study, with people, or with anything else: to let it all soak in, to let it mature slowly inside you until it has become a part of yourself. That, too, is a growing process. Everything is a growing process. And in between, emotions and sensations that strike you like lightning. But still the most important thing is the organic process of growing.

To be very unobtrusive, and very insignificant, always striving for more simplicity. Yes, to become simple and live simply, not only within yourself but also in your everyday dealings. Don't make ripples all around you, don't try so hard to be interesting, keep your distance, be honest, fight the desire to be thought fascinating by the outside world. Instead, reach for true simplicity in your inner life and in your surroundings, and also work. Yes, work. It doesn't matter at what, I still haven't found solid ground under my feet, but whether it's Russian essays or reading Dostoyevsky and Jung or having a talk, all of these can be work. And have confidence that it will all come together and everything will turn out all right in the end. That confidence is something I've had for a long time.

———

I keep remembering from my early student days how I would walk at night through the streets, my hands bunched into fists in the pocket of my coat, my head hunched deep into my collar, and how I used to say, "I want to work, I shall work"—and then I would come back home and be so exhausted by my determination that I had no strength left to do the actual work.

And so it went on for years. I remember Abrascha calling after the train that was taking me to Deventer, "You must work, child, work, work, always work."

And I could hear the rhythm in the wheels of the train: work-work, work-work, work-work.

And I wrote him a profound letter on that very subject, but I didn't do any work that year either because I simply couldn't. Later I came to see how it all fitted together. And now? As well as having the will, I now know how to put it into action. The will flows smoothly into the deed, the barriers I couldn't cross before have at last broken down. And I no longer say, "Yes, but I have not yet found my 'territory.' " I no longer suffer because I have not yet discovered the right "instrument," the right "object," as S. once put it to me. All that matters now is the "deep inner serenity for the sake of creation." Though whether I shall ever "create" is something I can't really tell. But I do believe that it is possible to create, even without ever writing a word or painting a picture, by simply molding one's inner life. And that too is a deed.

2 April [1942]. *Thursday morning, eight o'clock.* The morning lay ready-made outside my window. The green grass of the Skating Club and the Rijksmuseum seemed wide awake. And my two gaunt ascetics still pointed at the sky. It was a good awakening.

Last night at eight o'clock, Loekie turned up with an orange, which now lies there in all its gaudy roundness and perfection between the freesias and the three pine cones I gathered, how long ago? I really do like her so much, want to hang on to her and stop her from sliding down into the mire, which is where she will probably end up. If I help her conscientiously with her Russian now, it might perhaps give her a small toehold later for something better than the random adventures in which she keeps getting involved, almost despite herself. Eczema on her hands again, and a swelling on her foot; she can't get greens anywhere or buttermilk and other necessities, because she has no regular supplier. And yet she never complains and always shows the same dreamy face with the clear, childlike eyes. Yes, Loekie, one day I shall write a short story about you, and then you will walk with your long dancer's legs over oh, so many lines of my exercise book.

At 9:30 my latest pupil. And now that the first impression has had time to sink in—she is really like a charming young boy—I wonder: How are you and why did you turn out this way and how do you live and are you happy? Worked hard with her for an hour. And there was that remarkable invisible current between us. For me however, it had a human rather than an erotic bias. As for the latter, I am, of course, erotically receptive in all directions—to S.'s demonic mouth, to Liesl's trim little figure and waving blond hair, no less than to this girl with her slim and lively boy's face and bright, almost unnaturally bright, voice.

But the sexual and erotic element in me has gradually been conditioned to play a subordinate role to human warmth, although that warmth is intense and passionate enough. Typically, ever since I met this girl, this boy, I don't really know what to call her, I have had regular dreams about her. She is constantly in my dreams.

The first one went like this: I had just given her a Russian lesson, and we left together. She had two heavy suitcases, and I carried one of them. Suddenly, right in the middle of the street, she took leave of me and left me holding her luggage. I stood there feeling utterly confused and abandoned, and called after

*The Hillesum family, 1931.* From left to right: *Etty, Rebecca Hillesum-Bernstein, Mischa, Jaap, Louis Hillesum.*

*"In Deventer the days were like great sunny plains, each one a long, uninterrupted whole." Deventer, about 1925.*

*Etty, 1937.*

*Gabriël Metsustraat 6, about 1938. Etty's room is above the street lamp, slightly to the left.*

Amsterdam  Gabriel Metsustraat

*In the house; Etty is on the right.*

"One day when there is no more barbed wire left in the world, you must come and see my room. It is so beautiful and peaceful. I spend half my night at my desk reading and writing by the light of my small lamp. I have about 1,500 pages of a diary from last year, and one of these days I shall read it through. What a rich life leaps out at me from every page. To think that it was my life— and still is" [September 28, 1942].

*Maria Tuinzing in her room, about 1939.*

*Han Wegerif ("Father Han"), 1943.*

*"The man who is closest to me": Julius Spier, reading hands.*

Klaas Smelik, Sr.

Henny ("Tide") Tidemann.

Werner Levie, director of the
Jewish Theater.

Liesl Levie, Etty's best friend.

*At Julius Spier's house.* From left to
right: *Henny Tideman, Adri Holm,
Etty, Julius Spier.*

*Julius Spier.*

*Etty, taken by Han Wegerif.*

*Eight exercise books closely written in a small, hard-to-decipher hand: the diaries of Etty Hillesum.*

her, "We haven't fixed the next lesson," but she called back, "I'll give you a ring." I felt less than cheerful, alone in the middle of the street with the heavy suitcases.—S.'s interpretation was that I must have wanted to relieve her of her problems.

*Good Friday morning, 8:30.* Last night at 10:30 when I came back to my little room, where the curtains at the one large window are always left open,[32] there it stood, my poor, ravaged, lonely tree. A hesitant star climbed up its austere body, rested for a moment in the crook of one of its limbs (?!good!) and then lost itself in the wide sky, no longer caught up in the branches. The Rijksmuseum looked like a turreted city far away. Between S.'s bookcase, wide and deep, still a mysterious temple of wisdom, and my small monk's bed, there is just enough room for me to kneel down. Something I have been wanting to write down for days, perhaps for weeks, but which a sort of shyness—or perhaps false shame?—has prevented me from putting into words. A desire to kneel down sometimes pulses through my body, or rather it is as if my body had been meant and made for the act of kneeling. Sometimes, in moments of deep gratitude, kneeling down becomes an overwhelming urge, head deeply bowed, hands before my face.

It has become a gesture embedded in my body, needing to be expressed from time to time. And I remember: "The girl who could not kneel," and the rough coconut matting in the bathroom. When I write these things down, I still feel a little ashamed, as if I were writing about the most intimate of intimate matters. Much more bashful than if I had to write about my love life. But is there indeed anything as intimate as man's relationship to God?

*Saturday, nine o'clock.* We don't live under the same roof. I am separated from him by five streets, one very long one and four shorter ones, by a bridge and by a canal. And when I have cycled back home from seeing him, there on my desk is a small black telephone, and a similar marvel of modern technology stands on his overladen worktable. And we are connected by these two very often. That's how I know that he went to see that epileptic count with a copy of *Symbols of Transformation* and a volume of Rilke's letters, while I stayed behind on my sunny veranda with *Symbols of Transformation* and another volume of Rilke's letters. Quite by chance.

"It's really amazing," I said to him with great satisfaction on Thursday afternoon on the number 24 tram, when I went with him to the station. For days Jung's book had been beckoning me on my desk, and on a sudden impulse the night before I had picked it up and immersed myself in it for an hour. When I told him next morning, he said, astonished, "Would you believe it, I picked it up last night as well, on an impulse. It had been lying on my table for days, but I suddenly felt it was time to make a start with it."

And things like that happen quite often. Right now I am deep in Rilke. He is constantly in my thoughts, I have never experienced anything like it before—to become so completely absorbed in a writer as to lose oneself in him, so to speak. And then, there they were on top of his desk as well: Rilke's *Collected Works,* and in the evening he now and then reads me a line of Rilke over the telephone. Just like that, at random, without any prompting.

How did that discussion go again—on Thursday morning? When in the middle of saying something or other his fine, large hands slid along my bare thighs, and I suddenly said, "You know, only the other day I thought to myself that you are really a complete stranger." He looked rather taken aback and said, "And you really believe that? Because we have never seen each other naked? I don't feel like that at all." To him everything is of a piece, he does not separate the physical from the spiritual and feels so close and familiar to me precisely because his life is so much more coherent than mine. And I said to him that I was a bit afraid of the ultimate physical approach, that I would only want it if the body were the expression of the soul. And that it was for that reason that I had been so shy and withdrawn that evening with the haute Sauternes—that I had had the feeling that it was pure sensuality and that it could as well have been any other woman.

Then he became very serious and said that I was totally mistaken, that it was I and I alone who had "excited" him that time. Well, well. But I keep catching myself being irritable as I write this because I am really in two minds. For during our ultimate sexual contact, unknown sensations and emotions or even conflicts may easily arise. When I told him that, he said he was quite ready to face any consequences.

But he also said that he would always feel the same way about me even if that man-and-woman business shouldn't turn out to be a great success—he doesn't take it all that seriously and it isn't his first priority. But I still can't get the full flavor of our discussion properly onto paper. I only know that I love him, a bit more every day, and that I ripen beside him into a genuine and adult human being. A bit more every day.

Last night before falling asleep I asked myself if I did not live too reckless a life. In London there is a girl he intends to make his wife. Inwardly, I live in complete independence and freedom from him, and I tell myself that I go my own way in the world, but will I really be able to go on living away from the warmth of the rays that emanate from the very center of his being? When I thought about it very hard last night, in bed, shortly before falling asleep, I felt that I would not, and then my face was suddenly wet with tears and there was a longing in me that felt heavy as lead.

And this, too. In all the relationships I have had during my crowded young life, it always happened after a while that I looked back with nostalgia at the beginning, at the adventurous, fresh, promising beginning, and thought, "What a shame it is no longer like that, that it's never ever going to be as beautiful again." And now, with S., it's the other way round. With every new phase of our relationship I look back and say to myself, "The bond between us has never been as deep and as strong as it is now." With every fresh step the relationship seems to gain in intensity and all that went before seems to pale in comparison, so much more many-sided and colorful and eloquent and inward does our relationship become all the time.

I once said, after 3 February, when I had known him for a year, a whole year, "I don't believe it could ever grow better still." And yet it did, for all of a sudden a barren patch of our friendship came into blossom. And I have long since stopped saying, "It can't get any better." I know now that the two of us will grow in every possible direction.

*Wednesday, 9:30 P.M.* I reached for this paper suddenly, with a fierce gesture, between the typing of a few letters and with a violent headache. Such longing to jot down a few words! Such a strong sense of, Here on these pages I am spinning my thread. And a thread does run through my life, through my reality, like a continuous line. There is the Gospel of Saint Matthew morning and night, and now and then a few words on this paper. It's not so much the imperfect words on these faint blue lines as the feeling, time and again, of returning to a place from which one can continue to spin one and the same thread, where one can gradually create a continuum, a continuum that is really one's life.

Am I just writing this under the influence of the Rilke letters? Or do these letters affect me so much that I live in constant longing for them, drink them in with deep drafts, because I feel I have reached the same stage he describes in his letters of 1903 and 1904?

I still waste too much time, do not concentrate my mind nearly enough, am still too careless on the whole. Like a wave, the urge to kneel down sometimes floods through me, almost irresistibly, and then my head grows heavy, I sometimes think, heavy with devotion.

And now I still have to type S.'s letter to Mischa. I am very grateful to him for dictating it. He has entered Mischa's life with so much determination that Mischa will eventually be unable to shake him off and perhaps will even find him a sheet anchor at some catastrophic moment in his much too difficult life. S. never lets things go on by chance. Somewhere he always becomes part of your "destiny."

*Thursday morning, ten o'clock.* This morning, early, I kneeled down in the living room among all the bread crumbs on the carpet. And if I should have to say aloud what I said in my prayers, it would go something like this: "Oh, Lord, this day, this day—it seems so heavy to me, let me bear it well to its end, through the multitude of days. This day will probably be no heavier than any other day, but my strength to bear it is not so great. And then there is the anxiety and the burden of wondering what this summons to S. from Lippmann and Rosenthal really means. But Lord, help me not to waste a drop of my energy on fear and anxiety, but grant me all the resilience I need to bear this day." German soldiers were already drilling at the Skating Club. And so I also prayed, "God, do not let me dissipate my strength, not the least little bit of strength, on useless hatred against these soldiers. Let me save my strength for better things."

*15 April [1942]. Wednesday morning, 8:30.* A shout of joy, an impetuous shout of spring! I have partaken of his mouth and have sipped of his breath. He is back. Like exuberant children we ran about his sun-filled rooms these last few days, with so much love, so much warmth, so much childish joy. There is so much to write—well, the facts don't really matter. You have been going to bed too late again, Etty, these last few days; it'll end in tears.

I have lived just one life these last few days, this spring, with that dear, kind face always near me. And yet I have been attentive to so many other lovable faces. It was not physical food, there was hardly any physical contact, more the intense savoring of its promise for the future. I still have that length of gypsy material in my wardrobe. With Liesl's help I shall make a dress from it, open on all sides to the sun, the wind, and his caresses. And then in the summer, the heath, me in the gypsy dress with tanned bare legs and flowing gypsy hair, and then a small farmhouse with a low-beamed ceiling and the smell of apples and a view over the heath at night.

All that is still to come. Yesterday Lippmann and Rosenthal. Robbed and hunted, and yet? So much joy, human joy, more than that pale-faced, jittery, plundering official could ever imagine. And the recurrent feeling that one is complete master of one's inner resources, which grow stronger by the day, and the feeling of love, not just for one man, for one paltry man, but for everyone with whom one happens to share one's life. I have a thousand things more to note down, but I must first read my Saint Matthew and then, after breakfast, some Russian conversation, this afternoon the Freudian and Leonie, and then perhaps Liesl. In the evening to him, to do some more work. I have sipped of his breath.

It is now 11:30 at night, and I am lying in my bed. Han has just taken off his shirt, and once again I stretch out and relax along his familiar body. I have just taken an enchanted leave for the night of my two trees, my two dagger thrusts into the starry sky.

Just half an hour ago I was with S. We worked and chatted

under the small lamp, and there was just one, single, controlled caress. This afternoon I looked at his expressive mouth and whispered to it, "Tonight you will be the beaker from which I will sip his breath." The way he spoke of his work! I felt as if I were sitting beside a life-giving source, a source from which strength flowed into me. I love him so much. This evening I sat on the floor leaning against his legs, and he looked pensively down at me and said, "However do you manage it? Isn't it terribly hard for someone like you who is so used to living with men?"

And he also said, "Only eighteen months ago I could never have left a girl like you alone—I would have thought it a sin (or something like that) not to take her to bed." And he added, "I'm astonished how much I have changed. But otherwise I should never have been able to work as hard as I do now."

And I said, "I have complete respect for the way you live and hold it in high regard." And after a while: "One acquires more patience. I think physical intimacy is too often forced. I can live on a single caress from you for a long, long time." And so on. And now I am lying in bed beside Han, my bare legs between his thighs, looking at his profile and his closed eyes. There is an expectant expression on his face, he too is so familiar to me and so close. And I also know this: I now have the patience to wait for that loving caress from S. that has become so essential to me, and that patience I owe to Han. Life with him over the years has helped to assuage my appetite, life with him and his caressing hands, which were always round me.

And Han is taking an increasing, almost organic, place in my emotional life. I see and feel the difference between what was and what is more and more clearly and appreciate the important role he has played. Things used to be much more difficult, and he often irritated me, but that has all passed. And I love him very much, differently. For now there is something rounded off in our relationship, there are no fresh possibilities. Yet here I am lying by his side, stretched beside him in real affection, and watching his expectant profile to see whether he wants me again tonight, and I am ready for that as well—not for me, but for him. Out of a sense that he has a right to, but also out of genuine friendship. And S.? I have sipped his breath out of the beaker of his mouth, and perhaps this is the first time in my life that I have really kissed a man.

*Nine o'clock next morning.* By my faded hyacinth out on the veranda. It was, of course, not the whole truth when I wrote that I gave myself to him out of genuine friendship and because I felt he had a right after all the years we had spent together. That sounds so noble. There is something of that about it, of course. But it isn't just giving on my part; it also becomes an act of taking and of pleasure. Bodies that have known each other for so long suddenly begin to move with their own laws and rhythms. And now I look forward to a long day of steady work on this veranda.

Perhaps that is the only real way of kissing a man. Not just out of sensuality but also from a desire to breathe for one moment through a single mouth. So that a single breath passes through both. And it was with S. that I had this experience for the first time. Ever since, my kisses for Han have been platonic. But yes, bodies, they have their own laws. This Easter Monday, now, a good week ago. Early in the morning I was lying in bed with Han and felt the familiar touch of his caressing hands. Perhaps I had the somewhat coarser thought: if I give myself to him now, he'll be off to a good start and he'll probably be less upset at my being away for the rest of the day. But a thought like that is far too calculating, and never counts for much with me—human warmth invariably takes over.

Homo sum——. I remember, at the end of the day, which

comprised a whole life, as I lay in bed at two o'clock in the morning, being surprised at myself, perhaps even moved in a way, and asking myself: What sort of a person are you, really? At 11:30 on Easter morning I had gone to S. Lunch, intensity, warmth. And after lunch at the little table next to the window-sill with the flowering plants—he, like a patriarch, but with the radiant look of the lover, in his big armchair—we had moved easily on to his wide divan. And then for a short hour we had shared one breath as I had been wanting to do for many, many weeks. And I had rested so confidently and with so much sur-render in his arms and yet full of sensual tension. But above everything else there was that shared breath. And in that short hour so much strength flowed into me that I believed I could live on it my whole life long.

Then a walk along a country road for a few hours. A small brook, willows and meadows and in the distance the town. And his gesticulating hands and expressive head. And during our walk we passed a long, low-built house that came from a differ-ent century, and the house had a face of its own and it reached out to me. What I mean is that I felt in touch with everything round me, at one with the landscape through which I was walk-ing, and with an old house that suddenly came alive for me.

Rilke. The *Dinggedichte*. And in the evening that little dinner for just the three of us. My two friends, S. and Han, and green peas and fried eggs and substitute whipped cream. And a hectic girl, leaping about in the kitchen among all those pans, but everything came off beautifully! And after the meal he even dictated that letter to Mischa. Half-past nine at the Levies'. First time together. And then a new slice of life opened up and con-tinued until two o'clock in the morning. The struggle to stop Werner smoking. And when—I think it was about half past midnight and there had been a bit of an argument—I snatched away his umpteenth cigarette, he suddenly jumped on me like a frenzied, small black gypsy, and to his dismay I floored him. Then a wild wrestling match on the floor, Liesl looking on with a philosophical expression.

Next day at breakfast Werner said, "I feel marvelous, as if I've wrestled it all out of my system, so healthy." He cut down his smoking for two days, Liesl later told S., and the wrestling match had apparently given him a bit of a shock because he suddenly realized how very unfit he had become. He put that down to his smoking, too. And yesterday afternoon when he read me something from Maimonides, I said quite bluntly, "There's absolutely no point reading edifying things like that. Reading Maimonides and wanting to build a new world after the war when you are systematically, against your better knowledge, poisoning and destroying yourself with God knows how many packets of cigarettes a day!" And I know I am right. Unless every smallest detail in your daily life is in harmony with the high ideals you profess, then those ideals have no meaning.

My poor old father, the night before last. He said, "One should be thankful, nowadays, each day the sun shines and one is still at large." And he added a bit ruefully and ironically, "At least that's what I tell other people all the time." He really can't take much more. There is too much debris piled up over your well-spring to be cleared away by the time you are sixty years old. All we can do is to try to help others not to be so sad when they reach sixty. Much has been changed in my relationship with my parents, many tight bonds have snapped, and as a result I have gained the strength to love them more genuinely.

Well, that Monday, that Easter Monday. Liesl and Werner at two o'clock in the morning, like two Parisian street urchins sitting on the edge of their improvised gypsy beds in the living room. And me in Renate's bed. I took the blackout paper down from the window, and suddenly there were two stars at the head of the bed. They were not the same stars I see through my window, but I felt in touch with them all the same, and suddenly I was quite certain that no matter where I was in the world I would always find stars and be able to flop down on a bed, or on a floor, or anywhere else, and feel absolutely at home. And of this rich, oh, so rich Easter Monday, these were probably the two things that mattered most of all: the house that reached out to me and showed me its face, and those two stars at two o'clock in the morning. And now I really must get down to work.

*17 April. Friday morning, nine o'clock.* My God, what a character! Just look at her jumping about on that divan! She must be a Russian. We don't do that sort of thing in Holland, do we? An *enfant terrible*.

I am still assailed far too much by words like these. I prayed early this morning, "Lord, free me from all these petty vanities. They take up too much of my inner life, and I know only too well that other things matter much more than being thought nice and charming by one's fellows." What I mean is, that sort of thing mustn't take up too much of your time and imagination. For then you get carried away with: "What a nice person I am, what fun I am, how much everyone must like me."

In the past I used to play the fool almost despite myself, and felt terribly unhappy doing it. Now I am sometimes madly exuberant just out of a surplus of energy, particularly on those days when I am most serious and concentrated inside. Then some hidden sort of childish elation bubbles out of me, sometimes bordering on silliness. That's all right. But if it becomes obvious that others are applauding such behavior, then it's time to make sure it isn't going to one's head or tickling one's vanity, for if that is allowed, one's focus will once again be shifted from the inner life toward the outer. As it is, I have been living a life of pleasure these past few days, and it is on just such days that I must be even more collected and peaceful inside, for if I am not then everything gets dissipated in vanity and play-acting.

*22 April. Wednesday morning, noon.* My reply to Tide's postcard: You dear, I was so touched by what I found in my letterbox this morning.

At certain fixed times—though less and less often now—I have a tremendous need to cut myself off, to be quite alone for a time. On Sunday I found it very difficult to leave my desk and go over to your place. Was that very selfish and antisocial of me? However, I did enjoy the good atmosphere you create around you even though I didn't join in very much.

But last night I acted with shameless lack of consideration, just sitting in the corner and reading. I must still learn to find the courage it takes to say at times like these, "I am going to stay at home and keep myself to myself for a while." But I am still too afraid of hurting others, when it actually hurts them much more if I am with them in fact but not at all in spirit.

Recently, I think, I have been much too much of an extrovert—to use that imposing piece of jargon for once—and my really more introvert nature is being avenged. But I am no longer thrown off balance as badly as I used to be in the past. My inner peace never completely deserts me these days.

Your words first thing this morning were so very welcome and have done me so much good, Tide. A big hug.

*8:00 P.M.* This afternoon in his sunlit room I flung a pair of childish arms round his summery neck and nestled a little girl's face against that broad, kindly head of his, which radiates so much gentleness and generosity, and said, "I love you so much, so terribly much." At times like that he gives off such an all-encompassing goodness that I want to cry—no embrace is then enough to express my feelings for him.

He told me that during the lecture last night he had had to struggle with himself not to shout at me, "Leave the class." But then he had said to himself, "Is that really what you're like, getting hurt just because someone isn't listening to you?" And he had pulled himself together and had just been a bit cross for a few hours about my unseemly behavior, and then it had all blown over. And he said, "What would happen to my theories if I didn't live by them?" or something like that.

Leonie told me a little while ago that her friend said of S. in her sleep, "He's a real lady's man, you can sense it as soon as he takes your hand. He has that kind of aura."

What do people mean by a real lady's man? It's just another cliché. I think most of us get the wrong idea when we hear that phrase—we immediately think of sex. He is a lady's man, true enough, but only in the sense that, like Rilke, there is something about him to which women immediately respond and open up. And that is because he has so strong a feminine streak that he can understand how women feel—women whose souls can find no home since men will not join them to theirs. But in men like him the "soul" of a woman is given welcome and shelter. In that sense he is a lady's man, yes!

And Han. What am I to do about him? This afternoon, Leonie said with a guilty face, "I must speak to you, I think I've behaved very stupidly toward you." S. said, "I'll let the two of you have a chat. I'll disappear for a bit." And it was truly no small matter she confided in me. She had asked Han—tampering with my life—"Well, and what do you think of the relationship between Etty and S., it can't really be all that platonic?" But when she saw the surprised expression on Han's face, she had started backpedaling in a panic and seems to have saved the situation. At least I hope so. Right now Han is quietly ensconced on the veranda behind a cigar and a newspaper. And I said something like, "Leonie, why bother an old man with things he can't possibly cope with? Why should I tell him things that would upset him terribly but don't upset me in the least? Surely honesty doesn't entail telling everybody everything. All that matters is that you feel responsible for one another. And live your own life and not bother the other with it more than is necessary. And that doesn't mean living a life of frivolity." And so on.

And now there is so much more to write, but it won't come because of—forgive me—those accursed insides of mine.

This time it's really bad. Which also explains my odd behavior last night. Everything's due to those insides. My chemical composition suddenly changes, and I don't feel responsible any longer. The strangest processes ferment inside me during those few days of changed blood circulation. And there are also sudden bursts of creativity, but above all there is despair, so much despair at not being able to express any of the many vague and unclear things inside me. And finding that, though I'm getting quite old, I'm still without an "instrument" and without an "object." I must delve deep into myself and fetch up unformed slabs of granite and chisel them into shape. But no strength to lift them up as yet, no tool to hew the granite. And now a little homework for Becker's lesson tomorrow.

*11:00 P.M.* Typical that the telephone conversations we have, lasting an hour and a half or more at the end of the day, should be the most intense contacts I have with him. Then there are just our voices, the harmony of two voices in unison. No, that is badly put. Tonight his words were once again like a soothing hand laid upon my head. He said, "You should not be so dependent on your body, you must learn to get over these moods more quickly each time." But that's what I always try to do. This in connection with my insides, which turn everything upside down for a few days.

And we spoke of so much else, so much. And yet it's never an idle parade of words with him. Always aimed at the serious things of life. And always without pomp and circumstance—so ordinary, like life itself.

And his words also made me feel I really oughtn't to be thinking stupid things like, I am already so old, I'm twenty-eight and I haven't yet been able to express anything of all that lies buried in me and cries to be let out. One should just grow and mature and not think about the years. Perhaps it won't be until I'm sixty that I'll be able to say what I think I have to say.

Something else: at times I think that I will be able to write one day, to describe things, but then I suddenly grow tired and say to myself, "Why all these words?" I want every word I write to be born, truly born, none to be artificial, every one to be essential. For otherwise there is no point to it at all. And that is why I shall never be able to make a living by writing, why I must always have a job to earn my keep. Every word born of an inner necessity—writing must never be anything else.

*24 April, Friday morning, 9:30.* Eduard Veterman's face among a crowd of actors in the cafeteria: a gentle, friendly, mysterious moon, floating above a turbulent landscape. Or a Chinese lantern, casting a soft glow over all.

And as I stood, small and lost, in the center of that big stage, the gaping, empty chasm of the auditorium stretching out threateningly before me, I was suddenly hit by the realization that some people base their entire lives on applause from that gaping chasm.

Those were really the strongest impressions of the many hours I spent in the world of the theater. I found no real people, no one with whom I wanted to have a close friendship.

And it was at that time, too, that I realized that the last remnants of my snobbery had deserted me after all.

I was reminded all at once of a time when, at about the age of fifteen, I was sitting in my father's small study, untidy and impersonal as were all the rooms in all the different houses in which we ever lived—I sat there and suddenly needed to write. And I still remember what I wrote: "Red, green, black. Through the leaves of the green tree I see a girl in a bright red dress." Etcetera. That was the only way in which I could express all the vehement feelings inside me.

Later, too, on the train to Paris. Excited by the rhythm of the train, by the many impressions—there I sat with a miserable little notepad clutched in my fingers, and again needed to write. And I wrote something like: "Grey, dark, black, but inside it was bright orange and crimson." And then, in that hurtling train, I also wrote: "It is certain that the world dies a separate death for each one of us, and yet the world still exists." How odd. I remember that I thought this sentence immensely impressive and that, for a time, it relaxed me from my inner constriction.

I still need to write things down. I should like, as it were, to caress the paper with just the right word—I should like to write about yellow daffodils, tiny yellow marsh-marigolds, my chestnut twigs, which have stopped blooming now, their many small hands stretched out as gracefully as a dancer's and at the same time raised so defensively toward the sky. And so on. Many unconnected thoughts. But there is one good thing at least: my old asperity has gone. I could list a host of clever formulations overflowing with wit that I used to think up, but nowadays I've grown tired of all that. Indeed, I sometimes wonder whether I haven't been living too much on my "soul" of late—treating ideas with too much disdain. Sometimes I have a fleeting urge to express this or that in elegant words, but I kill the urge straightaway, finding all that now much too contrived. It will all balance out in the end. Have patience. Slowly, steadily, patiently.

Yesterday I woke up at six o'clock, and the first thing that struck me was that I'll have to study Dutch all over again and fashion myself an instrument out of that language. I probably place too much trust in the belief that the words will come by themselves when the time is ripe. Perhaps that is my great mistake. I am nothing and I know nothing.

When it comes to portraying character or atmosphere, I think I should get stuck at the first attempt. S. said to me one day, "You still savor your talent." I sometimes wonder if it is a talent at all. Perhaps I am really squandering everything I've got. No doubt I should be more energetic in concentrating my mind at this desk, my true hub. Sweep together all the scattered pieces from every corner and mold them into a whole. Perhaps I allow myself to be blown too easily with the wind. But I really don't know where to begin. Perhaps one day there will be a beginning, and then I shall know how to go on. But what of that beginning? Above all: be steadfast. Don't let the days crumble away between your clever fingers. Time passes so quickly. It's past ten o'clock already.

I got up at 7:30. Made breakfast. A few pages of Rilke, a page of the Bible, some awkward stammerings onto this paper, my latest pupil is due in forty-five minutes, this afternoon I shall have to sleep for an hour, because of my still rebellious insides—then work on Starreveld's papers, prepare the transl., write to Aimé, a bit more Russian, and tonight S.—a letter to Mischa. A lot happens to one on a day like this.

It is cold and chilly today—I have thrown my brightest shawl over my terracotta sweater to counter it. I am sitting here now so peaceful and absorbed and collected—in an hour's time I shall be another person altogether: animated and intense, and the stupid thing is that after lessons like that it is impossible to settle back straightaway into your earlier state of peaceful reflection—contacts with others invariably alter you, even if only a little. We are like chemicals: processed all day long and constantly compounded with other materials. One great, continuous process. But which part of you is the original element? It's almost frightening when you suddenly start to think about such matters. That you pass through the many hours of the day and at the end you are a different person from the one you were at the beginning. But here comes Käthe with the coffee.

*2:00 P.M.* Bit by bit you must learn this, too: on those days when you feel physically out of sorts, don't hit out and make trouble for those around you. People are really much too ready to do that. Feeling wretched and continually taking it out on those around them. We must find out how to come to terms with our own bad moods without making others suffer for them. I am gradually learning to control myself. Right now I feel like some animal that wants only to creep into a quiet corner and lie there hugging itself. That's quite a good feeling: not to want to hit out, but to stay quietly curled up in some corner. And also not to let your thoughts and feelings spill out on everything around you. I used to do that all the time. Then I would poison everything—everything that came near me, everything that came into my head, everything I set eyes on—with my bad feelings. Now I know how to isolate and accept that mood and make sure it causes no more trouble. Such days are really very trying. But one must grow more and more independent of one's body.

Last night. I kept him at arm's length. Earlier, when after an evening of work we were suddenly lying beside each other on the floor—I looked at his dear, kindly face, in which the mouth seemed so aggressive—and I said something like this, "We mustn't try to express physically all we feel for another." That's really why I am always so sad after we have had physical contact. One can often say much more with a very, very small gesture than in the wildest and most passionate night of love. And I flung myself against him almost desperately. And yet things are not nearly as bad as they used to be. I am happy in his caresses, although I am always fearful we may suddenly reach a limit, with no further possibilities. And I also said to him that sometimes on the telephone I feel much closer to him than in even the most passionate embrace. Is that some sort of over-sensibility on my part, I wonder? Yet here lies the eternal source of human suffering. I don't feel it as strongly in my body as I used to, but it follows me everywhere like a distant echo.

And this, too: how can I explain that, whenever I have had physical contact with S. in the evening, I spend the night with Han? Feelings of guilt? In the past, perhaps, but no longer.

Has S. unleashed things deep down inside me that can't yet come out but carry on their subterranean existence with Han? I can hardly believe that. Or is it perversity? A matter of convenience? To pass from the arms of one into those of the other? What sort of life am I leading?

Last night when I cycled home from S., I poured out all my tenderness, all the tenderness one cannot express for a man even when one loves him very, very much, I poured it all out into the great, all-embracing spring night. I stood on the little bridge and looked across the water; I melted into the landscape and offered all my tenderness up to the sky and the stars and the water and to the little bridge. And that was the best moment of the day.

And I felt this was the only way of transforming all the many and deep and tender feelings one carries for another into deeds: to entrust them to nature, to let them stream out under the open spring sky, and to realize that there is no other way of letting them go.

*26 April 1942.* Just a small red, faded anemone. But I like the idea that in years to come, I shall chance upon it again between these pages. By then I shall be a matron, and I shall hold this dried flower in my hands and say with a touch of sadness: "Look, this is the anemone I wore in my hair on the fifty-fifth birthday of the man who was the greatest and most unforgettable friend of my youth. It was during the third year of World War II, we ate under-the-counter macaroni and drank real coffee, on which Liesl got 'drunk,' we were all in such high spirits, wondering if the war would be over soon, and I wore the red anemone in my hair and somebody said, 'You look a mixture of Russian and Spanish,' and somebody else, the blond Swiss with the heavy eyebrows, said, 'A Russian Carmen,' and I asked him to recite a poem about William Tell for us in his funny Swiss burr."

And when it was all over we walked back through the familiar streets of South Amsterdam and climbed up to his roof garden. And Liesl had run ahead and put on a dress of shiny black silk, tight round her slender body, with full sleeves of a translucent sky blue and the same sky blue over her small white breasts. And she is the mother of two children! So thin and frail. Yet somewhere underneath runs a source of primitive strength. And Han looked so "natty" and go-ahead, and his card at table bore the inscription: "Eternally Youthful Lover, Father of Heroines," which titles Han accepted under protest. Liesl said to me later, "I could fall in love with that man."

But what made this evening stand out, at least for me, was this: it was about half past eleven, Liesl sat next to the piano and S. on a chair in front of her, and I stood leaning against him, and then Liesl asked something, and suddenly we were all talking psychology and S. assumed that intense expression and he began to speak with great vitality and spontaneity. For him the day had been one long rush of flowers and letters and people and to-ing and fro-ing and organizing a dinner and being the head of a table and later some wine and more wine, which he can't take all that well, and he must also have been terribly tired, but suddenly someone asked a question about something serious and immediately he was wide awake, missing nothing. He could have been standing on a platform in front of an attentive audience, and Liesl's little face above all that translucent sky blue was suddenly suffused with interest, and she looked at him with big eyes and stammered in the touching way that was so peculiarly her own, "I find it so moving that you are the way you are." And I leaned even closer against him and stroked his kind expressive head and said to Liesl, "Yes, that's really the greatest thing about S. He is always willing to talk and has an answer for you, and so the hours we spend with him are never a waste of time." And S. looked up in childlike astonishment, with an expression I can't hope to describe, and said, "But isn't that so with every human being?" He kissed little Liesl on her cheeks and forehead and pulled me tighter against his knee and I was suddenly brought to mind again of what Liesl had said a few weeks ago on her sunny roof, "I would so love to spend a few days with the two of you . . ."

S. said, "One must never seek to go to the limit, but leave some things to the imagination."

*29 April. Wednesday morning.* So much to write—and so little time, alas, so little time. What I need is an even tighter schedule. So as not to lose too much time in the fissures of the day, the gaps between my various busynesses. To switch over from one task to the next with a sure and firm movement. I still let too much time fritter away between one thing and another. Stead-fastness. My day sometimes seems like a complicated piece of machinery with many handles, and I must familiarize myself with their operation, work more steadily, assiduously and con-tinuously, above all continuously. There is such an awful lot to be done. A deep breath between two turns of the handle is rest enough. Such a mess has piled up on my desk. That, too, is due to misuse of the machine. And now to the Russian lesson.

*5:00 P.M. An ihm bin ich eigentlich erst schöpferisch geworden*—it is really with him that I became creative. How silly that I can't say that in Dutch but must put it into German! It is through being with him that my creative powers first awoke, and through him they will also take shape. Later on, he will have to thrust me away, push me toward my own inner space. In a flash of insight it is suddenly clear to me: I must not long to spend my whole life with him, nor seek to marry him. It is thanks to him that I have found a way of expressing myself, but he must release me again into a cosmic space where I can discover another expression, one that is purely my own.

*8:00 P.M.* There seemed to be a touch of nervousness just now in his voice, when he asked me somewhat ironically on the telephone, "Well, are you coming over here with your yellow star?" Only a few months ago I still believed that politics did not touch me and wondered if that was "unworldliness," a lack of real understanding. Now I don't ask such questions anymore. I have grown so much stronger, and I honestly feel I can cope with these frightful days, that I'll get through them, even make it my historical duty to get through them. A few months ago I was in two minds as to how I would choose, when it came to it, between this sunny veranda, my untroubled studies, and Han's faithful eyes on the one hand, and a concentration or some other camp where I could share my troubles with S. Now all that has ceased to matter. For something inside me has suddenly changed, and I know now that I shall follow S. wherever he goes and share his sorrows. And that, I believe, is because I have grown so much less dependent on him and so am able to tie my life to his, without feeling that I am sacrificing mine.

That must sound paradoxical, but it is the only wisdom there is between man and woman. And this too: a few months ago I was perhaps frightened that our dream would go sour on us in a life so full of care and pain. Yet somewhere inside me I now feel so at one with myself, and also with him, that the outer reality can do little damage to that bond. And as the emphasis shifts increasingly toward the inner life, so one grows less and less dependent on circumstances. I am writing this at my trusty desk, surrounded by books, chestnut twigs, and celandine plus the pencil sketch of S.'s head diagonally across from me on the wall.

I may be writing this in great comfort, but there is something inside me, tough and indestructible, that tells me I shall be able to bear different circumstances, too.

I am so glad that he is a Jew and I a Jewess. And I shall do what I can to remain with him so that we get through these times together. And I shall tell him this evening: I am not really frightened of anything, I feel so strong; it matters little whether you have to sleep on a hard floor, or whether you are only allowed to walk through certain specified streets, and so on— these are all minor vexations, so insignificant compared with the infinite riches and possibilities we carry within us. We must guard these and remain true to them and keep faith with them. And I shall help you and stay with you, and yet leave you entirely free. And one day I shall surrender you to the girl you mean to marry.

I shall support your every step, outwardly and inwardly. I think I have grown mature enough now to bear a great many hard things in life and yet not to grow too hard inside.

I feel so sure of myself and not in the least afraid and some-how so triumphant and unbreakable, and also so full of love and confidence. And whenever even the smallest vacillation, the tiniest fear should beset you, I shall be there to support you. An old dress, a couple of sandwiches, a little bit of sun, and now and then a kindly glance at each other. One hand is all we need to caress. And a little work. And our work can be done anywhere, wherever there is a human being, be he only a camp guard. I am coming over to your place right now. I have put on a beauty of a new pink wool blouse, and I have washed myself from top to toe with lilac soap.

I once quietly bemoaned the fact that there is so little space for our physical love in your two small rooms, and no chance of going elsewhere because of all those notices and prohibitions. And now it seems a veritable paradise of promise and freedom: your little rooms, your small table lamp, my lilac soap, and your gentle, caressing hands. God knows how much that means to our relationship, to all that may lie in store for us. Not that I worry unduly about the future. You can't tell how things will turn out in the long run, and so I don't bother too much about it. But if things are to be harder for us, I am quite ready to bear it.

*Thursday, six o'clock.* Never give up, never escape, take everything in, and perhaps suffer, that's not too awful either, but never, never give up.

Last night. At 8:45 P.M. I dropped in to see Liesl and Werner.[33] Werner sat by the coffee grinder in the corner of the kitchen, his gypsy face staring out defiantly above his yellow star—in its special honor he had bought two pounds of real coffee beans that afternoon, which must have cost him a whole week's wages at the very least—and Liesl was shuffling about with a stiff neck and a pale little white face from all that coughing. And I sat on the dresser and we were all nearly drunk with the smell of the coffee and I looked round the cheerful bright kitchen and at Werner's gypsy head, which can sometimes be so mischievous, and at Liesl's trim little figure, and sighed with a sense of well-being: Children, it's so neat and tidy here and everything is so clean and bright, and there you are, a couple of bohemians. What a fascinating combination! And then we flopped into armchairs and, with the steaming black coffee before us, reflected a bit on the Middle Ages and on history and yellow stars and psychology. In the years to come, children will be taught about ghettos and yellow stars and terror at school and it will make their hair stand on end.

But parallel with that textbook history, there also runs another. A few comfortable chairs, bought with the insurance money because all your possessions were wiped out of existence by bombs—a cup of coffee, a few good friends, a happy atmosphere, and a little philosophizing. And life being beautiful and worthwhile all the same. Or at least that was what I was bold enough to proclaim. Werner began to look serious then. But we were so contented, the three of us together that night—the very night on which the "yellow star" was issued.

And I said, "It is probably worth quite a bit being personally involved in the writing of history. You can really tell then what the history books leave out." That man in Beethovenstraat this afternoon won't get a mention in them. I looked at him as one might at the first crocus in spring, with pure enchantment. He was wearing a huge golden star, wearing it triumphantly on his chest. He was a procession and a demonstration all by himself as he cycled along so happily. And all that yellow—I suddenly had a poetic vision of the sun rising above him, so radiant and smiling did he look.

Come now, Etty my girl, things aren't all as congenial as you make out, and you really seem to gloss things over with your flights of poetry. Last night I wondered again if I was so unworldly simply because the German measures affect me so little personally. But I don't fool myself for one single moment about the gravity of it all. Yet sometimes I can take the broad historical view of the measures: each new regulation takes its little place in our century, and I try then to look at it from the viewpoint of a later age.

And the suffering, the ocean of human suffering, and the hatred and all the fighting? Yesterday I suddenly thought: there will always be suffering, and whether one suffers from this or from that really doesn't make much difference. It is the same with love. One should be less and less concerned with the love object and more and more with love itself, if it is to be real love. People may grieve more for a cat that has been run over than for the countless victims of a city that has been bombed out of existence. It is not the object but the suffering, the love, the emotions, and the quality of these emotions that count. And the big emotions, those basic harmonies, are always ablaze ("blazing harmonies" is not bad!), and every century may stoke the fire with fresh fuels, but all that matters is the warmth of the fire. And the fact that, nowadays, we have yellow stars and concentration camps and terror and war is of secondary importance. And I don't feel less militant because of this attitude of mine, for moral certainty and moral indignation are also part of the "big emotions."

But genuine moral indignation must run deep and not be petty personal hatred, for personal hatred usually means little more than using passing incidents as excuses for keeping alive personal hurts, perhaps suffered years ago. Call it psychology, but we can't let ourselves be led astray any longer; we must look at all that indignation we feel and discover whether its roots are genuine and deep and truly moral.—Heavens, how I am digressing! All this in connection with that quarter of an hour over a cup of fresh coffee. It is now 8:30. And there is still *soooooo* much to write.

I skipped off at 9:15, leaving my two bohemians in their tidy rooms, and rushed into S.'s place out of breath. Oh, yes. Werner said as I left, "I'd love to know what S. thinks about the yellow star." And at 10:30 I rang Werner from S.'s and asked, "Can you recommend a good lawyer in the Jewish Council? I want to ask him what happens if I marry a German refugee—that is, a stateless person. Will I be able to share his lot if, say, he is sent to Poland?" Etcetera. And Werner's voice suddenly very serious, "These are no small matters." And I, very resolutely, "Yes, I know, for it means living out one's destiny."

And in the many whirlpools into which I was being dragged after that, these few words almost got lost as well. But I keep finding them again, and each time they make me a little proud and very, very serious. Instead of living an accidental life, you feel deep down, that you have grown mature enough to accept your "destiny."

Mature enough to take your destiny upon yourself. And that

is the great change of the last year. I don't have to mess about with my thoughts anymore or tinker with my life, for an organic process is at work. Something in me is growing, and every time I look inside, something fresh has appeared and all I have to do is to accept it, to take it upon myself, to bear it forward, and to let it flourish. A few months ago I asked myself if I wanted to follow him into exile or wherever. And my imagination then enacted a host of heart-rending scenes. Deserting this beloved desk, the most dependable refuge I know, this sunny veranda and Han's levelheaded, ever-present succor—if I may put it like that—for an uprooted life in God knows what unfriendly spot on this earth, cut off from the past and from the future.

But nothing was decided at the time. True, I devised the most wonderful prayers for him against the day when he would be banished and far from me, and I wrote him letters in my thoughts that I certainly believed, had I written them, would have been among the most beautiful letters in world literature. But yesterday I suddenly felt oddly serious and grown-up and sure, and when I once again looked inside, lo!—something had matured in me during the past few months, was there, and all I had to do was to accept it.

Then I knew that I would bind my life to his, in a pretend marriage, just to be with him. One day, I would surrender him unharmed to his girlfriend, and I knew I could share a hard life with him precisely because I felt less bound to him than I had a few months ago. And now and then I looked round my room and said, "Oh, Etty, do you realize what you are doing?" But the room would be going with me; it had become a part of myself. And I couldn't have stayed in it all my life anyway, that I knew, and so long as I carry it in me I shall always be able to withdraw into it. It's part of my education, has stood loyally by me all these years, and has helped to make me, has always been so ready and open and receptive, and sometimes bathed in sunlight.

And Han? Isn't that a natural process as well? I shall slip

away from him very gradually until suddenly I shall be gone altogether, and I know that my heart will break many times when I think of him, about him, and also about me. But I shall always carry him with me; he, too, has become substance of my substance and has transformed it. And I felt so sure of myself. A pretend marriage, statelessness, banishment, or whatever, a marriage for friendship and also for love, but for a love of a different quality from the love needed for an ordinary marriage. And then to let him go and to depart from him and never want to burden him with my poor self, I don't seek the least curtailment of freedom for either of us. And it is just because I feel so free that I am not afraid to share his hardships. With all the risks they entail: the double danger that the bond will grow too tight or that we may drift apart and the intensity of our relationship die down.

But that doesn't matter, does it? What matters is that the two of us together will probably bear the hardship better than either of us alone. That we shall survive these difficult years. And that I shall be able to help him practically.

I told him all that during a long and serious and almost businesslike conversation.

And suddenly he looked down at me from his heights—I was sitting on the floor, my head against his knees—with searching and tender eyes, and said, "The marvelous way you have grown." And later, "You are a fantastic girl."

And it is right to feel sick and confused and unsettled for once, like today, full of cold fear and uncertainty, and a sigh of "Good God, child, what are you letting yourself in for?" But also a growing sense of self-certainty. I have matured enough to assume my destiny, to cease living an accidental life. But first I must have a chat with a lawyer. And with Tide. And my parents. And make absolutely sure that my inner certainty keeps growing stronger. And it helps that I am now twenty-eight and no longer twenty-two. Now I have a right to a destiny. It is no longer a romantic dream or the thirst for adventure, or for love, all of which can drive you to commit mad and irresponsible acts. No, it is a terrible, sacred, inner seriousness, difficult and at the same time inevitable.

And then the other side of the coin. Something quite different, much less factual. Weeks ago, I came into his place one evening. The bedroom caught a gleam of light from his study, the bed-clothes had been turned down for the night revealing white sheets and a white pillow, radiant yellow daffodils at the head of the bed, a heavy spray of orchids curving into the room over his bed, and I stood there stock-still in that small, half-lit bedroom and looked at the white pillow on which his head would be resting that night, alone—and then I turned back into his study and we worked hard the whole evening, perhaps there was the odd tender gesture between us, but those few minutes, when I stood there alone beside his turned-down bed with the spray of orchids, I felt as if I had just spent a night of love.

And yesterday I lay on that bed, for the first time naked in his arms, and it was less a night of love than that time. And yet it was good. It was not exciting, there was no ecstasy. But it was so sweet and so safe. The last inhibitions dropped away from me and it was so infinitely good to see his great, expressive hand resting on my white body, through my half-closed eyes. And he thought me beautiful. And placed his hand carefully on my breast and whispered almost with surprise, "So soft. And how gentle . . ."

*18 May 1942.* [ . . . ] The threat grows ever greater, and terror increases from day to day. I draw prayer round me like a dark protective wall, withdraw inside it as one might into a convent cell and then step outside again, calmer and stronger and more collected again. I can imagine times to come when I shall stay on my knees for days on end waiting until the protective walls are strong enough to prevent my going to pieces altogether, my being lost and utterly devastated.

*26 May, Tuesday, 9:30 A.M.* We walked along the quay in a balmy and refreshing breeze. We passed lilac trees and small rosebushes and German soldiers on patrol. We spoke about our future and how we would so like to stay together. Then I walked back home in the evening, through the soft night, feeling light and languid from the white Chianti, and I was suddenly absolutely certain of what I now again doubt: that I shall be a writer one day. Those long nights through which I would write and write would be the most beautiful nights of all.

*At night, after dinner.* [ . . . ] Michelangelo and Leonardo. They, too, are part of me, they inhabit my life. Dostoyevsky and Rilke and Saint Augustine. And the Apostles. I do seem to move in particularly exalted circles. But it is no longer a matter of my literary pretensions. These writers tell me something real and pertinent. Even on my saddest and most tired days I no longer let myself sink as deep as before. Life flows in a continuous and unbroken stream, at times a little more sluggishly, impeded by more obstacles, but nevertheless it flows on. Neither do I tell myself any longer, as I used to: I am so unhappy, I don't know what to do. All that has become completely alien to me. In the past I honestly thought I was the unhappiest person in the world.

"It is sometimes hard to take in and comprehend, oh God, what those created in Your likeness do to each other in these disjointed days. But I no longer shut myself away in my room, God, I try to look things straight in the face, even the worst crimes, and to discover the small, naked human being amid the monstrous wreckage caused by man's senseless deeds. I don't sit here in my peaceful flower-filled room, praising You through Your poets and thinkers. That would be too simple, and in any case I am not as unworldly as my friends so kindly think. Every human being has his own reality, I know that, but I am no fanciful visionary, God, no schoolgirl with a 'beautiful soul.' I try to face up to Your world, God, not to escape from reality into beautiful dreams—though I believe that beautiful dreams can exist beside the most horrible reality—and I continue to praise Your creation, God, despite everything." Parallel with the process of growing toward each other there runs a process of more and more freeing oneself of the other. But on those days when I feel altogether worn out and tired, I perhaps cling more desperately to his strength, as if I expect salvation from it. At the same time the energy that reaches me from him defeats me, for I cannot measure up to it. And neither is the proper reaction. My salvation must be wrought with my own strength, not his. His tremendous vitality can suddenly irritate me and frighten me, but that is probably what happens quite often when those who are sick come up against those in perfect health—they feel deprived.

*Saturday morning, 7:30.* [ . . . ] The bare trunks that climb past my window now shelter under a cover of young green leaves. A springy fleece along their naked, tough, ascetic limbs.

I went to bed early last night, and from my bed I stared out through the large open window. And it was once more as if life with all its mysteries was close to me, as if I could touch it. I had the feeling that I was resting against the naked breast of life, and could feel her gentle and regular heartbeat. I felt safe and protected. And I thought, How strange. It is wartime. There are concentration camps. I can say of so many of the houses I pass: here the son has been thrown into prison, there the father has been taken hostage, and an eighteen-year-old boy in that house over there has been sentenced to death. And these streets and houses are all so close to my own. I know how very nervous people are, I know about the mounting human suffering. I know the persecution and oppression and despotism and the impotent fury and the terrible sadism. I know it all.

And yet—at unguarded moments, when left to myself, I suddenly lie against the naked breast of life, and her arms round me are so gentle and so protective and my own heartbeat is difficult to describe: so slow and so regular and so soft, almost muffled, but so constant, as if it would never stop.

That is also my attitude to life, and I believe that neither war nor any other senseless human atrocity will ever be able to change it.

*Thursday morning, 9:30.* On a summer's day like this I lie in bed as if cradled in sweet arms. It makes one feel so indolent and languid. And when he sang "The Linden Tree" last time (I thought it so beautiful that I asked him to sing me a whole forest full of linden trees), the lines on his face looked like old, age-old, tracks through a landscape as ancient as creation itself.

At a small corner table at Geiger's recently, Münsterberg's young and finely cut face thrust itself between his and mine, and in a flash I realised to my dismay how old his face really looks. And I had a kind of snapshot realization then: I would definitely not want to tie my life to his for good. But really such reactions are so mean and unworthy. They all revolve about a convention, about marriage. My life is in any case bound to his forever, or rather it is united to his. And not only my life, but my soul as well. I admit I find that a grandiloquent word to use so early in the morning—probably because I have not yet fully acknowledged the fact that I have a soul.

It really is mean and petty and unworthy to think whenever you happen to be particularly pleased with his looks, "Yes, I will marry him and stay with him forever," and whenever he looks so old, so age-old, so ancient—and especially when a fresh young face appears beside his, to think, "No, it's no good." These attitudes simply must be rooted out. There are so many— how shall I put it?—impediments to truly deep feelings and relationships, relationships that transcend all the bounds of convention and marriage. And the real problem is not even the question of convention and marriage, but the preconceptions one carries about in one's own head.

*Friday evening, 7:30.* Looked at Japanese prints with Glassner this afternoon. That's how I want to write. With that much space round a few words. They should simply emphasize the silence. Just like that print with the sprig of blossom in the lower corner. A few delicate brush strokes—but with what attention to the smallest detail—and all around it space, not empty but inspired. The few great things that matter in life can be said in a few words. If I should ever write—but what?—I would like to brush in a few words against a wordless background. To describe the silence and the stillness and to inspire them. What matters is the right relationship between words and wordlessness, the wordlessness in which much more happens than in all the words one can string together. And the wordless background of each short story—or whatever it may be—must have a distinct hue and a discrete content, just like those Japanese prints. It is not some vague and incomprehensible silence, for silence too must have contours and form. All that words should do is to lend the silence form and contours. Each word is like a small milestone, a slight rise in the ground beside a flat, endless road across sweeping plains. It really is quite laughable: I can write whole chapters on how I would like to write, and it is quite possible that apart from these words of wisdom I shall never put pen to paper. But those Japanese prints suddenly showed me most graphically how I would really like to write. And one day I would love to walk through Japanese landscapes. In fact, I am sure that one day I shall go to the East.

*9 June [1942], Tuesday evening, 10:30.* This morning at breakfast reports about conditions in the Jewish district. Eight people in one small room, with all that entails.[34] It's still quite inconceivable, and to think that it's happening just a few streets away, almost on our own doorstep . . . And this evening, on our little walk from S.'s vegetarian Swiss friend back to his house with the proliferating geranium, I suddenly asked him, "Do tell me, what should I do about all those guilt feelings I have when I hear that eight people have to live in one tiny room, while I have this great sunny place all to myself?" He gave me a wicked, sidelong look and said, "There are two alternatives: either you move from your room" (and he glanced at me with an ironically searching expression that meant: I can just see you doing that) "or you must discover what really lurks behind your guilt. Perhaps the feeling that you don't work hard enough?" And then the truth suddenly dawned on me, and I replied, "Quite true, my work takes me into rarefied intellectual realms, and when I hear about such terrible housing conditions I probably wonder if I would be able to go on doing it with the same conviction and application if I were living with seven hungry people in one filthy room." I fear that I might not be able to pass that test. I still have to prove the validity of my way of life: I shall always have to earn my living as I do now, I am not cut out to be a social worker or a political reformer, even if my guilt feelings some day force me into becoming one or the other.

Of course I didn't say all this on our short walk. All I said was, "Perhaps it is the fear that I wouldn't be able to pass the test." And he, very seriously and very calmly, "This test is something all of us will have to face." And then he bought five little rosebuds and put them into my hands and said, "You never expect anything, and that's why you never go away empty-handed."

*Wednesday morning, 7:30.* It's so compelling, Saint Augustine on an empty stomach. Having a cold no longer throws me completely off balance, but it's far from pleasant all the same. Good morning, untidy desk! The duster has fallen carelessly across my five baby rosebuds, and Rilke's *Über Gott* lies half crushed under *Russian for Businessmen.* The crumpled anarchist Kropotkin rests neglected in a corner, he is no longer properly at home here. I fetched him down from a dusty shelf to reread his first reaction to the prison cell in which he was to spend several years. That account can still teach us how to cope with the measures by which our own freedom of movement is increasingly being restricted. To take what little space we are left with, to fathom its possibilities and to use them to the full.

And I thought: the first thing is to make sure that my system does not break down, I don't want to get sick here. I shall imagine I am on an expedition to the North Pole, forced to spend a few years in the Arctic. I shall move about as much as I possibly can, do my exercises, and not let conditions get me down. Ten steps from one end of my cell to another is better than nothing; doing it 150 times adds up to one Russian verst. I shall cover seven versts every day, about five miles; two versts in the morning, two before lunch, two after lunch, and one before I go to sleep.

The hour before breakfast. It is so quiet round me, although the neighbors have their radio on and Han is lying behind me snoring, even if pianissimo. There seems to be no sense of urgency.

*Friday.* [ . . . ] And now Jews may no longer visit greengrocers' shops, they will soon have to hand in their bicycles, they may no longer travel by tram, and they must be off the streets by eight o'clock at night.[35]

When I feel depressed about these measures—this morning they weighed on me like a menacing lead mass—it is not really the measures themselves that cause my anguish. Having to give some really awful lesson can torment me as much as the worst measures the occupying power can devise. It is never external events, it is always the feeling inside me—depression, uncertainty, or whatever—that lends these events their sad or menacing aspect. It always spreads from the inside outward with me, never the other way round. Generally the most ominous measures—and there are quite a few of those nowadays—have no power against my inner certainty and confidence and, once faced, lose much of their menace.

I shall have to come to terms with cold and discomfort, for they now take up too much of my energy and spoil my enthusiasm for work. I must get rid of the idea that because I suffer so much from the cold and from colds and have a stuffed-up nose I am justified in letting myself go a little and in working less hard. Just about the reverse is true, I would say, although even here I should not force it. And because food is getting increasingly scarce we shall have less and less resistance to colds, at least I shall. And then winter is still to come. But I must persevere and remain productive. I should be preparing myself even now for physical handicaps so that I don't come to a complete standstill every time I encounter some unexpected obstacle. I shall have to adapt myself in advance, make incapacity part of my daily life, of my whole self, the better to control and then dismiss it. Rather than come up against it anew every time and use up all my time and strength in the process. This may seem clumsily put, but I know what I mean.

*Saturday morning.* As tired and discouraged and worn out as an old maid. And as dreary as the chill drizzle outside. And as ineffectual. But no one made me sit in the bathroom reading until one o'clock in the morning when I could barely keep my eyes open with fatigue. That's not the real reason, of course. A growing sense of unease and exhaustion. Perhaps it's purely physical after all? Or is it the many splinters of my ego that bar the way?

The more tired and ineffectual I feel, the more astonished I am by his energy and by the love he has for everyone at all times. Then I resent the fact that he has so much strength even in times like these. We could be ordered at any moment to those barracks in Drenthe Province, and the greengrocers have signs in their shops saying, "No Jews." The average person has more than enough on his plate these days. But he still sees six patients a day and gives all he has to each one. He breaks them open and draws out the poison and delves down to the sources where God hides Himself away. And he works with such intensity that, in the end, the water of life begins to flow again in dried-up souls; each day the life stories pile up on his little table, almost every one ending with, "Please help me." And there he is ready and willing to help each one. Last night I read the following passage about a priest: "He was a mediator between God and men. Nothing worldly ever touched him. And that was why he understood the need of all who were still busy growing."

There are days when I can no longer carry on, from fatigue or something. That is when I want his attention and his love for myself alone. Then I am nothing but my cramped little ego, and the cosmic spaces inside me are locked away. And, of course, I also lose contact with him. Then I want him, too, to be nothing but ego, "cramped" and there for me only. A very understandable and feminine wish. But I have come quite a long way and shall have to persevere. And suffer relapses on the way. In the past I would sometimes write on the spur of the moment, "I hold him so dear, so infinitely dear." That feeling has now gone. Perhaps that is why I am so heavy at heart, so sad and so worn out. I have not been able to pray these last few days either. And I don't like myself. These three things are doubtless interconnected. And then I become suddenly as obstinate as a mule, refusing to take another step on a rocky path. When I get this dead feeling—no space within me and no energy left for him—then I suddenly wonder: has he let go of me as well? Are his energies so used up by the many who need him each day that he simply had to turn away from me? Etty, I loathe you. So selfish and so mean. Instead of supporting him with your love and caring, you fret like a spoiled child because he isn't paying enough attention to you. It is a petty woman indeed who wants all a man's attention and love for herself alone. Just had a very factual and bland telephone conversation with him. And I believe that he can see what is happening to me, that I am working myself into a "tragic" mood. And it's not just a question of being unhappy all the time, but a question of being more unhappy than ever before. Bringing a dramatic situation to a head and then suffering from it with relish. A remnant of my masochism? And it doesn't help being so reasonable and adult on the surface when poisonous plants have taken root and are proliferating underneath. He would probably laugh out loud if he heard all these fantasies about my dead feelings for him. He would simply say gravely in a matter-of-fact and resigned tone of voice, "That happens in every relationship, that sort of withdrawal. One must leave it alone, and one day everything will be all right again."

I take such moments much too seriously. It is all so stupid of me, and in times like these, too, which sap one's strength so. Feeling unhappy just because the bonds between you and a man seem to have slackened. You, who don't have to stand in queues for hours on end. And have enough food every day—Käthe sees to that. And your desk and books waiting for you each morning. And the most important man in your life lives only a few streets away and hasn't been carted off yet. Just have a good night's sleep and stop carrying on so. You should be ashamed of yourself.

*19 June, Friday morning, 9:30.* I am sometimes afraid to call a spade a spade. Because nothing will then be left to the imagination? No, things ought to be called by their proper name. If they can't stand it, then they have no right to be. We try to save so much in life with a vague sort of mysticism. Mysticism must rest on crystal-clear honesty, can only come after things have been stripped down to their naked reality.

I often find when I come home at night that I want to record the wonderful experiences I have had. Not in the plain and necessarily clumsy words befitting a diary, no, what I would like best is to be able to produce immediate aphorisms and eternal truths from the simplest experiences. Less than that will not do. That's where all my vagueness and my generalizations come in. It seems quite beneath my dignity to write about my belly (what a singularly plump and crude name for so important a part of the body!). If I were to write the whole truth about last night's mood, I would have to admit honestly and factually: it was the day before I started menstruating, and I am only half responsible for my actions then. If Han had not chased me to bed at half past twelve, I would probably still be sitting at my desk. I don't think that I have any truly creative ideas at times like those, just pseudo-creative ones at best. I am all turmoil and commotion inside. And then I am overwhelmed by a sort of agitation and disruption and sometimes a recklessness as well, and all because of the female, with me, alas, three-weekly, process south of my midriff. So much for my reactions last night.

Soon you'll have grease spots all over your books and ink spots all over your sandwiches, said Pa Han. The others are still at lunch, I have pushed my plate to one side and am copying out bits of Rilke between the extremely good strawberries and the odd kind of rabbit food we are eating . . . And now the room is empty, and I am writing amid crumbs on the tablecloth, a lonely radish, and dirty napkins. Käthe is already washing up in the kitchen. It is half past one. I shall take a nap for an hour until the worst of my stomachache has gone. At five o'clock Becker is sending me a man who wants to take Russian lessons. Tonight I must read Pushkin for one hour. I don't have to stand in queues and have few worries about the housekeeping. I don't think there's another person in all Holland who has it as easy, at least that's how it seems to me. I feel a very strong obligation to make full use of all this time I have to myself, not to waste one minute of it. And yet I still don't work with enough concentration and energy. I really have obligations, moral obligations.

*Saturday night, 12:30.* [ . . . ] Humiliation always involves two. The one who does the humiliating, and the one who allows himself to be humiliated. If the second is missing, that is, if the passive party is immune to humiliation, then the humiliation vanishes into thin air. All that remains are vexatious measures that interfere with daily life but are not humiliations that weigh heavily on the soul. We Jews should remember that. This morning I cycled along the Station Quay enjoying the broad sweep of the sky at the edge of the city and breathing in the fresh, unrationed air. And everywhere signs barring Jews from the paths and the open country. But above the one narrow path still left to us stretches the sky, intact. They can't do anything to us, they really can't. They can harass us, they can rob us of our material goods, of our freedom of movement, but we ourselves forfeit our greatest assets by our misguided compliance. By our feelings of being persecuted, humiliated, and oppressed. By our own hatred. By our swagger, which hides our fear. We may of course be sad and depressed by what has been done to us; that is only human and understandable. However: our greatest injury is one we inflict upon ourselves. I find life beautiful, and I feel free. The sky within me is as wide as the one stretching above my head. I believe in God and I believe in man, and I say so without embarrassment. Life is hard, but that is no bad thing. If one starts by taking one's own importance seriously, the rest follows. It is not morbid individualism to work on oneself. True peace will come only when every individual finds peace within himself; when we have all vanquished and transformed our hatred for our fellow human beings of whatever race—even into love one day, although perhaps that is asking too much. It is, however, the only solution. I am a happy person and I hold life dear indeed, in this year of Our Lord 1942, the umpteenth year of the war.

*Sunday morning, eight o'clock.* [ . . . ] My breakfast is at my elbow: a glass of buttermilk, two grayish slices of bread with cucumber and tomato. I have dispensed with the cup of hot chocolate to which I used to treat myself surreptitiously on a Sunday morning, in order to train myself in more frugal habits. I pursue my appetites to their most secret and hidden lairs and try to root them out. More and more we must learn to do without those of our physical necessities that are not absolutely vital. We must train our bodies until they expect no more than the absolutely essential, especially when it comes to food, for it looks as if we are going to face some very lean times. Not "going to face"; those times are here already. And still my feeling is that we are wonderfully well off. But it is easier to train oneself to go without in times of abundance, voluntarily, than in scarce times, through necessity. What one does freely of one's own accord is always more soundly based and longer lasting than what has been forced upon one. (I shall never forget Professor Becker and his little box of cigarette stubs.) We must grow so independent of material and external things that whatever the circumstances our spirit can continue to do its work. And so: buttermilk instead of hot chocolate.

What a lot there is to deal with on my desk. Tide's geranium, which she gave me last week (was it only a week ago?) after that sudden flood of tears, is still standing there. And then the pine cones, I remember when I picked those up. It was on the heath, just behind Mrs. Rümke's country cottage. I think it was the first time I had spent the whole day with S. out in the country. We had a talk about the demonic and the angelic. Well, we shan't be seeing any heath for a very long time, and every so often I find it a great deprivation, although I know that as long as one small street is left to us, the whole sky still stretches above it. And the three pine cones will, if need be, go with me even to Poland. Goodness me, my desk looks just like the world on the first day of creation. As well as exotic Japanese lilies, a geranium, faded tea roses, pine cones that are now holy relics, that Moorish statue, there are also Saint Augustine and the Bible and Russian grammars and dictionaries and Rilke and countless little scribbling blocks, a bottle of ersatz lemonade, typing paper and carbons and more Rilke, all jumbled together, and of course Jung. And this is only what just happens to be lying about.

*Tuesday morning, 8:30.* [ . . . ] A few days ago, I still felt a bit maligned and vindictive, but this morning I suddenly lay there laughing aloud in my bed at my infantile reactions. I had been staring at Hertha's ever-smiling face on his chest of drawers. I was standing by the door, ready to leave, and looking with one eye at that face that has smiled unceasingly for the past sixteen months and with the other at his bed already turned down for the night, and I felt desolate and sad and lonely all over again, thinking, "Yes, that inviting bed over there is for that deadly dull girl with her lifeless smile." His thundering laughter would probably re-echo from all the walls if he ever read these tormented womanly outpourings of mine. Poor Hertha, how unfair

I have been to you. I often wonder what sort of life you live in London, sometimes even as I cycle down the quiet street and see from afar his figure leaning out of the window, bending over that straggly geranium shedding its lifeblood, and the impatient waving of his arm. I run up the stone steps to the front door, which he has usually opened for me by then, and tumble into his two small rooms quite out of breath. Sometimes he stands there looking as powerful and imposing as if he were hewn from some primeval, weathered stone. And sometimes he looks not nearly so impressive, but good-natured and plump like a cuddly toy, so much so that I find it hard to believe that a man who looks like that could be anything but boring or effeminate. And then a sudden thought will shape his features, and he will say, "Look here . . ." and then come out with something from which I can usually learn a thing or two. And always his hands, his large, fine hands, continuous conductors of a tenderness that flows straight from his soul. Poor Hertha, in faraway London. I have the lion's share of our common bond. Later I shall be able to tell you so much about him. Through suffering I have learned that we must share our love with the whole of creation. Only thus can we gain admittance to it. But the price is high: much blood and tears. But all the suffering is worth it. And it is all still in store for you. By then I no doubt shall be tearing frenetically through the world, insignificant woman that I shall never cease to be.

You will probably have to travel a similar path to mine, for this man is so steeped in eternity that he is unlikely to change. And I think that you and I have much in common, for otherwise this friendship between him and me would never have been. You are probably a little more difficult and lonely than I am now. And no doubt you are more serious, where he finds me a little outlandish. And my sense of loss will begin with your welcome entrance into our lives. He will think these words stupid, for he has enough love for us all; with him none of us has to go short. But we women have such a strange makeup. My life is intertwined with yours, but what will that mean when we all come together? If we are ever to meet then it would be best to agree right now to be kind to each other, no matter what. Are you not desperate sometimes over there, across the Channel? Of course you are, I have read all your letters. A young girl all on her own in that big battered city. How do you do it? Really, deep down I admire you, and once I give in to my compassion for you it will overflow.

There is one woman in Amsterdam who prays for you every evening. This is really noble of Tide, for she too loves him, next to God, with a love that is the first and last in her life. I am glad there is somebody who prays for you, your life is better protected for it. I can't do it yet. I'm not really generous enough, except perhaps in odd flashes, but in the main I am full of all the vices—jealousy and obstinacy and what have you. Perhaps there will come a night when I, too, shall pray for you. And that same night you will suddenly feel so good and more reconciled with life than you have been for a long time, and you won't be able to tell where all these new feelings come from. But I haven't yet reached that point. What are you doing at this moment? Your daily struggle is so much harder than mine that I might easily come to feel guilty about you, as I feel guilty about all who must slave for their daily food, who must stand in long queues, and so on. It places great moral obligations and responsibilities upon me. For all I have to do is study Russian and learn more about the great and beloved country in which that language is spoken. The moment you step ashore I shall rush wildly to the station and take a ticket straight to the heart of that country. What do you think of so much childish romanticism in the early morning? In times like these? Yes, it makes me ashamed of myself, but that is precisely what goes on in my imagination. Oh, Hertha, if you only knew under how grave a threat we live here.

I write on this sunny morning so blithely about "stepping ashore" and "meeting each other," but who knows if we shall not have perished in some ghastly camp long before that ever happens? Our life here is more and more menaced from day to day, and what the end of all this will be nobody can tell.

*Thursday afternoon.* From a letter from my father with his inimitable sense of humor: "Today we have entered the cycleless age. I have delivered up Mischa's bicycle personally. In Amsterdam, I see from the paper, the Jews may still cycle about. What a privilege! At least we need fear no longer that our bicycles will be stolen. That is some balm for the nerves. In the wilderness we also had to do without bicycles, for forty long years."

*27 June, Saturday morning, 8:30.* If we have to share a prison cell with several others, isn't it our duty to keep our bodies and souls clean and fresh?

Yesterday at our musical afternoon, S. said after a Schubert piece for four hands followed by Mozart, "Schubert reminds me of the limitations of the piano, Mozart of its virtues."

And Mischa, hesitant and fumbling for the right words, "Yes, Schubert abuses the piano in this piece in order to make music." Later I walked a short way with him along the quay. Suddenly I was overwhelmed by the presentiment of imminent parting and said, "Perhaps we really have no future . . ." And he replied, "Perhaps, but only if you take a materialist view . . ."

One can live without coffee and without cigarettes, Liesl said rebelliously, but not without nature, that's impossible, no one should be allowed to deprive you of that. I said, "Think of it as if we'd got to spend a prison sentence here, for a few years perhaps, and learn to look at the couple of trees over there across the road as if they were a forest. And for prisoners, we still have a good deal of freedom of movement."

Liesl, that small elf, a moonlight bather on warm summer nights, also cleans spinach for three hours a day and queues for potatoes to the point of passing out. And little sighs escape her at times, sighs that start deep down inside her and make her small body tremble from head to toe. She seems cloaked in shyness and chastity, although the facts of her life don't sound altogether chaste, and at the same time there is something powerful, an original natural force, in her. And she would be utterly amazed if she could see what I have written here: really she is my only girlfriend.

*Monday morning, ten o'clock.* [ . . . ] God is not accountable to us, but we are to Him. I know what may lie in wait for us. Even now I am cut off from my parents and cannot reach them, although they are only two hours away by train.[36] But I know exactly where they are, and that they're not going short of food, and that there are many kind people all round them. And they know where I am, too. But I am also aware that there may come a time when I shan't know where they are, when they might be deported to perish miserably in some unknown place. I know this is perfectly possible. The latest news is that all Jews will be transported out of Holland through Drenthe Province and then on to Poland. And the English radio has reported that 700,000 Jews perished last year alone, in Germany and the occupied territories. And even if we stay alive, we shall carry the wounds with us throughout our lives. And yet I don't think life is meaningless. And God is not accountable to us for the senseless harm we cause one another. We are accountable to Him! I have already died a thousand deaths in a thousand concentration camps. I know about everything and am no longer appalled by the latest reports. In one way or another I know it all. And yet I find life beautiful and meaningful. From minute to minute.

*1 July [1942], morning.* My mind has assimilated everything that has happened in these last few days. So far the rumors have been infinitely worse than the reality, for us in Holland at least, since in Poland the killers seem to be in full cry. But though my mind has come to terms with it all, my body hasn't. It has disintegrated into a thousand pieces, and each piece has a different pain.

And now I can rouse neither body nor soul, I am so shattered physically. It is almost one o'clock. After I've had my coffee I shall try to get a bit of sleep. And at 4:45 to S.'s. My day is sometimes made up of a hundred days. But now I am completely exhausted. Last night at seven o'clock I was cast into a hell of alarm and despondency brought on by the new regulations. It was all to the good, I suppose, since it helped me to get some idea of the fear felt by so many others—for fear was something I had almost forgotten. Then at eight o'clock I was all peace again. And I was almost proud of the fact that, exhausted though I was, I could still give one and a half hours of Russian conversation. In the past I would have telephoned to cancel it with some excuse about feeling unwell. And tonight it'll be a new day and I'll be seeing somebody else in trouble, a Catholic girl. For a Jew to be able to help a non-Jew these days gives one a peculiar sense of power.

*3:45 in the afternoon.* Sun on the balcony and a light breeze through the jasmine. As I said, a new day has dawned—how many of them have there been since seven o'clock this morning? I shall linger another ten minutes with the jasmine, and then on the household bicycle—for which we have a permit—to see the friend who has been part of my life for sixteen months and whom I feel I have known for a thousand years, yet who can still suddenly present me with an aspect so new that I catch my breath with surprise. How exotic the jasmine looks, so delicate and dazzling against the mud-brown walls.

I can't take in how beautiful this jasmine is. But there is no need to. It is enough simply to believe in miracles in the twentieth century. And I do, even though the lice will be eating me up in Poland before long.

It is possible to suffer with dignity and without. I mean: most of us in the West don't understand the art of suffering and experience a thousand fears instead. We cease to be alive, being full of fear, bitterness, hatred, and despair. God knows, it's only too easy to understand why. But when we are deprived of our lives, are we really deprived of very much? We have to accept death as part of life, even the most horrible of deaths. And don't we live an entire life each one of our days, and does it really matter if we live a few days more or less? I am in Poland every day, on the battlefields, if that's what one can call them. I often see visions of poisonous green smoke; I am with the hungry, with the ill-treated and the dying, every day, but I am also with the jasmine and with that piece of sky beyond my window; there is room for everything in a single life. For belief in God and for a miserable end. When I say, I have come to terms with life, I don't mean I have lost hope. What I feel is not hopelessness, far from it. I have lived this life a thousand times over already, and I have died a thousand deaths. Am I blasé then? No. It is a question of living life from minute to minute and taking suffering into the bargain. And it is certainly no small bargain these days. But does it matter if it is the Inquisition that causes people to suffer in one century, and war and pogroms in another? To suffer senselessly, as the victims would put it? Suffering has always been with us, does it really matter in what form it comes? All that matters is how we bear it and how we fit it into our lives. Am I merely an armchair theorist safely ensconced behind my desk, with my familiar books around me and the jasmine outside? Is it all theory, never tested in practice? I don't think so. All our conversations are now interlarded with sentences such as, "I hope he'll still be there to enjoy these strawberries with us." I know that Mischa, with his delicate physique, has been ordered to report at Central Station, and I think of Miriam's and Renate's[37] pale little faces, and of many, many worried people, and I know it all, everything, every moment, and I sometimes bow my head under the great burden that weighs down on me, but even as I bow my head I also feel the need, almost mechanically, to fold my hands. And so I can sit for hours and know everything and bear everything and grow stronger in the bearing of it, and at the same time feel sure that life is beautiful and worth living and meaningful. Despite everything. But that does not mean I am always filled with joy and exaltation. I am often dog-tired after standing about in queues, but I know that this too is part of life, and *somewhere there is something inside me that will never desert me again.*

*3 July 1942, Friday evening, 8:30.* Yes, I am still at the same desk, but it seems to me that I am going to have to draw a line under everything and continue in a different tone. I must admit a new insight into my life and find a place for it: what is at stake is our impending destruction and annihilation, we can have no more illusions about that. They are out to destroy us completely, we must accept that and go on from there. Today I was filled with terrible despair, and I shall have to come to terms with that as well. Even if we are consigned to hell, let us go there as gracefully as we can. I did not really want to put it so blandly.

Why this mood at this particular moment? Is it because I have a blister on my foot from walking through the hot town, because so many people have had sore feet ever since they were stopped from using the trams, because of Renate's pale little face, because she has to walk to school on her short little legs through the heat, one hour there and one hour back? Because Liesl stood in a queue and didn't get any vegetables after all? It is for such an awful lot of reasons, all of them petty in themselves, but all of them part of the great campaign to destroy us. Some are merely grotesque by comparison, though equally hard to grasp: that S. may no longer visit this house, no longer has access to the piano or to his books. That I may not visit Tide, and so on.[38]

Very well then, this new certainty, that what they are after is our total destruction, I accept it. I know it now, and I shall not burden others with my fears. I shall not be bitter if others fail to grasp what is happening to us Jews. I work and continue to live with the same conviction, and I find life meaningful—yes, meaningful—although I hardly dare say so in company these days.

Living and dying, sorrow and joy, the blisters on my feet and the jasmine behind the house, the persecution, the unspeakable horrors—it is all as one in me, and I accept it all as one mighty whole and begin to grasp it better if only for myself, without being able to explain to anyone else how it all hangs together. I wish I could live for a long time so that one day I may know how to explain it, and if I am not granted that wish, well, then somebody else will perhaps do it, carry on from where my life has been cut short. And that is why I must try to live a good and faithful life to my last breath: so that those who come after me do not have to start all over again, need not face the same difficulties. Isn't that doing something for future generations? Bernard's Jewish friend had them ask me after the latest promulgations, "Didn't I now agree that all Germans should be done away with, preferably hung, drawn, and quartered?"

Yes, we carry everything within us, God and Heaven and Hell and Earth and Life and Death and all of history. The externals are simply so many props; everything we need is within us. And we have to take everything that comes: the bad with the good, which does not mean we cannot devote our life to curing the bad. But we must know what motives inspire our struggle, and we must begin with ourselves, every day anew.

There was a time when I thought that I had to come up with a host of brilliant ideas each day, and now I sometimes feel like a barren stretch of land on which nothing grows, but which is nevertheless spanned by a high, wide sky. And this way is by far the better. Something has crystallized. I have looked our destruction, our miserable end, which has already begun in so many small ways in our daily life, straight in the eye and accepted it into my life, and my love of life has not been diminished. I am not bitter or rebellious, or in any way discouraged. I continue to grow from day to day, even with the likelihood of destruction staring me in the face. I shall no longer flirt with words, for words merely evoke misunderstandings: I have come to terms with life, nothing can happen to me, and after all my personal fate is not the issue; it doesn't really matter if it is I who perish or another. What matters is that we are all marked men.

By "coming to terms with life" I mean: the reality of death has become a definite part of my life; my life has, so to speak, been extended by death, by my looking death in the eye and accepting it, by accepting destruction as part of life and no longer wasting my energies on fear of death or the refusal to acknowledge its inevitability. It sounds paradoxical: by excluding death from our life we cannot live a full life, and by admitting death into our life we enlarge and enrich it. This has been my first real confrontation with death. I never knew what to make of it before. I had such a virginal attitude toward it. I have never seen a dead person. Just imagine: a world sown with a million corpses, and in twenty-seven years I have never seen a single one. I have often wondered what my attitude to death really is. I never delved deeply into the question: there was no need for that. And now death has come as large as life, and I greet him as an old acquaintance. Everything is so simple. You don't have to have any profound thoughts on the subject. There death suddenly stands, large as life and part of it.

And so I can go to sleep peacefully. It is ten o'clock. I didn't do very much today. I fell behind, what with having to walk hot pavements on my blistered feet and similar petty annoyances. Then I was overcome with despair and uncertainty. And then I went to see S. He had a headache, and that worried him, for normally everything works so smoothly in his powerful body. I lay in his arms, and he was so gentle and so sweet, almost wistful. I feel a new period is beginning in our lives, more serious and more intense, one in which we shall concentrate on the essentials. Every day we shed more trivia. "We are moving toward our destruction, that is quite plain now, we mustn't fool ourselves about that." Tomorrow night I shall borrow Dicky's[39] bed; she will sleep on the ground floor and come up to wake me in the morning. We can still do that. And I know that we shall support one another often in these hard times.

*A little later:* And if this day has brought me nothing else—not yet that fine and final confrontation with death and extinction— then I am nevertheless grateful for that kosher German soldier at the kiosk with his bag of carrots and cauliflowers. First he pushed that note into Liesl's hand on the tram, and then came the letter that I had to read and reread: she reminded him so much of the late rabbi's daughter whom he had nursed on her deathbed for days and nights on end. And tonight he is paying a visit.

And when Liesl told me all this, I knew at once: I shall have to pray for this German soldier. Out of all those uniforms one has been given a face now. There will be other faces, too, in which we shall be able to read something we understand: that German soldiers suffer as well. There are no frontiers between suffering people, and we must pray for them all. Goodnight.

*Saturday morning, nine o'clock*. It feels as if great changes are taking place in me, and I believe it is more than a passing mood.

Last night was a great breakthrough: a new insight, at least if one can call something like that insight, and this morning I was filled with peace again and with an assurance I have not felt for a long time. And all this because of one little blister on my left foot.

My body is a home for many pains; they lie hidden in every corner, with first this one making itself felt and then the next. I have become reconciled to that, too. And I wonder how I can work so well and even concentrate with all my aches and pains. But I also have to accept that intellectual powers alone do not get one very far when things get really serious. The walk to and from the tax office has taught me that. We walked the pavements of this sunny, beautiful town like happy tourists. His hand caught mine, and they felt so good together, our hands. And when at one point I was overcome with tiredness and had this sudden peculiar feeling about not being allowed to take a tram anywhere in this great city with its long streets, and not even being allowed to sit down at one of the little pavement cafés (I could tell him something about so many pavement cafés: "Look, that's where I went with my friends two years ago, after I took my finals"), then I thought, or rather I didn't really think it, it welled up somewhere inside me: throughout the ages people have been tired and have worn their feet out on God's earth, in the cold and the heat, and that, too, is part of life. This sort of feeling has been growing much stronger in me: a hint of eternity steals through my smallest daily activities and perceptions. I am not alone in my tiredness or sickness or fears, but at one with millions of others from many centuries, and it is all part of life.

And at the end of our long walk there was a room waiting for us with a divan on which to fling ourselves after having kicked off our shoes, and then such a wonderful treat sent by friends—

a basket of cherries from the Betuwe. A good lunch, which used to be something we took for granted, is now a special treat. As life becomes harder and more threatening, it also becomes richer, because the fewer expectations we have, the more the good things of life become unexpected gifts that we accept with gratitude. At least, that's how I feel, and he as well, and we can tell each other from time to time how strange it is that we feel no hatred or indignation or bitterness, but we can't say that openly in company, for no one would understand.

During our walk I knew that a house was waiting for us at the end, but I also knew that a time would come when there would be nothing like that and all our walks would end in some barracks. I knew this while we were walking, knew it would be true not only for myself but also for all the others, and I accepted that too. And one more thing I learned from this walk: those short two hours on the pavements gave me such a bad headache that my skull threatened to burst its seams. And my feet were so sore that I thought to myself, How will I ever be able to walk again? And all the aspirins I swallowed when we got back (I felt I had to take them because otherwise I would have had to go to bed, but shouldn't one gradually learn to bear pain without artificial aids?) made me feel foul and poisoned all next day. Yet I did not let it get me down, not for one moment, though I had to tell myself, "You're in a poor state, Etty. Your body is completely unfit and has no resistance; in a labor camp you'd break down inside three days, and all the intellectual power in the world will not be able to save you if a companionable walk lasting less than two hours, with every possible comfort awaiting you at the end, makes you so tired." I don't mind so much for myself—I can stretch out on the floor and relax, and when it is all past I praise life and God. But I'm afraid of being a burden to others. In the past I never let on that I had overdone things: I kept on walking, kept on playing, went to bed very late, joined in everything. But wasn't it all just showing off? Being afraid that others wouldn't find me much fun and that they might drop me if they had to bear the weight of my tired body as well as their own? Just part of my inferiority complex. In any case, we arranged to meet again today and to look up a few addresses in the Jewish district where we might perhaps be able to help, and that means walking much farther than we did on Thursday morning.

By last night I had not plucked up enough courage to say that I could not walk so far, for I know that to him such walks are relaxing. And I also thought something like: Tide can walk with him for hours, so I should be able to do it, too. It is that same old childish fear of losing another's love if one doesn't meet all his expectations. But I am ridding myself more and more of these feelings. One must be able to admit one's inadequacies, even in the physical sphere. And one must also be able to accept the fact that one may not always be for another just what one would have liked to be.

To admit one's weaknesses is not the same as complaining about them, for complaining means shifting the misery onto others. And I'm sure that this was why just before eight o'clock last night, as I was actually on my way to see him, I rang up a pupil and canceled a lesson, which is something I rarely do. And as I was lying next to him on the divan I suddenly said that I was so sorry that the walk had made me so tired, because it made me realize just what poor physical shape I was in. And he immediately replied, as if it was the most obvious thing in the world, "Then it would probably be much better if we didn't go on that walk." And then I said that I would take my bicycle with us so that I could ride back home. It seems such a small thing, but for me it was quite an achievement. Normally I would probably have ruined my feet rather than give him the slightest cause to think I might spoil his walk.

It's all in my mind, of course, but now I say, quite simply and candidly, "Look, my strength isn't up to it, I can't go any farther, there's nothing I can do about it, you must take me as I am." This is just one more step toward maturity and independence, and I seem to be getting a little closer every day.

Many who are indignant about injustices are only indignant because the injustices are being inflicted on them. Their indignation is skin-deep.

In a labor camp I should die within three days. I should lie down and die and still not find life unfair.

*Late morning.* Every pretty blouse I put on is a kind of celebration. And so is every occasion I have to wash with scented soap in a bathroom all to myself for half an hour. It's as if I were reveling in these civilized luxuries for the last time. But even if I have to forgo them one day, I shall always know that they exist and that they can make life pleasant, and I shall think of them as a great boon even if I can't share in them any longer. For whether or not I share in them isn't really the point, is it?

One must face up to everything that happens, even when someone in the shape of a fellow human being comes up to you just as you are leaving the pharmacy with a tube of toothpaste, pokes you with his finger, and demands inquisitorially, "Are you allowed to buy that?" "Yes sir," you say softly but firmly in your customary pleasant manner, "this is a pharmacy." "I see," he says, curtly and suspiciously, and walks on. I am no good at such exchanges. I can be sharp in intellectual debate, but when it comes to bullies in the street, to put it bluntly, I am completely at a loss. I become embarrassed and sad and upset that people can behave like that to each other, but I am quite incapable of quick repartee, of giving as good as I get. That man should not have been allowed to question me like that. He probably thinks he's a great idealist; no doubt he'll do his bit one day to clear society of all "Jewish elements." These brushes with the outside world still make me sad. But I am not the slightest bit concerned about cutting a fine figure in the eyes of this persecutor or that. Let them see my sadness and my utter defenselessness, too. There is no need to put on a show, I have my inner strength and that is enough, the rest doesn't matter.

*8:30 A.M.* He wore a pair of light blue pajamas and an embarrassed expression when he came in. He looked very sweet. And he sat for a while on the edge of the bed talking to me. Now he has gone, and it will be another hour before he's finished: washing, exercises, "reading." "Reading" is something I am allowed to do with him. When he said, "I'll be another hour still," I felt as sad as if I had just said farewell for good. A sudden wave of sadness washed through me. Oh, to let someone you love go entirely free, to leave him to live his own life, is the most difficult thing there is in this world. I am learning it for his sake.

There was a riot of bird song on the flat, graveled roof, and a pigeon outside my wide-open window. And the early-morning sun.

He woke up at 5:30. At 7:30 I stripped and washed, did a few exercises, and then went back under the bedclothes. He came in hesitantly in his light blue pajamas, looked embarrassed. He was coughing and still has that pain in his head, and he said, "We won't be going to Adri's for that meal. I've had a really bad nightmare, a 'dream-omen.' I'm in a state of exhaustion." And so we are off to the doctor's this morning instead of going for a walk. I shall retire for the day into my own stillness, accepting the hospitality of that calm space for one whole day. Perhaps I shall be rested then. Body and mind are very tired and out of condition. But I won't do any work today, and everything should be all right.

There is sun outside, and this room now feels so welcoming

that I should be able to pray in it. The two of us have done a lot of living, after all, he with women, I with men, and yet there he sat in his light blue pajamas at the edge of my bed and just leaned his head against my bare arm, and we spoke a little, and then he went away again. It was really very touching. Neither of us is tasteless enough to take advantage of the other. We have had wild and unfettered lives in many strange beds, and we are nevertheless shy all over again, each time. I find this very beautiful and delight in it. Now I shall put on my brightly colored dressing gown and go downstairs to read the Bible with him. Then I shall spend the whole day sitting in a corner of the silent space I carry within me. I still lead a very privileged life. I need do nothing today, not even housework, and I have no lessons. My breakfast is wrapped in a napkin, and Adri will bring us a hot meal. I am left alone in my still corner, squatting like a Buddha and smiling like one as well, deep within, that is.

*9:45.* Those psalms that have become part of my daily life were excellent fare on an empty stomach.

We shared the beginning of the day together, and that was very lovely. And very sustaining. There was that silly stab in my heart again when he said, "Now I'm going to do my exercises, and then I'll get dressed." And I felt as if I was forsaken and all alone in the world. I remember thinking I would love to share my toothbrush with him, feeling the desire to be with someone, to share in his smallest everyday activity. And yet this distance is good and fruitful: one discovers the other anew each time. Soon he will come up to fetch me for breakfast at his small round table beside the geranium, which is still shedding more petals each day. Oh, those birds and the sun of the gravel-covered roof! And in myself so much meekness and acceptance. And a contentment that rests in God. Something elemental flows out of the Old Testament, and something homely as well. Splendid people live in its pages, poetic and austere. The Bible is so rugged and tender, simple and wise. And so full of wonderful characters, too.

*10:00 P.M.* Just one thing more: every minute of this day seems one great gift and consolation, a memory I shall carry within me as an ever-present reality. And each phase of it has been followed by another that makes everything that has gone before seem pale. We must count neither on being preserved nor on being destroyed. These are the extreme possibilities, but neither is a certainty. What matter are the concerns of daily life. Last night we talked about the labor camps. I said, "I don't have any illusions about them, I know that I shall be dead within three days because my body is so useless." Werner was sure he would fare no better. But Liesl said, "I don't know, I have a feeling that I'll come through." I can sympathize with that feeling of hers, I used to have it myself. A feeling of indestructible resilience. And I still have it now, that's the whole point, but no longer in a purely material sense. It doesn't matter whether my untrained body will be able to carry on, that is really of secondary importance; the main thing is that even as we die a terrible death we are able to feel right up to the very last moment that life has meaning and beauty, that we have realized our potential and lived a good life. I can't really put it into words.

*Monday, 11:00 A.M.* Perhaps I can now write for a few uninterrupted hours about the essentials. Rilke wrote somewhere to his paralyzed friend Ewald of "days in which the minutes pass like years." That is how yesterday felt to us. When we said good-bye I leaned against him and said, "I want to stay with you as long as I possibly can." And his mouth looked so soft and defenseless and sad, and he said, almost dreamily, "Yes, which one of us does not have his wishes?"

And I wondered: must we say good-bye to these wishes as well? When one begins to accept, must one not try to accept everything? He leaned against the wall of Dicky's room, and I leaned gently and lightly against him, just as I had done on countless similar occasions in the past, but this time it suddenly felt as if the sky had fallen as in a Greek tragedy. For a moment my senses were totally confused, and I felt as though I was standing with him in the center of infinite space—pervaded by threats but also filled with eternity. In that moment a great change took place within us, forever. He remained leaning against the wall for a little and said in an almost plaintive voice, "I must write to my girlfriend tonight, it will be her birthday soon. But what am I to say to her? I haven't the heart for it or the inspiration." And I said to him, "You must start even now and try to reconcile her to the fact that she will never see you again, you must give her something to hold on to for the future. Tell her how the two of you, though physically apart for all these years, have nevertheless been as one, and that she has a duty to carry on if only to keep something of your spirit alive." Yes, that's how people talk to each other these days, and it doesn't even sound unreal anymore. We have embraced a new reality, and everything has taken on new colors and new emphases. And between our eyes and hands and mouths there now flows a constant stream of tenderness, a stream in which all petty desires seem to have been extinguished. All that matters now is to be kind to each other with all the goodness that is in us. And every encounter is also a farewell. This morning he rang me up and said almost dreamily, "It was so beautiful yesterday, and we must be together as much as possible."

In the afternoon, when the two of us, spoiled "bachelors" that we still are, sat over a copious lunch at his small round table, a lunch in which the world outside ceased to matter, and I said that I didn't want to leave him, he suddenly became stern and solemn and said, "Don't forget what you always preach. Never forget it." And I did not even have the old feeling that I was a little girl acting a role in a play far beyond my understanding, but felt instead that my very life and fate were at stake, and I could accept that, with all the threats, the uncertainties, the faith, and the love, for it seemed to fit me like some garment specially made to measure. I love him with all the unselfishness I am capable of, and I shall not burden him with even the smallest weight of my fears and demands. I shall even relinquish the wish to stay with him to the last moment. My whole being has become one great prayer for him. And why only for him? Why not for all the others as well? Girls of sixteen are being sent to the labor camps as well. We older ones shall have to take them under our wing when it is the turn of us Dutch girls. Last night I suddenly felt like saying to Han, Do you know that sixteen-year-old girls are being picked up as well? And I kept it back and thought to myself, Why add to his already heavy burden? Everyone surely knows what is going on, but we must be kind to others and not always saddle them with what we can perfectly well carry alone.

A few days ago I still thought to myself: the worst thing for me will be when I am no longer allowed pencil and paper to clarify my thoughts—they are absolutely indispensable to me, for without them I shall fall apart and be utterly destroyed.

But now I know that once you begin to lower your demands and your expectations, you can let go of everything. It took me just a few days to learn that.

Perhaps I shall be able to stay on here for another month, but by that time any loophole in the regulations will surely have been closed.[40] Every day I shall put my papers in order, and every day I shall say farewell. And the real farewell, when it comes, will only be a small outward confirmation of what has been accomplished within me from day to day.

I feel so strange. Am I really sitting here writing things down so calmly? Would anybody understand me if I told them that I feel so strangely happy, not bursting with it, but just plain happy, because I can sense a new gentleness and a new confidence growing stronger inside me from day to day? That all the confusing and threatening and dreadful things that assail me do not drive me out of my mind for even one moment? I dare hardly write on, I don't know how to put it, it is as if I had gone almost too far in my dissociation from all that drives most people out of their minds. If I knew for certain that I should die next week, I would still be able to sit at my desk all week and study with perfect equanimity, for I know now that life and death make a meaningful whole. Death is a gentle slipping away, even when gloom and abominations are its trappings.

We still have to go through a great deal. We shall become poor, then destitute, until in the end our strength will go, not only because of all the fears and uncertainties but also, very simply, because we are banned from more and more shops and therefore have to cover longer distances on foot, which is already undermining the health of many people I know. From all sides our destruction creeps up on us, and soon the ring will be closed and no one at all will be able to come to our aid. All the little loopholes that are still left will soon be stopped up. Life is so strange: it is cold and wet just now. As if you had suddenly been thrown from the peaks of a sultry summer night down a steep drop into a dark and chilly valley. Last time I spent a night with Han, it was also on the razor edge of heat and cold. Yesterday when we talked before an open window about the latest developments and I looked into his tortured face, I had the feeling: tonight we shall lie in each other's arms and sob. We did indeed lie in each other's arms, but we did not sob. Only in our final ecstasy did a flood tide of despair, of elemental human sorrow, rise up from deep within me and submerge me, and there was so much pity for myself and for everyone else, and after that a feeling that everything had to be just as it was. But in the dark I was able to bury my head between his naked shoulders and weep my tears in secret. And then I suddenly thought of Mrs. W.'s cake in the afternoon, and how it was covered with strawberries, and I couldn't help grinning and giving way to a feeling of radiant good humor. And now I must see to lunch, and at two o'clock I am going over to see S. I should add that my stomach is upset but I have decided not to dwell on my health any longer, it takes up too much paper and I'll cope with it somehow. In the past I used to write a great deal about it because I couldn't manage it properly, but now I have got the better of it. At least that's what I think. Am I being frivolous and reckless? I can't really tell.

*7 July, Tuesday morning, 9:30.* Mien[41] just rang to say that Mischa had been selected for Drenthe yesterday. Outcome unknown. Mother is up and about, she said, and Father reads a lot, he really has great inner resources.

The streets through which we cycle are not what they used to be, the sky hangs so low and so threatening over them and there seem to be storm signals even when the sun is shining. We now live side by side with destiny, or whatever you want to call it, we rub shoulders with it daily, and nothing is how we learned it from our books.

This much I know: you have to forget your own worries for the sake of others, for the sake of those whom you love. All the strength and love and faith in God that one possesses, and which have grown so miraculously in me of late, must be there for everyone who chances to cross one's path and who needs it. "I have become so terribly used to you," he said yesterday. And God knows how "terribly" I have become "used to" him. And yet I must let him go. I mean: out of my love for him I must draw strength and love for everyone who needs it, but my love and concern for him must not be allowed to become too egocentric. And you can draw strength even from suffering. You have to be consistent to the end. You can say, I can bear everything else, but if something were to happen to him or if I had to leave him, then I couldn't go on. But even in that case you simply have to go on. You must learn to forgo all personal desires and to surrender completely. And surrender does not mean giving up the ghost, fading away with grief, but offering what little assistance I can wherever it has pleased God to place me. I feel so strange, as if I were floating on air, as if I were divorced from reality, had no precise awareness of what was going on.

A few days ago I wrote: I long to sit at my desk and get on with my studies. That is no longer true. It may indeed be granted to me, but I must stop longing for it. Werner said yesterday, "We shan't be moving house, it's not worth it any longer." And he looked at me and said, "If only they let all of us go together." The little Weyl girl peered sadly at her thin legs and said to me, "I must try and get myself two pairs of long underpants this week, but how am I going to do it?" And to the others, "If only I could share a compartment with you." They are leaving by train one night next week at half past one, and the journey is free, oh yes, free, and they are not allowed to take any pets with them. That was all in the call-up notice. Also that they had to take working shoes and two pairs of socks and a spoon, but no gold or silver or platinum, no, nothing like that, except for wedding rings—quite a generous concession, that. And I shan't take a hat, said F——,[42] a cap will be much more becoming.

Yes, that's how we carry on in the evenings. Last night when I was walking home to mull over the latest news with the others, I thought to myself, "How in heaven's name will I be able to give a lesson tonight?"—I could write a book about those lessons with that girl with her sleek boy's head and her great questioning eyes. I hope I shall remember everything that happens to us so that one day I'll be able to retell it all. It is so different from everything you read in books, altogether different. So I make a mental note of every small gesture, every utterance, every facial expression, and I do so with almost cold detachment. I approach things like an artist and expect that later, when I feel the need to tell everything, I shall have what talent it takes to do so.

*Afternoon.* One of Bernard's friends met a German soldier in the street who asked him for a cigarette. A conversation started up, and it appeared that the soldier was an Austrian teacher who had worked in Paris. I must record one remark he made as quoted by Bernard. He said, "In Germany more soldiers die in their barracks than are killed by the enemy."

That broker turned up on Leo Krijn's terrace on Sunday morning and said, "We must pray for better things with all our hearts, as long as there still is hope. If we allow our hatred to turn us into savage beasts like them then there is no hope for anyone."

My biggest worry is what to do with my useless feet. I just hope my blister heals up in time, or else I'm bound to be a nuisance when we are all herded together. And I must go to the dentist soon—so many essentials that I have put off endlessly but are now, I think, urgent. I shall stop all that messing about with Russian grammar, too, I know enough to keep my pupils going for the next few months, and I'll be better occupied finishing *The Idiot.*

I won't copy things out anymore either, because it takes up too much time, and I won't be allowed to drag all this paper around with me in any case. I shall simply try to store away the essential bits in my mind against the lean days. And I had better get used to the fact that I shan't be about much longer, and prepare for my leave-taking in all sorts of little ways so as to be sure I am not hit too hard by the finale when it comes: getting rid of letters and papers and other old junk in my desk. I really do think that Mischa will be rejected as unfit.

I must go to bed earlier, otherwise I feel sleepy all day and that's no good. I must try to get hold of that letter from our kosher German soldier before Liesl goes to Drenthe, and preserve it as a *document humain*. After dealing out crushing blows, history often takes the strangest of turns. Life is so odd and so surprising and so infinitely varied, and at every twist of the road the whole vista changes all of a sudden. Most people carry stereotyped ideas about life in their heads. We have to rid ourselves of all preconceptions, of all slogans, of all sense of security, find the courage to let go of everything, every standard, every conventional bulwark. Only then will life become infinitely rich and overflowing, even in the suffering it deals out to us.

I would so much like to read everything of Rilke's before the time comes when I won't perhaps be able to lay my hands on books for a long time. I feel very much at one with a small group of people I met by chance at Werner and Liesl's. All are being deported next week to work in Germany under police guard. Tonight I dreamed that I had to pack my case. I tossed and turned, fretting about what shoes to take—all of them hurt my feet. And how was I to pack all my underwear and food for three days and blankets into one suitcase or rucksack? And I had to find room somewhere for the Bible. And if possible for Rilke's *Book of Hours* and *Letters to a Young Poet*. And I very much wanted to take along my two small Russian dictionaries and *The Idiot* so as to keep up the language. It's going to be strange during registration when I give my occupation: teacher of Russian. Presumably that will make me a "special case." For all I know they might decide to make use of my linguistic expertise once I'm in their clutches, in which case I could still end up in Russia, although God alone knows by what circuitous route.

*Eight o'clock.* Well, now, let's put a lid on all today's tumult, and I'll have this evening to myself in peace and quiet concentration.

A yellow tea rose on my desk is flanked by two small vases of violets. After our regular evening conversation with the others S. looked utterly worn out and said, "How on earth do the Levies stand it? I can't take any more, I feel absolutely awful." As for me, I am able to put everything, fact and rumor, behind me and study and read all evening. How odd: not a single one of the day's worries and alarms has followed me here; I sit at my desk "untouched," immersed in my studies as if nothing were happening in the world outside. Everything has simply fallen away from me, leaving no trace, and I feel more "receptive" than ever before. Next week no doubt it will be the turn of the Dutch Jews. With each minute that passes I shed more wishes and desires and attachments. There are moments when I can see right through life and the human heart, when I understand more and more and become calmer and calmer and am filled with a faith in God that has grown so quickly inside me that it frightened me at first but has now become inseparable from me. And now to work.

*Thursday morning, 9:30.* Such words as "god" and "death" and "suffering" and "eternity" are best forgotten. We have to become as simple and as wordless as the growing corn or the falling rain. We must just be.

Have I really made so much progress that I can say with complete honesty, I hope they will send me to a labor camp so that I can do something for the sixteen-year-old girls who will also be going? And to reassure the distracted parents who are kept behind, saying, "Don't worry, I'll look after your children"?

When I tell others, Fleeing or hiding is pointless, there is no escape, so let's just do what we can for others, it sounds too much like defeatism, like something I don't mean at all. I cannot find the right words either for that radiant feeling inside me, which encompasses but is untouched by all the suffering and all the violence. But I am still talking in much too philosophical, much too bookish a way, as if I had thought it all up just to make life more pleasant for myself.

*Friday morning.* One moment it is Hitler, the next it is Ivan the Terrible; one moment it is resignation and the next war, pestilence, earthquake, or famine. Ultimately what matters most is to bear the pain, to cope with it, and to keep a small corner of one's soul unsullied, come what may.

*Later.* I keep fretting and brooding and trying to do the most urgent daily chores as quickly as possible, and there is a knot inside that makes it hard to breathe and I rack my brains and have to give up my studies for part of the morning, pace up and down the room, have a stomachache, and so on, and suddenly my confidence floods back: later, when I have survived it all, I shall write stories about these times that will be like faint brush strokes against the great wordless background of God, Life, Death, Suffering, and Eternity. Your worries leap up on you like vermin. All right, so you have to do some scratching, and your looks suffer as a result, but in the end you manage to shake them off. I shall treasure the short time I still have to stay here as one might a bonus, as a holiday.

A hard day, a very hard day. We must learn to shoulder our common fate; everyone who seeks to save himself must surely realize that if he does not go another must take his place. As if it really mattered which of us goes. Ours is now a common destiny, and that is something we must not forget. A very hard day. But I keep finding myself in prayer. And that is something I shall always be able to do, even in the smallest space: pray. And that part of our common destiny that I must shoulder myself, I strap tightly and firmly to my back, it becomes part of me, as I walk through the streets even now.

And I shall wield this slender fountain pen as if it were a

hammer, and my words will have to be so many hammer strokes with which to beat out the story of our fate and of a piece of history as it is and never was before. Not in this totalitarian, massively organized form, spanning the whole of Europe. Still, a few people must survive if only to be the chroniclers of this age. I would very much like to become one of their number.

S.'s quivering mouth when he said, "Adri and Dicky won't be allowed to bring me my food anymore."

*11 July 1942, Saturday morning, eleven o'clock.* We must only speak about the ultimate and most serious things in life when the words well up inside us as simply and as naturally as water from a spring.

And if God does not help me to go on, then I shall have to help God. The surface of the earth is gradually turning into one great prison camp, and soon there will be nobody left outside. The Jews here are telling each other lovely stories: they say that the Germans are burying us alive or exterminating us with gas. But what is the point of repeating such things, even if they should be true?

It hasn't stopped pouring with rain since last night. I have already cleared out one of the drawers in my desk. I rediscovered the one photograph I have of S., which I mislaid nearly a year ago. I have always been absolutely convinced that it would turn up again. And there it suddenly was, at the bottom of that untidy drawer. That's typical of me: I just know with some things, big or small, that they will turn out all right in the end. I never worry about tomorrow. For instance I know I am going to have to leave here very soon, and I haven't the faintest idea where I'll end up or how I shall earn my living, but I know that something will turn up. If one burdens the future with one's worries, it cannot grow organically. I am filled with confidence, not that I shall succeed in worldly things, but that even when things go badly for me I shall still find life good and worth living.

I catch myself making all sorts of minor but telling adjustments in anticipation of life in a labor camp. Last night when I was walking along the quay beside him in a pair of comfortable sandals, I suddenly thought, "I shall take these sandals along as well, I can wear them instead of the heavier shoes from time to time." What goes on in my head at moments like that? Such lighthearted, almost playful good humor. Yesterday was a hard, a very hard day, when I suffered agonies. Yet once more I was able to brave it all, everything that came storming at me, and now I can bear a little more than I was able to bear yesterday. And that probably explains my cheerfulness and inner peace: that I am able, time after time, to cope all by myself, that my heart does not shrivel up with the bitterness of it all, and that even the moments of deepest sadness and black despair finally make me stronger. I don't fool myself about the real state of affairs, and I've even dropped the pretense that I'm out to help others. I shall merely try to help God as best I can, and if I succeed in doing that, then I shall be of use to others as well. But I mustn't have heroic illusions about that either.

But how shall I really feel and act, I keep wondering, with a call-up card for Germany in my bag and orders to leave in a week's time? Supposing the card came tomorrow, how would I act then? I wouldn't tell a soul at first but retire to the quietest spot in the house, withdraw into myself and gather what strength I could from every cranny of my body and soul. I would have my hair cut short and throw my lipstick away. I would try to finish reading the Rilke letters before the week was out. And I'd have a pair of trousers and a jacket made out of that heavy winter coat material I've got left over. I would try to see my parents, of course, and do my best to reassure them, and every spare minute I would want to write to him, to the man I shall always long for—I now know that for certain. Yes, when I think about having to leave him and never being able to know what is happening to him, I feel as if I were dying already.

In a few days' time I shall go to the dentist and have lots and lots of holes in my teeth filled. For that really would be awful: suffering from toothache out there. I shall try to get hold of a rucksack and pack only what is absolutely essential, though everything must be of good quality. I shall take a Bible along and that slim volume *Letters to a Young Poet,* and surely I'll be able to find some corner for the *Book of Hours.* I won't take along any photographs of those I love; I'll just take all the faces and familiar gestures I have collected and hang them up along the walls of my inner space so that they will always be with me.

And even now I keep telling my heart that we two will have to carry on even if I am separated from those without whom I now think I cannot live. Each moment I free myself more from dependence on external props and draw closer inwardly to those from whom I cannot be separated however far apart we happen to be. And yet, when I walk with him hand in hand along the quay, which looked so autumnal and stormy last night, and then warm myself in his little room on his open and loving gestures, I am flooded with human, oh so human, hopes and desires: why can't we stay together after all? Nothing else would really matter if only we could be together. I don't ever want to leave him. Yet sometimes I say to myself, It is probably easier to pray for someone far away than to witness him suffering by your side.

In this tempestuous, havoc-ridden world of ours, all real communication comes from the heart. Outwardly we are being torn apart, and the paths to each other lie buried under so much debris that we often fail to find the person we seek. We can only continue to live together in our hearts, and hope that one day we may walk hand in hand again.

I cannot tell, of course, how I shall react when I really do have to leave him. His voice over the telephone this morning still rings in my ear; tonight we shall have a meal together; tomorrow morning we shall work together and then lunch at Liesl and Werner's, and in the afternoon we shall play music together. He is still here. And perhaps in my heart of hearts I do not really accept that all of us are about to be separated. A human being, after all, is only human.

Many accuse me of indifference and passivity when I refuse to go into hiding; they say that I have given up. They say everyone who can must try to stay out of their clutches, it's our bounden duty to try. But that argument is specious. For while everyone tries to save himself, vast numbers are nevertheless disappearing. And the funny thing is I don't feel I'm in their clutches anyway, whether I stay or am sent away. I find all that talk so cliché-ridden and naive and can't go along with it anymore. I don't feel in anybody's clutches; I feel safe in God's arms, to put it rhetorically, and no matter whether I am sitting at this beloved old desk now, or in a bare room in the Jewish district, or perhaps in a labor camp under SS guards in a month's time—I shall always feel safe in God's arms. They may well succeed in breaking me physically, but no more than that. I may face cruelty and deprivation the likes of which I cannot imagine in even my wildest fantasies. Yet all this is as nothing to the immeasurable expanse of my faith in God and my inner receptiveness.

I shall always be able to stand on my own two feet even when they are planted on the hardest soil of the harshest reality. And my acceptance is not indifference or helplessness. I feel deep moral indignation at a regime that treats human beings in such a way. But events have become too overwhelming and too demonic to be stemmed with personal resentment and bitterness. These responses strike me as being utterly childish and unequal to the fateful course of events.

People often get worked up when I say it doesn't really matter whether I go or somebody else does, the main thing is that so many thousands *have* to go. It is not as if I want to fall into the arms of destruction with a resigned smile—far from it. I am only bowing to the inevitable, and even as I do so I am sustained by the certain knowledge that ultimately they cannot rob us of anything that matters. But I don't think I would feel happy if I were exempted from what so many others have to suffer. They keep telling me that someone like me has a duty to go into hiding, because I have so many things to do in life, so much to give. But I know that whatever I may have to give to others, I can give it no matter where I am, here in the circle of my friends or over there, in a concentration camp. And it is sheer arrogance to think oneself too good to share the fate of the masses.

And if God Himself should feel that I still have a great deal to do, well then, I shall do it after I have suffered what all the others have to suffer. And whether or not I am a valuable human being will only become clear from my behavior in more arduous circumstances. And if I should not survive, how I die will show me who I really am. Of course that doesn't mean I will turn down a medical exemption if they give me one on account of my inflamed kidneys and bladder. And I have been recommended for some sort of soft job with the Jewish Council. They had permission to hire 180 people last week, and the desperate are thronging there in droves, as shipwrecked people might cling for dear life to a piece of driftwood. But that is as far as I am prepared to go, and beyond that I am not willing to pull any strings. In any case, the Jewish Council seems to have become a hotbed of intrigue, and resentment against this strange agency is growing by the hour. And sooner or later it will be their turn to go, anyway.

But, of course, by then the English may have landed. At least that's what those people say who have not yet abandoned all political hope. I believe that we must rid ourselves of all expectations of help from the outside world, that we must stop guessing about the duration of the war and so on. And now I am going to set the table.

*Sunday morning prayer.* "Dear God, these are anxious times. Tonight for the first time I lay in the dark with burning eyes as scene after scene of human suffering passed before me. I shall promise You one thing, God, just one very small thing: I shall never burden my today with cares about my tomorrow, although that takes some practice. Each day is sufficient unto itself. I shall try to help You, God, to stop my strength ebbing away, though I cannot vouch for it in advance. But one thing is becoming increasingly clear to me: that You cannot help us, that we must help You to help ourselves. And that is all we can manage these days and also all that really matters: that we safeguard that little piece of You, God, in ourselves. And perhaps in others as well. Alas, there doesn't seem to be much You Yourself can do about our circumstances, about our lives. Neither do I hold You responsible. You cannot help us, but we must help You and defend Your dwelling place inside us to the last. There are, it is true, some who, even at this late stage, are putting their vacuum cleaners and silver forks and spoons in safekeeping instead of guarding You, dear God. And there are those who want to put their bodies in safekeeping but who are nothing more now than a shelter for a thousand fears and bitter feelings. And they say, 'I shan't let them get me into their clutches.' But they forget that no one is in their clutches who is in Your arms. I am beginning to feel a little more peaceful, God, thanks to this conversation with You. I shall have many more conversations with You. You are sure to go through lean times with me now and then, when my faith weakens a little, but believe me, I shall always labor for You and remain faithful to You and I shall never drive You from my presence.

"I have strength enough, God, for suffering on a grand scale, but there are more than a thousand everyday cares that leap up on me without warning like so many fleas. So I scratch away desperately and tell myself, 'This day has been taken care of now, the protective walls of a hospitable home still surround me like a well-worn, familiar piece of clothing, there is food enough for today, and the bed with the white sheets and the warm blankets stands waiting for me tonight, so don't let me waste even one atom of my strength on petty material cares. Let me use and spend every minute and turn this into a fruitful day, one stone more in the foundations on which to build our so-uncertain future.' The jasmine behind my house has been completely ruined by the rains and storms of the last few days; its white blossoms are floating about in muddy black pools on the low garage roof. But somewhere inside me the jasmine continues to blossom undisturbed, just as profusely and delicately as ever it did. And it spreads its scent round the House in which You dwell, oh God. You can see, I look after You, I bring You not only my tears and my forebodings on this stormy, gray Sunday morning, I even bring you scented jasmine. And I shall bring You all the flowers I shall meet on my way, and truly there are many of those. I shall try to make You at home always. Even if I should be locked up in a narrow cell and a cloud should drift past my small barred window, then I shall bring you that cloud, oh God, while there is still the strength in me to do so. I cannot promise You anything for tomorrow, but my intentions are good, You can see."

And now I shall venture out upon this day. I shall meet a great many people today, and evil rumors and threats will again assault me like so many enemy soldiers besieging an inviolable fortress.

*14 July, Tuesday evening.* Everyone must follow the way of life that suits him best. I simply cannot make active preparations to save myself, it seems so pointless to me and would make me nervous and unhappy. My letter of application to the Jewish Council on Jaap's urgent advice has upset my cheerful yet deadly serious equilibrium. As if I had done something underhand. Like crowding onto a small piece of wood adrift on an endless ocean after a shipwreck and then saving oneself by pushing others into the water and watching them drown. It is all so ugly. And I don't think much of this particular crowd, either. I would much rather join those who prefer to float on their backs for a while, drifting on the ocean with their eyes turned toward heaven, and who then go down with a prayer. I cannot help myself. My battles are fought out inside, with my own demons; it is not in my nature to tilt against the savage, cold-blooded fanatics who clamor for our destruction. I am not afraid of them either, I don't know why; I am so calm it is sometimes as if I were standing on the parapets of the palace of history looking down over far-distant lands. This bit of history we are experiencing right now is something I know I can stand up to. I know what is happening, and yet my head is clear. But sometimes I feel as if a layer of ashes were being sprinkled over my heart, as if my face were withering and decaying before my very eyes, and as if everything were falling apart in front of me and my heart were letting everything go. But these are brief moments; then everything falls back into place, my head is clear again, and I can once more bear and stand up to this piece of history that is ours. For once you have begun to walk with God, you need only keep on walking with Him and all of life becomes one long stroll—such a marvelous feeling.

We go too far in fearing for our unhappy bodies, while our forgotten spirit shrivels up in some corner. Our lives are going wrong, we conduct ourselves without dignity. We lack a historical sense, forget that even those about to perish are part of history. I hate nobody. I am not embittered. And once the love of mankind has germinated in you, it will grow without measure.

Many would call me an unrealistic fool if they so much as suspected what I feel and think. And yet there exists in me all the reality the day can bring. I must look up those sentences in Rathenau's letter I copied out some time ago. That is what I shall miss later: here, I need only stretch out my hand to put my finger on so many words and passages. Out there, I shall simply have to carry everything inside me. One ought to be able to live without books, without anything. There will always be a small patch of sky above, and there will always be enough space to fold two hands in prayer.

It is now 11:30 P.M. Weyl straps on his rucksack, which is much too heavy for his slight back, and starts walking toward Central Station. I go along with him. One ought really to stay up all night and do nothing but pray.

*Wednesday morning.* I'm afraid I did not pray hard enough last night. When I read S.'s note this morning, something broke inside me and overwhelmed me. I was busy laying the breakfast table, and suddenly I had to stop in the middle of the room and fold my hands and bow my head, and the tears that had been locked up inside me for so long welled up from my heart.

It must sound odd, but these few faint, untidy pencil scrawls are the first real love letter I have ever received. I have suitcases full of others, of the so-called love letters men have written me in the past. Passionate and tender, pleading and demanding, so many words with which they tried to warm themselves and me, and so often it was all a flash in the pan.

But these words of his, yesterday, "Oh you, my heart is so heavy," and this morning, "Dear one, I so want to go on praying." They are the most precious presents ever laid before my spoiled heart.

*Evening.* No, I don't think I shall perish. This afternoon a brief spell of so much despair and sadness, not for everything that is happening but simply for myself. And the thought that I will have to leave S., not even grief about the longing I shall feel for him but grief about the longing he will feel for me. A few days ago I thought that nothing more could happen to me, that I had suffered everything in anticipation, but today I suddenly realized that things can indeed weigh more heavily on me than ever I thought possible. And they were very, very heavy. "I was unfaithful to You, God, but not entirely." It is good to have such moments of despair and of temporary extinction; continuous calm would be superhuman. But now I know again that I shall always get the better of despair. This afternoon I should not have thought it possible that, by this evening, I would be so calm again and so hard at work at my desk. But now my head is clearer than ever before. Tomorrow I must speak to S. at length about our fate and our attitude. I must!

The Rilke letters have come, those covering the years 1907–1914 and 1914–1921; I hope I shall be allowed to finish them. And the Schubert, too. Jopie brought them. And like a second Saint Martin, she took off her pure wool sweater, which wards off the rain and the cold, and gave it to me. Just the garment for a long journey. Will I be able to pack the two parts of *The Idiot* and my small Langenscheidt dictionary between the blankets? I would gladly make do with a little less food if only I could get the books in. Fewer blankets won't do, for I'm bound to freeze to death as it is. Han's rucksack was lying in the passage this afternoon, I tried it out on the sly, there wasn't very much in it, but to be honest the thing was much too heavy for me. Well, I am in God's hands. My body with all its aches and pains as well. If I should ever feel utterly crushed and bewildered, I will surely remember in some tiny corner of my mind that I shall surely be able to get up again.

I walk along a path even while I am led along it. I look to my memory, and it tells me clearly how I must act. Or not how I must act, but that I will know how to act when the time comes.

"Dear one, I so want to go on praying."

I love him so much.

Now I must go and do some reading.

When I pray, I never pray for myself, always for others, or else I hold a silly, naive, or deadly serious dialogue with what is deepest inside me, which for the sake of convenience I call God. Praying to God for something for yourself strikes me as being too childish for words. Tomorrow I must ask S. if he ever prays for himself. To pray for another's well-being is something I find childish as well; one should only pray that another should have enough strength to shoulder his burden. If you do that, you lend him some of your own strength.

The greatest cause of suffering in so many of our people is their utter lack of inner preparation, which makes them give up long before they even set foot in a camp. They believe our fate is sealed already, our catastrophe complete. Really, Dante's *Inferno* is comic opera by comparison. "Ours is the real hell," S. said recently, very simply and drily. There are moments when my head spins with the wailing and the howling and the screeching all around. And the sky looms so low and so threatening. And yet now and then that bright and bubbling good humor of mine rises to the surface again, it never really leaves me, and it isn't gallows humor either, I'm quite sure. I have grown so used to the times in which we live that few things baffle me now or obscure my view. After all, it has not been "literature" and "aesthetics" alone I have been busy with here at my desk during these last few years.

No, what I have collected here has helped me to ride over these past eighteen months. It has become part of me and will help me brave what other storms life may still have in store for me.

*Later*. I must remember something for my most difficult moments: the fact that Dostoyevsky spent four years in a Siberian jail with the Bible as his only reading matter. He was never allowed to be alone, and the sanitary arrangements were not particularly marvelous.

*[On 15 July 1942 Etty was given a job in the Cultural Affairs Department of the Jewish Council.]*

*16 July, 9:30 P.M.* "Have You any other plans for me, oh God?" Tomorrow I must betake myself to hell, and if I am to do the work properly, I shall have to get in a good night's sleep. It would take me a whole year to describe just this one day. Jaap and Loopuit, my old friend, who said, "I shan't let our Etty be dragged off to G." And I said to Jaap, after Leo de Wolff[43] had once again saved us from having to hang about for a few hours, "I shall have to do a great many favors for a great many people after this." It is all most irregular and certainly not fair. Liesl said very breezily, "You happen to be a victim of patronage."

And yet there in the passage, amid all the gloom and the bustle, I was able to read a few Rilke letters, to continue living my own life. Despite the deadly fear I saw in all those faces. All those faces, my God, those faces!

I am going to bed now. I hope to be a center of peace in that madhouse. I shall get up early in order to brace myself. "Oh God, what are Your plans for me?" It took me quite a few hours to get over that offer of a job. How did it all happen so quickly? S. said, "I read your diary this afternoon, and as soon as I read it I knew: nothing will happen to you." I must do something for Liesl and Werner, I really must. Not rashly but after a lot of reflection.

A miracle has happened, and that too is something I must accept and learn to bear.

*19 July, Sunday evening, 9:50.* "I need to talk to You so much, oh God," but I must go to bed. I feel as if I were drugged, and if I am not in bed by ten o'clock I shan't be able to get through another day like this one. Indeed I shall have to invent an entirely new language to express everything that has moved my heart these last few days. And this night. He is breathing as if he were running a race. And I think under the blankets, "Let us pray together." No, I can't put it into words, everything that happened the last few days and last night.

"And yet I am one of Your chosen, oh God, for You allow me to experience so many things and have given me enough strength to bear them all." Last night when I finally went up to Dicky's room at two o'clock and kneeled down, almost naked, in the middle of the floor, completely undone, I suddenly said, "I have been through such great things, today and tonight, my God, I thank You for helping me to bear everything and for letting so little pass me by." And now I simply must go to bed.

*20 July, Monday morning, 9:30.* They are merciless, totally without pity. And we must be all the more merciful ourselves. That's why I prayed early this morning:

"Oh God, times are too hard for frail people like myself. I know that a new and kinder day will come. I would so much like to live on, if only to express all the love I carry within me. And there is only one way of preparing the new age, by living it even now in our hearts. Somewhere in me I feel so light, without the least bitterness and so full of strength and love. I would so much like to help prepare the new age."

That's how it went, more or less, my prayer this morning. I suddenly had to kneel down on the hard coconut matting in the bathroom, and the tears poured down my face.

And that prayer gave me enough strength for the rest of the day.

And now I must still read a short story. I shall try to preserve my lifestyle come what may, even if I have to type a thousand letters a day from 10:00 A.M. until 7:00 P.M. and get back home, sorefooted, at eight, and then still have to get some food down. I shall always find an hour for myself, never let circumstances grind me down. I should be quite unable to do the work were I not able to draw each day on that great reservoir of peace and maturity.

"Yes, God, I am faithful to You, through thick and thin."

*21 July, Tuesday evening, seven o'clock.* This afternoon on my long walk home, when worries assailed me wildly and refused to go away, I suddenly said to myself, If you really believe in God, then you must surrender yourself completely and live in faith. Never worry about tomorrow. And as I was walking along the quay with him—and I thank You, oh God, for making that possible, even if it is only for five minutes a day, I am still grateful—he said, "Oh, the worries we all have." And I said to him, "We must be consistent, if we have any faith at all then we must have faith all the time."

I feel as if I were the guardian of a precious slice of life, with all the responsibility that entails. There are moments when I feel like giving up or giving in, but I soon rally again and do my duty as I see it: to keep the spark of life inside me ablaze. I shall now read a few Rilke letters and then very early to bed. When it comes to my personal life I am still so infinitely better off than most.

And between the urgent petitions I typed out today in surroundings best described as midway between hell and a madhouse, I still found time to read Rilke, and he said as much to me as he would had I read him in the seclusion of my quiet room.

And I want to add something: I believe I have gradually managed to attain the simplicity for which I have always longed.

*22 July, 8:00 A.M.* "God give me strength, not only spiritual strength but physical strength as well. In a moment of weakness I must make You a candid confession: if I have to leave this house I shall be totally lost. But I don't want to worry about that in advance. Take these worries from me, please, for if I have to bear them as well as all the others, I shall scarcely be able to go on living.

"I am so terribly tired, my whole body aches, and I have no energy for today's work. I don't really believe in it, and if it goes on for long I shall probably end up completely worn out. Still, I am grateful to You for driving me from my peaceful desk into the midst of the cares and sufferings of this age. It wouldn't do, would it, to live an idyllic life with You in a sheltered study? Still I confess it truly is difficult to carry You intact with me and to remain faithful to You through everything, as I have always promised.

"As I walk through the streets I am forced to think a great deal about Your world. *Think* is not really the right word, it is more an attempt to plumb its mystery with a new sense. It often seems to me that I can already discern the beginning and the end of this one phase of history, already see it in perspective.

"And I am deeply grateful to You for leaving me so free of bitterness and hate, with so much calm acceptance, which is not at all the same as defeatism, and also with some understanding for our age, strange though that may sound. One must understand one's age just as one understands one's contemporaries, for after all, it is of their making, it is what it is and must be understood as such, however perplexing it may be."

*[On 22 July 1942, Etty volunteered at the Jewish Council for deportation to Westerbork.]*

*Wednesday, 2:00 P.M.* My heart failed a few times again today, but each time it came back to life. I say my good-byes from minute to minute, shaking myself free of all outer things. I cut through the ropes that still hold me bound, I load up with everything I need to set out on my journey. I am sitting now by a quiet canal, my legs dangling over the stone wall, and I wonder whether one day my heart will be so weary and worn that it will no longer fly where it wants, free as a bird.[44]

*23 July, Thursday, 9:00 P.M.* My red and yellow roses are now fully open. While I sat there working in that hell, they quietly went on blossoming. Many say, "How can you still think of flowers!"

Last night, walking that long way home through the rain with the blister on my foot, I still made a short detour to seek out a flower stall, and went home with a large bunch of roses. They are just as real as all the misery I witness each day. "There is room for many things in my life, so much room, oh God." As I walked down those overcrowded corridors today, I suddenly felt the urge to kneel down right there, on the stone floor, among all those people. The only adequate gesture left to us in these times: "kneeling down before You." Each day I learn something new about people and realize more and more that the only strength comes, not from others, but from within.

"Living is not the sole meaning of life," S. said when we discussed the problem of how to make sense of all that happens.

It is all a great big mess, I think to myself quite often, against my will as it were. But today I suddenly wondered why I used the word *mess* in the first place. It is so much hot air and doesn't make things any better.

The most depressing thing of all is that the mental horizon of all the people I work with is so narrow. They don't even suffer deep down. They just hate and blind themselves to their own pettiness, they intrigue, they are still ambitious to get on, it is all a great big, dirty mess, and there are moments when I would like to lay my head down on my typewriter and say in despair, "I can't go on like this." But I do go on, learning more about people all the time.

It is now ten o'clock. By rights I ought to be in bed. But I must do a little reading first. I am still so fantastically well off. Liesl, brave little Liesl, sits up until three o'clock in the morning making little bags as an outworker for some factory. Werner hasn't taken his clothes off for sixty hours, all sorts of strange things have been happening in our lives, God grant us strength. But above all, let S. get well and don't take him away from me yet. Today I was suddenly filled with fears that he was about to be torn from me.

"Dear God, I have promised to trust You and to banish all my fears and anxieties. I am supposed to be with him on Saturday night. I can't thank You enough for making that possible even now." This day was another very black day, I was only just able to bear it, but I feel like ending it on a happy note, I don't know why, with something about the roses or about my love for him. I am going to read a few more Rilke poems and then to bed.

I shall take Saturday off.

Odd, isn't it, I am so healthy these days, no headaches, no stomachaches, etc. Sometimes I feel tiny twinges of them, but then I summon up all the inner calm I possess until my blood courses quietly through my veins again. Most of my aches are imaginary, I now realize. Neither is my new inner calm put on, as many think it is. Had all of this happened to me only a year ago, I should certainly have collapsed within three days, committed suicide, or pretended to a false kind of cheerfulness. But now I am filled with such equanimity, endurance, and calmness that I can see things very clearly and have an inkling of how they fit together.

Today when both of us kept saying how much we wanted to stay together, I thought to myself once again, "You look so ill, so terribly tired, and loving you as much as I do, the worst thing that could happen to me would be to sit by and watch you suffering. I would much sooner pray for you from a distance." I shall accept whatever lies in store for me. I don't much believe in help from the outside, nor do I count on it. On the English or the Americans or a revolution or God knows what. No one should put his trust in that sort of help. Whatever happens is for the best. Goodnight.

*24 July, Friday morning, 7:30.* I would very much like to do an hour's hard studying before I start on this day. I feel a great need to do so, and I also have the necessary concentration. When worries started to assail me again early this morning, I simply jumped out of bed. "God, take them away from me, please."

I don't know what I shall do if they send for him, what influence I can use on his behalf.

We must accept everything as it comes and be prepared for the worst. Don't brood and don't be afraid, but be calm and think clearly. When the crucial moment comes, you will surely know what you have to do.

My roses are still in bloom. I shall take that half-pound of butter to Jaap.

If I should survive and keep saying, "Life is beautiful and meaningful," then they will have to believe me.

If all this suffering does not help us to broaden our horizon, to attain a greater humanity by shedding all trifling and irrelevant issues, then it will all have been for nothing.

Tonight I shall dine with him in the Café de Paris. It is

almost grotesque, an outing like that. Liesl said, "It is a great privilege, isn't it, that we have been chosen to bear all this?" Liesl is a great woman, a truly great woman, I would like to write about her one day. We shall come through, no doubt.

*25 July, Saturday morning, nine o'clock.* I started the day stupidly. By talking about the "situation," as if words could be found to describe it.

This precious gift, this one free day, is something I must use well. Not by chattering or bothering those around me, but by sustaining my spirit: I have noticed a growing need to proffer my unruly spirit all the material it can digest. This last week has brought clear proof of how much stronger I have become. I keep following my own inner voice even in the madhouse in which I work, with a hundred people chattering together in one small room, typewriters clattering, and me, sitting in a corner reading Rilke. Yesterday we were all moved out suddenly in the middle of the morning; tables and chairs were pulled from under us, people thronged about giving orders and counter-orders, even about the smallest chair, but Etty just sat down in a corner on the dirty floor between her typewriter and a packet of sandwiches and read Rilke. I make my own rules and do as I like. In all this chaos and misery I follow my own rhythm, so much so that at any given moment between typing letters I can immerse myself in the things that matter to me. It is not that I am cutting myself off from all the suffering around me, nor is it a dulling of the senses. I take everything in and store it away, but I go my own way. Yesterday was a silly day. A day in which my sardonic humor asserted itself and I suddenly felt like an exuberant child.

God save me from one thing: don't let me be sent to a camp with the people with whom I now work every day. I could write a hundred satires about them. Still, life continues to be full of pleasant surprises: yesterday I ate fried flounders with S., unforgettable both as to cost and quality. And this afternoon at five o'clock I am going over to his place, and I shall stay there until the morning. We shall read a little and write a little and be together for one evening, one night, and one breakfast. Yes, such things still happen. I have been feeling strong and happy since yesterday. So free of fears and anxieties. And I am developing very strong leg muscles thanks to all the walking I do. Perhaps I shall walk right across Russia one day, who knows?

It is now 9:30. I want to sit here at this desk until noon; the rose petals lie scattered among my books. A yellow rose has opened as far as it can and now looks at me large and wide. The two and a half hours I have left seem to me like a year's seclusion. There is a vast silence in me that continues to grow.

*27 July 1942.* One should be prepared at all times to review one's life and to start all over again in a different place. I am spoiled and undisciplined.

Despite all that has happened, my desire to enjoy life to the full is probably still much too great. When I consider the mood I have been in since last night I cannot but say to myself, "You are an ungrateful wretch." There was so much that was good this weekend. So much that ought to sustain me for weeks even if those weeks had brought little but disaster. Instead I behave inconsiderately toward my colleagues, the other typists. It's just that I find the work so utterly monotonous. I am more querulous and sad and dissatisfied this early morning than I have been for a long time, and not because of the great "suffering" but because of all sorts of petty resentments and grievances. And I am very sad that so much that was precious and fine about this weekend has been buried and stifled beneath such unimportant things. That a somewhat vulgar and bossy girl said to me, when I tried to slip away at five o'clock, "No, you don't, you can't possibly go before that guide has been typed out, you're being inconsiderate." And since my machine can only manage five copies at a time and we need ten, I had to type everything out twice.

And I was dying to be with my friends, and I had a pain in my back, and every cell in my body was rebelling. You have the wrong attitude altogether, Etty, my girl. You should remember that your typing is what allows you to stay on in Amsterdam with the people you love. But yesterday afternoon it suddenly struck me how depressing, dreary, demeaning, and without any real point this whole business really is: "I humbly beg for exemption from labor service in Germany, because I am already working for the Wehrmacht here and am indispensable." The whole thing is hopeless. And I firmly believe unless we provide an alternative, a dazzling and dynamic alternative with which to start afresh somewhere else, then we are lost, lost permanently and for all time.

I am tired and depressed. I still have half an hour, and I would like to write for days, until all of my sudden depression has been shaken off.

Yesterday afternoon I sat in a narrow, overcrowded corridor and waited for Werner for one and a half hours. I sat on a stool against the wall, and people walked on me, over me, and past me. I sat there with Rilke on my lap and read. And I really read, concentrated on every word. And I found something that could suffice for many days. I copied it down immediately. And later I found a dustbin in the sun in the yard behind our most recent place of employment, and I sat down there and read more Rilke.

And Saturday night: the ring of our relationship was closed so simply and manifestly. As if nothing more ever covered me at night than a flowered blanket.

And there are always the canals beside which I walk and which I engrave ever more deeply on my memory, so that I need never again be without them. And can working just one short hour longer, even if it is monotonous work, really deprive you of anything that matters? Should you let it get you into such a state? My fears obviously run deeper than I thought, and I shall no doubt get to the bottom of them, but I haven't the time to do it now.

I shall soon be walking along the canals again, and I shall try to be very quiet and to listen to what has really happened inside me. I really shall have to change a great deal.

And another thing: I still believe I have an inner regulator, which warns me every time I take the wrong path by bringing on a "depression." If only I remain honest and open with myself and determined enough to become what I must be and to do what my conscience commands, then everything will turn out all right.

*28 July, Tuesday morning, 7:30.* I shall allow the chain of this day to unwind link by link, I shall not intervene but shall simply have faith. "I shall let You make Your own decisions, oh God." This morning I found a buff envelope in my letter box. I could see there was a white paper inside. I was quite calm and thought, "My call-up notice, what a pity, now I won't have time to try repacking my rucksack." Later I noticed that my knees were shaking. It was simply a form to be filled in by the staff of the Jewish Council. They haven't even issued me with an identity number yet. I shall take the few steps I have to. My turn may not come for a long time. Jung and Rilke will go with me in any case. And if my mind should be unable to retain very much later on, nevertheless these last two years will shine at the edge of my memory like a glorious landscape in which I was once at home and which will always remain part of me. I feel that I am still tied by a thousand threads to everything I treasure here. I will have to tear myself away bit by bit and store everything inside me, so that when I have to leave I shall not abandon anything but carry it all with me.

There are moments when I feel like a little bird, tucked away in a great protective hand.

Yesterday my heart was a sparrow, caught in a vise. It is on the wing again, flying wherever the fancy takes it. And now I shall make some sandwiches and be on my way.

I shall become the chronicler of our adventures. I shall forge them into a new language and store them inside me should I have no chance to write things down. I shall grow dull and come to life again, fall down and rise up again, and one day I may perhaps discover a peaceful space round me that is mine alone, and then I shall sit there for as long as it takes, even if it should be a year, until life begins to bubble up in me again and I find the words that bear witness where witness needs to be borne.

*8:30 P.M.* This was a day of gaiety, neglect of duty, and sunshine. I played truant along the canals, and I crouched in a corner of his room facing his bed. There were five tea roses in a small tin vase.

There is a difference between hardy and hard. It is often forgotten nowadays. I believe that I get hardier every day, except for the recalcitrant blister of mine, but I shall never grow hard. All sorts of things are becoming clear to me. For instance, this: I don't want to be S.'s wife. To put it quite soberly and bluntly, the difference in our ages is too great. I have seen a man change before my eyes in a few years. I see him changing even now. He is an old man whom I love, love infinitely, and to whom I shall always be united by an inner bond. But "marry," what the worthy citizen calls marry, I must, in all seriousness and honesty, say finally that I do not want to. And the fact that I am going to have to go my own way all by myself gives me a great feeling of strength. Sustained hourly by the love I bear him and others. So many couples rush off to be married at the last moment, in haste and desperation. I would rather be alone and there for everyone.

Nothing can ever atone for the fact, of course, that one section of the Jewish population is helping to transport the majority out of the country. History will pass judgment in due course.

And yet there it always is again: life remains so "interesting" through it all. Ever-present in me is an almost demonic urge to watch everything that happens. A wish to see and to hear and to be present, to worm out all of life's secrets, to observe with detachment what people look like in their last convulsions. And also, suddenly, to be forced to face oneself and to learn what one can from the spectacle that one's own soul enacts in these times. And later to be able to find the right words for it.

I shall read through my old diaries. I have decided not to tear them up after all. Perhaps later on they will help reacquaint me with my former self.

We have had more than enough time to prepare for our present catastrophe: two whole years. And the last of these has proved to be the most crucial of my life, my most beautiful year. And I know for certain that there will be a continuity between the life I have led and the life about to begin. Because my life is increasingly an inner one, and the outer setting matters less and less.

*29 July, Wednesday morning, eight o'clock.* On Sunday morning I was curled up on his floor in my big striped dressing gown, darning socks. Water can be so clear that you can see right through it and distinguish everything on the bottom. What a basic way of putting things I have.

What I really wanted to say is: it suddenly felt as if life in its thousand details, twists, and turns had become perfectly clear and transparent. Just like a crystal-clear sea.

You huddle in the corner on the floor in the room of the man you love and darn his socks, and at the same time you are sitting by the shore of a mighty ocean so transparent that you can see to the bottom. And that is an unforgettable experience.

And now I think I am getting flu or something very much like it. It shouldn't be allowed, I am against it on principle. And my unfit legs are still very tired today from yesterday's long walk. And today I must get Werner's identity papers. I shall stand there in that little room with the same friendly smile and dogged determination I displayed yesterday on my own behalf. And it is high time I saw the dentist as well. And will there be a lot of work today? One can never tell what the day will bring, but it doesn't matter, for one doesn't have to depend on what the day brings, not even in these times. Am I exaggerating? What if my call-up papers come tomorrow? It looks as if transportations from Amsterdam have stopped for the time being. They are now starting in Rotterdam. "Help them, oh God, help the Rotterdam Jews."

*[It would seem that Etty kept no diary between 29 July and 5 September, when there was a dramatic change in her circumstances: she voluntarily accompanied the first group of Jews being sent to Westerbork camp.*

*Her life was also drastically changed by the sudden illness and death of Spier on 15 September 1942, the very day the Gestapo came to take him to Westerbork. At the end of August 1942 Etty had been given leave to return to Amsterdam for a few days. She was ill when she arrived and stayed there for over a month.*

*Her last notes were written in the aftermath of Spier's death, before she returned to Westerbork.]*

*15 September 1942, Tuesday morning, 10:30.* "Perhaps, oh God, everything happening together like that was a little hard. I am reminded daily of the fact that a human being has a body, too. I had thought that my spirit and heart alone would be able to sustain me through everything. But now my body has spoken up for itself and called a halt. I now realize, God, how much You have given me. So much that was beautiful and so much that was hard to bear. Yet whenever I showed myself ready to bear it, the hard was directly transformed into the beautiful. And the beautiful was sometimes much harder to bear, so overpowering did it seem. To think that one small human heart can experience so much, oh God, so much suffering and so much love, I am so grateful to You, God, for having chosen my heart, in these times, to experience all the things it has experienced. Perhaps it is all to the good that I fell ill. I am not yet reconciled to that fact, I am a little numb and bewildered and helpless, but at the same time I am trying to scrape together what patience I have from all the corners of my being, and I shall have to find a new kind of patience to meet this entirely new state of affairs. I shall follow the tried and tested old method, talking to myself now and again on these faint blue lines. And talking to You, God. Is that all right? With the passing of people, I feel a growing need to speak to You alone. I love people so terribly, because in every human being I love something of You. And I seek You every-where in them and often do find something of You. But now I need so much patience, patience and thought, and things will be very difficult. And now I have to do everything by myself. The best and the noblest part of my friend, of the man whose light You kindled in me, is now with You. What was left behind was a childish, worn-out husk in the two small rooms in which I experienced the greatest and deepest happiness of my life. I stood beside his bed and found myself standing before one of Your last mysteries, my God."

*3:00 p.m.* The tree is still there, the tree that could write my life story. But it is no longer the same tree, or is it I who am no longer the same? And there is the bookcase, within reach of my bed. I have only to stretch out my left hand to touch Dostoyev-sky or Shakespeare or Kierkegaard. But I do not stretch out my hand. I feel so dizzy. "You have placed me before Your ultimate mystery, oh God. I am grateful to You for that, I even have the strength to accept it and to know there is no answer. That we must be able to bear Your mysteries."

I am sure it would be good for me to sleep for days, to let go completely. The doctor said yesterday that my inner life is too intense, that I must come down to earth, that I keep knocking at the gates of heaven, and that my physique simply cannot stand it. Perhaps he is right. Oh God, the last one and a half years! And the last two months, which were a whole life in themselves. But have I not had hours of which I could say, "This one hour is like a whole life, and if I should suddenly die, it would still have been worth it?" And there have been many such hours. Why should heaven not be like them? But it is really the other way round: heaven is inside one, like Rilke's "cosmic interior."

And now I must sleep and let everything go. I am so dizzy. Nothing in my body feels right. I want so badly to get well again. "But I accept everything from Your hands, oh God."

But I still suffer from the same old complaint. I cannot stop searching for the great redeeming formula. For the one word that sums up everything within me, the overflowing and rich sense of life. "Why did You not make me a poet, oh God? But perhaps You did, and so I shall wait patiently until the words have grown inside me, the words that proclaim how good and beautiful it is to live in Your world, oh God, despite everything we human beings do to one another."

*The thinking heart of the barracks.*


*Tuesday night, 1:00 A.M.* I once thought that I wanted to read your life up to and including the last page. Now I have done just that.

There you lie now in your two small rooms, you dear, great, good man. I once wrote to you, "My heart will always fly to you like a bird, from any place on earth, and it will surely find you."

And this is what I wrote in Tide's diary, "that you had become so much a part of the heaven that stretches above me that I had only to raise up my eyes to be by your side. And even if they flung me into a dungeon, that piece of heaven would still spread out within me and my heart would fly up to it like a bird, and that is why everything is so simple, so terribly simple and beautiful and full of meaning."

I had a thousand things to ask you and to learn from you; now I will have to do everything by myself. But I feel so strong that I'm sure I'll manage. What energies I possess have been set free inside me. You taught me to speak the name of God without embarrassment. You were the mediator between God and me, and now you, the mediator, have gone, and my path leads straight to God. It is right that it should be so. And I shall be the mediator for any other soul I can reach.

I am sitting at my desk lit by my small lamp. I have written to you so often from this very place and written about you as well. I must tell you something quite remarkable. I have never seen a dead person. In this world, where thousands die every day, I have never seen a corpse. Tide says, "It is only a 'shell.' " I know that's true. But you are the first dead man I shall have seen, and I cannot help feeling that that must be highly significant.

People seem to fritter away what could be their last moments. So many make themselves ill or refuse to get better for fear of being dragged away. Many even take their own lives, again out of fear. I am so grateful that his life has come to a natural end. He has been spared the suffering that his fellow humans would have inflicted upon him. You, dear spoiled man, would have been quite unable to bear that. I can bear it much better, and even as I suffer I shall continue to live your life and pass it on.

When one has once reached the point of experiencing life as something significant and beautiful, even in these times, or rather precisely in these times, then it is as if everything that happens has to happen just as it does and in no other way. To think that I am back at my desk again! And I shan't be going back to Westerbork tomorrow, but shall be with all our friends as we lower your body into the ground.

Oh well, that's the way things are, you know, one of man's more hygienic habits. Still, we shall all be together again and your spirit will be with us and Tide will sing for you. If only you knew how happy I am that I can be there. I came back just in time, I was still able to kiss your withered, dying mouth, for the last time you took my hand and led it to your lips. You once said when I came into your room, "The wandering girl." And you also once said, "I have such strange dreams, I dreamed that Christ himself came to baptize me." Now I stood with Tide beside your bed, and for a moment we thought that you were dying and that the light in your eyes was breaking. Tide put her arms round me, and I kissed her dear, pure mouth, and she said very gently, "We have found each other." We stood beside your bed, how happy you would have been to see the two of us there like that. Perhaps you did see us, just when we thought you were dying?

And I am grateful that your last words should have been, "Hertha, I hope . . ." What a struggle you waged to remain faithful to her, and how faithful you remained above everything else! And I myself made it very difficult for you, I know, but I, too, learned from you what true faithfulness is, and struggle and weakness.

All the bad and all the good that can be found in a man were in you—all the demons, all the passions, all the goodness, all the love—great discerner, God-seeker, and God-finder that you were. You sought God in every human heart that opened up before you—and how many there were!—and found a little bit of Him in each one. You never gave up, you could be so impatient about small things, but about the important things you were so patient, so infinitely patient.

I am glad that it should have been Tide herself who came to

tell me, Tide, with her dear and radiant face. We sat together in the kitchen. And Father Han came in later and stood at the back. And Tide touched the keys of your piano, and she sang a short song, "Lift up mine heart with gladness." It is now two o'clock in the morning. It is so quiet in the house. I must tell you something strange, but I think you'll probably understand. A portrait of yours hangs on my wall. I want to tear it up and throw it away. To be closer to you. We did not call each other by our first names. We used the formal *Sie* for a long time, and later, much later, we said *Du*. And your *Du* was to me one of the most caressing any man had ever used toward me. And as you know, there had been quite a few. You always signed your letters with a question mark, and I mine as well. You began your letters with, "Just listen to this . . . ," with your characteristic, *"Hören Sie mal,"* but across your last letter you wrote, "Dearest." To me, you are nameless, as nameless as the heavens above. And I want to put all your portraits away and never look at them again, for they are so much dead matter. I want to carry you in me, nameless, and pass you on with a new and tender gesture I did not know before.

*Wednesday morning, nine o'clock (in the doctor's waiting room).* I often used to think to myself as I walked about in Westerbork among the noisily bickering, all too energetic members of the Jewish Council: if only I could enter a small piece of their soul. If only I could be the receptacle of their better nature, which is sure to be present in all of them. Let me be rather than do. Let me be the soul in that body. And I would now and then discover in each one of them a gesture or a glance that took them out of themselves and of which they seemed barely aware. And I felt I was the guardian of that gesture or glance.

*16 September, Wednesday, 3:00 P.M.* I'm off once more to that street. I was always separated from him by three streets, a canal, and a little bridge. He died at 7:15 yesterday, the day my pass ran out.[45] Now I am going to visit him one more time. Just now in the bathroom, I thought, "I shall be seeing my first dead person." But it didn't seem to mean anything to me. I thought: I must do something solemn, something out of the ordinary. And I kneeled down on the coconut matting. And then I thought, "This is so conventional." How full of conventions we are, full of preconceptions about what we think ought to happen in certain situations. Sometimes, when I least expect it, someone suddenly kneels down in some corner of my being. When I'm out walking or just talking to people. And that someone, the one who kneels down, is myself.

And now a mortal shell lies on that more than familiar bed. Oh, that cretonne coverlet! I hardly need to go back there again. It's all being played out somewhere inside me, everything; there are wide plains inside me beyond time and space, and everything is played out there. And now I walk along those few streets again. How often I have walked them with him, always engaged in absorbing and worthwhile dialogue. And how often will I be walking there again, no matter in what corner of the earth I happen to be? Am I expected to put on a sad or solemn face? I am not really sad, am I? I would like to fold my hands and say, "Friends, I am happy and grateful, and I find life very beautiful and meaningful. Yes, even as I stand here by the body of my dead companion, one who died much too soon, and just when I may be deported to some unknown destination. And yet, God, I am grateful for everything. I shall live on with that part of the dead that lives forever, and I shall rekindle into life that of the living that is now dead, until there is nothing but life, one great life, oh God."

Tide will sing for him once again, and I already rejoice in the moment when I shall hear her vibrant voice.

Joop,[46] old friend, I am by your side, not physically, but you are much in my thoughts, and I am so grateful that I can give you something of what I cannot help handing on.

It is significant that you should have entered my life. It could not have been otherwise. Hello!

*17 September, Thursday morning, eight o'clock.* What he called "reposing in oneself." And that probably best expresses my own love of life: I repose in myself. And that part of myself, that deepest and richest part in which I repose, is what I call "God." In Tide's diary I often read, "Take him gently into Your arms, Father." And that is how I feel, always and without cease: "As if I were lying in Your arms, oh God, so protected and sheltered and so steeped in eternity." As if every breath I take were filled with it and as if my smallest acts and words had a deeper source and a deeper meaning. In one of his first letters to me he wrote, "If I can pass on a little of this overflowing strength, then I am happy."

"It is all to the good that my body has called a halt, oh God." For I must rest a while if I am to do what I have to do. Or perhaps that is just another conventional idea. Even if one's body aches, the spirit can continue to do its work, can it not? It can love and *hineinhorchen*—"hearken unto"—itself and unto others and unto what binds us to life. *Hineinhorchen*—I so wish I could find a Dutch equivalent for that German word. Truly, my life is one long hearkening unto my self and unto others, unto God. And if I say that I hearken, it is really God who hearkens inside me. The most essential and the deepest in me hearkening unto the most essential and deepest in the other. God to God.

"How great are the needs of Your creatures on this earth, oh God. They sit there, talking quietly and quite unsuspecting, and suddenly their need erupts in all its nakedness. Then, there they are, bundles of human misery, desperate and unable to face life. And that's when my task begins. It is not enough simply to proclaim You, God, to commend You to the hearts of others. One must also clear the path toward You in them, God, and to do that one has to be a keen judge of the human soul. A trained psychologist. Ties to father and mother, youthful memories, dreams, guilt feelings, inferiority complexes, and all the rest block the way. I embark on a slow voyage of exploration with everyone who comes to me. And I thank You for the great gift of being able to read people. Sometimes they seem to me like houses with open doors. I walk in and roam through passages and rooms, and every house is furnished a little differently, and yet they are all of them the same, and every one must be turned into a dwelling dedicated to You, oh God. And I promise You, yes, I promise that I shall try to find a dwelling and a refuge for You in as many houses as possible. There are so many empty houses, and I shall prepare them all for You, the most honored lodger. Please forgive this poor metaphor."

*At night, 10:30.* "God, give me calm and let me face everything squarely." There is so much to face. First I must start living a disciplined life. At this moment, the lights are being turned off in the men's barracks. But was there ever a real light in them? Where were you this evening, Jopie, little comrade? I have moments when I am suddenly filled with sadness: sadness that I cannot walk out of my barracks and onto the great moor outside. I take a short walk around the camp and before long find my comrade, with his tanned face and that straight furrow between his eyes, by my side. And as it grows dark I can hear in the distance the first chords of Beethoven's Fifth.

I so wish I could put it all into words. Those two months behind barbed wire have been the two richest and most intense months of my life, in which my highest values were so deeply confirmed. I have learned to love Westerbork. Yet when I fell asleep on my narrow plank bed there, what I dreamed of was the desk behind which I now sit and write. "I am so grateful to You, God, for having made my life so rich, but no matter where You place me, I always long for that desk of mine." But it does make life rather difficult and hard at times. It is now past 10:30, the time when they turn out the lights in the barracks, and when I myself must turn in. "The patient is advised to lead a quiet life," it says on my impressive certificate. And that I have to eat rice and honey and other such fabulous delicacies.

I am suddenly reminded of that woman with the snow-white hair and the fine oval face. She carried a packet of toast in her knapsack, all she had for the long journey to Poland, for she was on a strict diet. She was so incredibly lovely and so serene with her tall, girlish figure. One afternoon I was sitting out in the sun with her just in front of the transit barracks. I gave her a little book from Spier's library, Johanna Müller's *Die Liebe,* and she seemed very glad to have it. She said later to some young girls who came over to join us, "Remember, when we leave early tomorrow morning each of us may cry just three times." And one of the girls replied, "I haven't been issued with a ration book for that."

It is about eleven o'clock now. How quickly the day has passed. I shall have to go to bed after all. Tomorrow Tide will put on her light gray suit and sing, "Lift up mine heart with gladness" at the cemetery chapel. I shall ride in a car with little black curtains for the first time in my life. I have still so much to write down, enough to keep me busy for many days and nights. "Give me patience, oh God. An entirely new kind of patience. This desk seems so much part of my life once again, and the tree outside my window no longer makes me feel giddy with delight. By leading me back to my desk, You probably intended me to do my best." And now really goodnight.

I am so afraid you will have a hard time of it, Jopie, and I would so much love to help you. And I will certainly do what I can. Goodnight.

*Sunday night.* Verbalize, vocalize, visualize.

Many people are still hieroglyphs to me, but gradually I am learning to decipher them. It is the best I can do: to read life from people.

In Westerbork it was as if I stood before the bare palisade of life. Life's innermost framework, stripped of all outer trappings. "Thank You, God, for teaching me to read better and better."

I talk a great deal to people, more than ever of late. I still speak much more expressively and clearly than I can write. Sometimes I feel that I shouldn't dissipate my strength on the spoken word, that I should withdraw and go my own quiet, searching way on paper. A part of me wants to do just that. But another part wavers and loses itself in words among people.

Max, did you see that deaf and dumb woman in her eighth month, with her epileptic husband? I wonder, Max, how many women in their ninth month are being driven from their homes in Russia this very moment and still reach for their guns?

My heart is a floodgate for a never-ending tide of misery.

Jopie on the heath sitting under the great, big starry sky, talking about nostalgia. I have no nostalgia left, I feel at home. I have learned so much about it here. We *are* "at home." Under the sky. In every place on earth, if only we carry everything within] us.

I have often felt, and I still feel, like a ship with a precious cargo; the moorings have been slipped, and now the ship is free to take its load to any place on earth. We must be our own country. It took me two nights before I could bring myself to speak of it to him, this most intimate of all intimate feelings. And all the time I was dying to make him a present of it. And then, then I knelt down on the great heath and told him about God.

The doctor is wrong, of course. In the past words like his would probably have made me feel insecure, but now I have learned to see through people and to illumine their words with my own insight. "You live too cerebral a life. You don't let yourself go enough. You ignore the basic rules of life." I nearly asked, "Do you want me to lie down with you here on this couch?" It wouldn't have been a very sensitive remark, but that's what he really wanted. And later, "You don't live in the real world." And I thought to myself, "He really doesn't make sense." The real world! All over the real world men and women are being kept apart. The men are at the front. In camps. In prisons. Men and women separated from each other. That is the real world. And you have to come to terms with that. And not just stoke your desires and retreat into Onan's sin. Why not turn the love that cannot be bestowed on another, or on the other sex, into a force that benefits the whole community and that might still be love? And if we attempt that transformation, are we not standing on the solid ground of the real world, of reality? A reality as tangible as a bed with a man or a woman in it. And there are other realities, too, are there not? There is something childish and lacking about an older man who, in these times, my God, in these times, goes on about living life to the full. I wish so much that he had come right out with exactly what he really meant.

"After this war, two torrents will be unleashed on the world: a torrent of loving-kindness and a torrent of hatred." And then I knew: I should take the field against hatred.

*22 September.* I would love to be like the lilies of the field. Someone who managed to read this age correctly would surely have learned just this: to be like a lily of the field.

I once thought, "I would like to feel the contours of these times with my fingertips." I was sitting at my desk with no idea what to make of life. That was because I had not yet arrived at the life in myself, was still sitting at this desk. And then I was suddenly flung into one of many flashpoints of human suffering. And there, in the faces of people, in a thousand gestures, small changes of expression, life stories, I was suddenly able to read our age—and much more than our age alone. And then it suddenly happened: I was able to feel the contours of these times with my fingertips. How is it that this stretch of heathland surrounded by barbed wire, through which so much human misery has flooded, nevertheless remains inscribed in my memory as something almost lovely? How is it that my spirit, far from being oppressed, seemed to grow lighter and brighter there? It is because I read the signs of the times and they did not seem meaningless to me. Surrounded by my writers and poets and the flowers on my desk, I loved life. And there among the barracks, full of hunted and persecuted people, I found confirmation of my love of life. Life in those drafty barracks was no other than life in this protected, peaceful room. Not for one moment was I cut off from the life I was said to have left behind. There was simply one great, meaningful whole. Will I be able to describe all that one day? So that others can feel too how lovely and worth living and just—yes, just—life really is? Perhaps one day God will give me the few simple words I need. And bright and fervent and serious words as well. But above all simple words. How can I draw this small village of barracks between heath and sky with a few rapid, delicate, and yet powerful, strokes of the pen? And how can I let others see the many inmates, who have to be deciphered like hieroglyphs, stroke by stroke, until they finally form one great readable and comprehensible whole?

One thing I now know for certain: I shall never be able to put down in writing what life itself has spelled out for me in living letters. I have read it all, with my own eyes, and felt it with many senses.

This house, I feel, is slowly losing its hold on me. It's a good thing to be able to cut all ties with it. Very carefully, with great sorrow, but also in the certainty that it is all for the best and that there can be no other way, I let go, day by day.

And with one shirt on my back and another in my rucksack—how did that fairy tale go, the one about the king who searches his kingdom for the shirt of his happiest subject, and finds in the end that the man does not own a shirt—and with a very small Bible, perhaps my Russian dictionaries and Tolstoy's folk tales, and no doubt, no doubt at all, there will be room for one volume of Rilke's letters. And then the pure lambswool sweater, knitted by a friend—what a lot of possessions I have, oh God, and someone like me wants to be a lily of the field!

And with that one shirt in my rucksack I am off to an "unknown destination." That's what they call it. But wherever I go, won't there be the same earth under my roving feet and the same sky with now the moon and now the sun, not to mention all the stars, above my grateful head? So why speak of an unknown destination?

*23 September.* We shan't get anywhere with hatred, Klaas.[47] Appearances are so often deceptive. Take one of my colleagues. I see him often in my thoughts. The most striking thing about him is his inflexible, rigid neck. He hates our persecutors with an undying hatred, presumably with good reason. But he himself is a bully. He would make a model concentration camp guard. I often watched him standing beside the camp entrance to admit his hunted fellow Jews, never a pleasant sight. I also remember his throwing a few grubby pieces of licorice to a sobbing three-year-old across the table and saying gruffly, "See you don't get it all over your face." Thinking back, I'm sure it was more awkwardness and shyness than lack of goodwill that made him seem curt—he simply couldn't hit the right tone. When I saw him walking about among the others with his rigid neck and imperious look and his ever-present short pipe, I always thought, All he needs is a whip in his hand, it would suit him to perfection. But still I never hated him, I found him much too fascinating for that. Now and then I really felt terribly sorry for him. He had such an unhappy, miserable mouth, if the truth be told. The mouth of a three-year-old who has been unable to get his way with his mother. He himself had meanwhile passed the thirty-year mark, a clever fellow, a successful lawyer—one of the most able in Holland—and the father of two children. But the mouth of a dissatisfied three-year-old had been stamped on his face. There was never any real contact between him and others, and he would give such covert, hungry looks whenever other people were friendly to each other. (I could always see him do it, for we lived a life without walls there.) Later I heard a few things about him from a colleague who had known him for years. During the German invasion he jumped into the street from a third-floor window but failed to kill himself. Later, he threw himself under a car, but again to no avail. He then spent a few months in a mental institution. It was fear, just fear. I also learned that his wife had had to walk on tiptoe in the house because he could not bear the slightest noise and that he used to storm at his terrified children. I felt such deep, deep pity for him. What sort of life was that? In the end he hanged himself. (I must make sure his name is taken off the card index.)

Klaas, all I really wanted to say is this: we have so much work to do on ourselves that we shouldn't even be thinking of hating our so-called enemies. We are hurtful enough to one another as it is. And I don't really know what I mean when I say that there are bullies and bad characters among our own people, for no one is really "bad" deep down. I should have liked to reach out to that man with all his fears, I should have liked to trace the source of his panic, to drive him ever deeper into himself, that is the only thing we can do, Klaas, in times like these.

And you, Klaas, give a tired and despondent wave and say, "But what you propose to do takes such a long time, and we don't really have all that much time, do we?" And I reply, "What you want is something people have been trying to get for the last two thousand years, and for many more thousand years before that, in fact, ever since mankind has existed on earth." "And what do you think the result has been, if I may ask?" you say.

And I repeat with the same old passion, although I am gradually beginning to think that I am being tiresome, "It is the only thing we can do, Klaas, I see no alternative, each of us must turn inward and destroy in himself all that he thinks he ought to destroy in others. And remember that every atom of hate we add to this world makes it still more inhospitable."

And you, Klaas, dogged old class fighter that you have always been, dismayed and astonished at the same time, say, "But that—that is nothing but Christianity!"

And I, amused by your confusion, retort quite coolly, "Yes, Christianity, and why ever not?"

At night the barracks sometimes lay in the moonlight, made out of silver and eternity: like a plaything that had slipped from God's preoccupied hand.

*24 September.* "There is just one consolation," said Max with his awkward, lopsided grin. "In winter, the snow will pile up so high that it'll cover the barrack windows, so it will be dark all day as well." He thought he was being rather witty. "But at least we'll be nice and warm, the temperature will never drop below zero. And they've put two little tiled stoves in the workshop," he added delightedly. "The men who brought them told us that they are such good burners that they'll explode the first time they're lit."

We shall have to suffer and to share a great deal this winter; let us help one another to bear it: the cold, the darkness, and the hunger.

We shall be housed in wooden barracks under a bare sky, with bunks from the Maginot Line in tiers of three, and no lights because Paris has not sent the wiring. And even if there were lights, there still isn't any blackout paper.

I have had to cut things short, and now it is evening again. My body is behaving most disagreeably today. A small, rose-red cyclamen stands under my steel lamp. Tonight I spent a great deal of time thinking of S. I suddenly felt the first twinges of grief, and that, too, is a part of life. And tonight I suddenly found that there were so many questions I would have liked to ask him, not least about himself, that so much has been left unclear. Now I shall have to find the answers myself. Stupid, but whenever the telephone rings it will never again be his voice at the other end, half bossy, half tender, saying, "Listen here." Things are bound to be very hard now and then. How long it is since I last saw Tide!

My latest treasure: the birds of the heavens and the lilies of the fields in Matthew 6:33: But seek ye first the kingdom of God, and his righteousness; and all these things shall be added unto you.

And tomorrow a date with Ru Cohen in the Café de Paris. There were five people in Adema van Scheltema Square[48] dressed in nothing but nightshirts and slippers, and it has turned so chilly, and now they have also taken someone in the last stages of cancer, and last night a Jew was shot in Van Baerl Straat, just round the corner from here, "while trying to escape."

Many people are being killed this very moment, all over the world, while I sit here writing beside my rose-red cyclamen under my steel office lamp. My left hand rests on a small open Bible, I have a headache and a stomachache, and the sunny summer days on the heath and the field of yellow lupins stretching as far as the delousing barracks are buried deep in my heart. It was not a month ago, on 27 August, that Jopie wrote to me, "Here I sit again with my legs dangling out of the window listening to the tremendous stillness, while the lupin field, now stripped of its jubilant colors, is bathed in comforting sunlight. Now everything is so solemn and so peaceful that I am very calm and serious, too. I drop down from the window and take a few steps in the loose sand and stare at the moon." And then he ended his letter, written in his tight, close handwriting on cheap paper, "I can understand why one might say, Only one gesture will do here: to drop to one's knees. No, I didn't do it myself, I didn't think it was necessary, I did my kneeling even while I sat on the windowsill, and then I went to sleep."

It is odd how this man has sprung so suddenly, almost noiselessly, into my life, vital and inspiring, even while my great friend, the one who had attended at the birth of my soul, lay in his bed full of pain and turning into a child. "At difficult moments like these, I often wonder what You intend with me, oh God, and therefore what I intend with You."

With a sharp pang, all of suffering mankind's nocturnal distress and loneliness passes now through my small heart. What shall I be taking upon myself this winter?

"One day, I would love to travel through all the world, oh God; I feel drawn right across all frontiers and feel a bond with all Your warring creatures." And I would like to proclaim that bond in a small, still voice but also compellingly and without pause. But first I must be present on every battlefront and at the center of all human suffering.

"Give me a small line of verse from time to time, oh God, and if I cannot write it down for lack of paper or light, then let me address it softly in the evening to Your great Heaven. But please give me a small line of verse now and then."

*25 September, 11:00 P.M.* Tide told me that a girlfriend once said after the death of her husband, "God has moved me up into a more advanced class; the desks are still a little too big for me."

And when we spoke about his not being there anymore and how strange it was that neither of us felt empty inside, indeed had a sense of fulfillment, Tide simply ducked her head and shrugged her shoulders and said with a brave little laugh, "Yes, the desks are still a little too big, things are bound to be a bit difficult now and then."

Matthew 5:23: Therefore if thou bring thy gift to the altar, and there rememberest that thy brother hath ought against thee; 24: Leave there thy gift before the altar, and go thy way; first be reconciled to thy brother, and then come and offer thy gift.

I was hurrying along at Ru's side, and after a very long conversation in which we broached all the "ultimate questions" once again, I suddenly stopped beside him in the middle of narrow, dreary Govert Flinck Straat, and said, "But you know, Ru, like a child I still feel that life is beautiful, and this helps me to bear everything." Ru looked at me full of expectation, and I said, as if it were the most ordinary thing in the world—and it really is, "Yes, you see, I believe in God." And, I think, he was rather taken aback, then, searching my face for some mysterious sign, appeared to like what he found there. Perhaps that is why I felt so radiant and so strong for the rest of the day? Because it came out so spontaneously and so simply in the middle of that drab working-class district, "Yes, you see, I believe in God."

I'm glad I've been able to stay on in Amsterdam for a few weeks. I am going back refreshed and reinvigorated. I used to be much too unsociable, much too indolent. I really ought to have gone to see those old people, the Bodenheimers, and not have let myself off with the excuse that there's nothing I can do for them. And there were so many other things like that where I fell short. I pursued my own pleasure too much. I was so ready, of an evening on the heath, to gaze into a friendly pair of eyes. That was lovely, and yet I fell short in so many ways. Even with the girls in my dormitory. From time to time I would fling them a little piece of myself and then run away. It was not nearly good enough. And yet I am thankful it was like that and that I shall be able to make amends when I get back. I'm sure I'll be returning in a more serious and more concentrated frame of mind, less in pursuit of my own pleasure. If one wants to exert a moral influence on others, one must start with one's own morals. I keep talking about God the whole day long, and it is high time that I lived accordingly. I still have a long way to go, oh yes, a long way, and yet sometimes I behave as if I were there already. I am frivolous and easygoing, and I often look on things that happen as if I were an artist, a mere observer. There is something bizarre and fickle and adventurous in me. But as I sit here at my desk, late at night, I also feel a compelling, directive force deep down, a great and growing seriousness, a soundless voice that tells me what to do and forces me to confess: I have fallen short in all ways, my real work has not even begun. So far I have done little more than play about.

*26 September, 9:30.* I shall have to surrender much more of me to You, oh God. And also stop making conditions: if only I remain healthy, and so on . . . Even if I am not healthy, life goes on, doesn't it? I have no right to lay down conditions. I will not do so in future. And the moment I made that resolution, my stomachache suddenly became quite a lot better.

I leafed a little through my diary this morning. Thousands of memories flooded back. What a rich year it has been!

*27 September.* For what shall it profit me if I should bestow all my worldly goods to feed the poor and have not love . . .

At least you don't have to suffer with me, S., spoiled darling that you were, I am able to face it alone: that little bit of cold and that little bit of barbed wire, and yet you continue to live in my heart. And I carry on what is immortal in you.

We always end up with some material token: that small broken pink comb of his Tide gave me. I really don't want to keep any photographs of him, perhaps I won't ever speak his name again, but that grubby little pink comb, which I have seen him use to comb his thin hair for one and a half years, now lies in my briefcase among my most important papers, and how wild with grief I should be if I were ever to lose it! We human beings are strange creatures, are we not?

*28 September.* It made quite an impression on me that time, when that flirt of a doctor with his melancholy eyes said to me, "You live too cerebral a life, it's bad for your health, your constitution isn't up to it." When I told Jopie about it, he said reflectively, "He's probably right." I worried about it for quite a long time, but then I realized with ever-greater certainty: he wasn't right. True, I may think too much, sometimes with a demonic and ecstatic intensity, but I refresh myself from day to day at the original source, life itself, and I rest from time to time in prayer. And what those who say "You live too intensely" do not know is that one can withdraw into a prayer as into a convent cell and leave again with renewed strength and with peace regained.

I think what weakens people most is fear of wasting their

strength. If after a long and arduous process, day in, day out, you manage to come to grips with your inner sources, with God, in short, and if only you make certain that your path to God is unblocked—which you can do by "working on yourself"—then you can keep renewing yourself at these inner sources and need never again be afraid of wasting your strength.

*29 September.* You often said, "This is a sin against the spirit, it will be avenged." Every sin against the spirit will be avenged, in man himself and in the world outside.

Let me just note down one more thing for myself: Matthew 6:34: Take therefore no thought for the morrow: for the morrow shall take thought for the things of itself. Sufficient unto the day is the evil thereof.

We have to fight them daily, like fleas, those many small worries about the morrow, for they sap our energies. We make mental provision for the days to come, and everything turns out differently, quite differently. Sufficient unto the day. The things that have to be done must be done, and for the rest we must not allow ourselves to become infested with thousands of petty fears and worries, so many motions of no confidence in God. Everything will turn out all right with my residence permit and with my ration book; right now there's no point in brooding about it, and I would do much better to write a Russian essay. Ultimately, we have just one moral duty: to reclaim large areas of peace in ourselves, more and more peace, and to reflect it toward others. And the more peace there is in us, the more peace there will also be in our troubled world.

Just had a short telephone conversation with Toos. Jopie writes, "Don't send any more parcels. Everything is in turmoil." Haanen sent a letter to his wife: too short to make sense but long enough to make everyone nervous. Nasty. And it set off a bad reaction in me as well. We have to fight that. Must turn our backs on all these pointless rumors, which spread like an infectious disease. Now and then I get an inkling of what goes on in all these unhappy people. Their lives are so impoverished and so empty. And then they say what I have heard from so many of them, "I can't read any books these days, I just can't concentrate any longer. In the past my house was always full of flowers, but now, well, I no longer care for that sort of thing." Impoverished, empty lives. Can they be taught to work on themselves, to find peace in themselves? To live a productive and confident life despite all these fears and rumors? To know that one can fling oneself down on one's knees in the farthest and quietest corner of one's inner life and stay there kneeling until the sky above looks sunny and clear again? I felt it once more in the flesh, last night, what human beings have to suffer these days. It is good to be reminded of that from time to time, if only to learn how to fight it. And then to continue undisturbed through the wide and open landscape that is one's own heart. But I haven't reached that point yet. First to the dentist, and this afternoon to my appointment at the Jewish Council in Keizersgracht.

*30 September.* To be true to one's own spontaneity, to what one set out to do in an all too spontaneous moment.

To be true to every feeling and thought that has started to germinate.

To be true in the fullest sense of the word, to be true to God, to one's own best moments.

If I have one duty in these times, it is to bear witness. I think I have learned to take it all in, to read life in one long stretch. And in my youthful arrogance I am often sure that I can remember every least thing I see and that I shall be able to relate it all one day. Still, I must try to put it down now.

I seem able to see ever more clearly the gaping chasms that swallow up man's creative powers and joie de vivre. They are holes in our own mind. Sufficient unto the day is the evil thereof. And: man suffers most through his fears of suffering. The body keeps leading the spirit, when it should be the other way round. "You live too cerebral a life." And why now? Because I would not surrender my body to your greedy hands? How strange men are! How much I want to write. Somewhere deep inside me is a workshop in which Titans are forging a new world. I once wrote in despair, "It is inside my little skull that this world must be rethought, that it must be given fresh clarity." I still occasionally think so, with the same, almost diabolical, presumption. I know how to free my creative powers more and more from the snares of material concerns, from the idea of hunger and cold and danger. They are, after all, imaginary phantoms, not the reality. Reality is something one shoulders together with all the suffering that goes with it, and with all the difficulties. And as one shoulders them, so one's resilience grows stronger. But the *idea* of suffering (which is not the reality, for real suffering is always fruitful and can turn life into a precious thing) must be destroyed. And if you destroy the ideas behind which life lies imprisoned as behind bars, then you liberate your true life, its real mainsprings, and then you will also have the strength to bear real suffering, your own and the world's.

*Friday morning, in bed.* I have not been entirely honest with myself. I shall have to learn this lesson, too, and it will be the most difficult of all: "Oh God, to bear the suffering you have imposed on me and not just the suffering I have chosen for myself."

I have been using so many words these last few days to convince myself and others that I must go back to Westerbork and that my stomach is not really all that bad—perhaps it really isn't, either.

It seems to me that I have only to stretch out the fingers of my hand to hold all Europe and Russia in my grasp. So compact, so easily surveyed and familiar have they become for me. Everything seems to be so near—even in this bed. Remember: even in this bed. Even if I had to lie still and motionless for weeks. But I still find it hard to bear the thought that I may not be able to get up.

"I promise You to live as fully as I can wherever it should please You to put me. But I should so much like to go back on Wednesday, if only for the two weeks." Yes, I know perfectly well, there is a risk: there are more and more SS men in the camp, and there is more and more barbed wire all round, and everything is getting stricter, it's possible they won't even let me out again in two weeks' time, that's always on the cards. Can I take that risk?

I give myself until Sunday, and if it then turns out that it wasn't just a passing spell of giddiness, then I will have to be reasonable and stay. I give myself three days. But I must keep calm, not do anything silly. Not try to compress a whole life into a few weeks. The people I have to see won't run away. It really doesn't have to be done in a rush, no need to throw my precious life away. Don't let me provoke the gods wantonly, they have arranged everything so wonderfully well, don't let me go and spoil their work for them now. I give myself another three days.

*Later.* I have the feeling that my life is not yet finished, that it is not yet a rounded whole. A book, and what a book, in which I have got stuck halfway. I would so much like to read on. There have been moments when I have felt as if my whole life had been one great preparation for community living, when in fact I have always led a very private life.

*Later.* Flowers and fruit grow wherever they are planted, isn't that what it all means? And shouldn't we affirm that meaning?

I am sure I shall learn to do it. We must learn to dispense with labels. You don't have to know whether it is called an intestinal hemorrhage or a stomach ulcer or anemia to know what it is. It looks as if I shall probably have to lie flat on my back for a time, I don't want to admit it yet, I still split hairs to convince myself that it isn't too bad and that I'll be able to leave here on Wednesday. I have made up my mind: I shall give myself another three days, and if I still feel trapped in this armor of weakness then I shall just have to give in. And if I should feel fit again by Monday? Then I shall call on Neuberg and say in my most prepossessing way—yes, I can see it already, a smile revealing the new porcelain tooth with its gold edge—"Doctor, I have come to speak to you as one friend to another. Look, I would so much like to go, do you think I could?" And I know already that he will say yes, because that's what I will make him say. I shall make him give me the answer I want to hear.

I think I still have a lot to learn before I can shoulder my burden, whatever that might turn out to be.

I am rather gratified when I find that yet another well-laid plan turns out to have been nothing but vain speculation. We used to feel so certain that we would help each other bear the sorrows of our age. Now he lies a wasted corpse under a stone—what does the stone really look like, I wonder—in the farthest corner of flower-filled Zorgvlied cemetery, and I lie, encased in weakness, in the little room that has been my own now for almost six years. Vanity of vanities—but what was not vain was my discovery that I was able to commit myself unreservedly to another, to bind myself to him and to share his sorrow. And did he not lead me to God, after first paving the way with his imperfect human hand?

No, my girl, the way your body feels under the blankets, I don't like it one little bit.

Not to be mobile is a very bad business. "And how mobile I used to be, my God, how mobile! How many of Your unknown highways and byways did I not walk with a rucksack on my back! It was like a miracle. Gateways suddenly opened up for me everywhere and led me on to roads I had always thought closed. How much space there was for me! But now I am really ill, truly I am. I give You another two and a half days."

I want to pay them all a visit some day, one by one, the thousands who passed through my hands on their way to that patch of heath. And if I do not find them, then I shall look up their graves. I shall never again be able to sit quietly at a desk. I want to travel all over the world and see with my own eyes and hear with my own ears how they fared, all those we sent on their way.

*Late afternoon.* Walked a little indoors. Who knows, perhaps it will be all right after all, perhaps it's just anemia and I'll get over it with a bit of medicine.

And now it seems that I have been "exempted." "Am I expected to jump for joy?" I asked the lawyer with the short leg. I don't want that scrap of paper for which most Jews would give their right arm, I don't want it in the least, so why should it have dropped into mine of all laps? I want to be sent to every one of the camps that lie scattered all over Europe, I want to be at every front, I don't ever want to be what they call "safe," I want to be there, I want to fraternize with all my so-called enemies, I want to understand what is happening and share my knowledge with as many as I can possibly reach—and I can, if You will only let me get healthy, oh Lord!

*Saturday morning, 6:30, in the bathroom.* I am beginning to suffer from insomnia, and that's not allowed. I jumped out of bed at the crack of dawn and kneeled down at my window. The tree stood motionless out there in the gray, still morning. And I prayed, "God, grant me the great and mighty calm that pervades all nature. If it is Your wish to let me suffer, then let it be one great, all-consuming suffering, not the thousand petty anxieties that can break a human being. Give me peace and confidence. Let every day be something more than the thousand everyday cares. All those worries about food, about clothing, about the cold, about our health—are they not so many denials of You, my God? And don't You come down on us hard in punishment? With insomnia and with lives that have ceased to be worth living?" I want to lie here quietly for another few days, but then I would wish my life to turn into one great prayer. One great peace. To carry my peace about with me once again. "The patient must live a peaceful life." "Give me peace, Lord, wherever I may be. Perhaps I no longer feel Your peace because I am doing wrong. Perhaps, but I don't know." I brood far too much about my health these days, and that is no good. "Let there be the same great calm in me that pervaded Your gray morning today. Let my day be more than just looking after the body."

It is now close on seven o'clock. I shall go and wash from head to toe in cold water, and then I shall lie down quietly in my bed, dead still, I shall no longer write in this exercise book, I shall simply lie down and try to be a prayer. I have felt it so often, all misery for a few days and thinking I wouldn't get over it for weeks, and then suddenly the clouds were lifted from me. But now I don't live as I should, for I try to force things. If at all possible I would so much like to leave on Wednesday. But I know perfectly well I am not much good to anyone as I am now. I would so love to be just a little bit better again. But I ought not to make any demands. I must let things take their course, and that's what I am trying to do with all my might.

"Not my will, but Thy will be done."

*A little later.* Of course, it is our complete destruction they want! But let us bear it with grace.

There is no hidden poet in me, just a little piece of God that might grow into poetry.

And a camp needs a poet, one who experiences life there, even there, as a bard and is able to sing about it.

At night, as I lay in the camp on my plank bed, surrounded by women and girls gently snoring, dreaming aloud, quietly sobbing and tossing and turning, women and girls who often told me during the day, "We don't want to think, we don't want to feel, otherwise we are sure to go out of our minds," I was sometimes filled with an infinite tenderness, and lay awake for hours letting all the many, too many impressions of a much-too-long day wash over me, and I prayed, "Let me be the thinking heart of these barracks." And that is what I want to be again. The thinking heart of a whole concentration camp. I lie here so patiently and now so calmly again, that I feel quite a bit better already. I feel my strength returning to me; I have stopped making plans and worrying about risks. Happen what may, it is bound to be for the good.

*Saturday, 4:00 P.M.* I must really stop being so impatient. Why am I in such a hurry to share the deprivations of those behind barbed wire? And what are six weeks in a lifetime? There is an iron band round my skull, and the debris of a whole city weighs down on my head. I really do not want to be a sick, dry leaf dropping from the stem of the community.

*3 October, Saturday evening, nine o'clock.* One ought to pray, day and night, for the thousands. One ought not to be without prayer for even a single minute.

*4 October [1942], Sunday evening.* Tide this morning, then Professor Becker in the afternoon. Later Jopie Smelik.[49] Ate with Han. Giddy and weak. "God, You have entrusted me with so many precious gifts, let me guard them well and use them properly." All this talking with friends is bad for me right now. I am worn to a frazzle. I lack the strength it takes to leave it all behind, to strike a balance between my inner and my outer worlds. That is my main task. They are both equally strong in me. I so love being with people. It is as if my own intensity draws what is best and deepest right out of them: they open up before me, every human being a new story, told to me by life itself. And my eyes simply read on joyfully. Life has confided so many stories to me, I shall have to retell them to people who cannot read the book of life itself.

Alone for once in the middle of the night. God and I have been left together, and I feel all the richer and at peace for it.

*8 October, Thursday afternoon.* I am still sick. I can do nothing about it. I shall have to wait a little longer to gather up all their tears and fears. Though I can really do it here just as well, here in bed. Perhaps that's why I feel so giddy and hot. I don't want to become a chronicler of horrors. Or of sensations. This morning I said to Jopie, "It still all comes down to the same thing: life is beautiful. And I believe in God. And I want to be there right in the thick of what people call 'horror' and still be able to say: life is beautiful." And now here I lie in some corner, dizzy and feverish and unable to do a thing. When I woke up just now I was parched, reached for my glass of water, and, grateful for that one sip, thought to myself, "If I could only be there to give some of those parched thousands just one sip of water." And all the time I keep telling myself, "Don't worry, things aren't all that bad." Whenever yet another poor woman broke down at one of our registration tables, or a hungry child started crying, I would go over to them and stand beside them protectively, arms folded across my chest, force a smile for those huddled, shattered scraps of humanity, and tell myself, "Things aren't all that bad, they really aren't that bad." And all I did was just stand there, for what else could one do? Sometimes I might sit down beside someone, put an arm round a shoulder, say very little and just look into their eyes. Nothing was alien to me, not one single expression of human sorrow. Everything seemed so familiar, as if I knew it all and had gone through it all before. People said to me, "You must have nerves of steel to stand up to it." I don't think I have nerves of steel, far from it, but I can certainly stand up to things. I am not afraid to look suffering straight in the eyes. And at the end of each day, there was always the feeling: I love people so much. Never any bitterness about what was done to them, but always love for those who knew how to bear so much although nothing had prepared them for such burdens. Blond Max with his shaven head, always with a little fresh stubble, and his gentle, blue dreamer's eyes. He had been so mistreated in Amersfoort that he could not be "transported" anywhere but had to be left behind in a hospital. One night, he gave us an exact account of what they did to him. Others will record such stories in all their minutiae one day, something that will presumably be necessary if the history of these times is to be handed down in full to the next generation. I have no need for these details.

*Next day.* Father suddenly turned up, and there was great excitement. "My little abbess" and "what quixoticism" and "Lord, make me less eager to be understood by others but make me understand them."

It is now 11:00 A.M. Jopie must have reached Westerbork by now. It feels just as if a piece of myself were there. I am having to battle with impatience and dejection all the time today, brought on by pains in my back and that leaden feeling in my legs, which want so much to travel the world but cannot yet do so. It will come. But one should not be so materialistic. For even while I lie here, am I not traveling through the world?

The earth is in me, and the sky. And I well know that something like hell can also be in one, though I no longer experience it in myself, but I can still feel it in others with great intensity. And that is as it should be, or else I might grow too complacent.

Paradoxical though it may sound: whenever one tries too desperately to be physically close to some beloved person, whenever one throws all one has into one's longing for that person, one is really giving him short change. For one has no reserves left then for a true encounter.

I am going to read Saint Augustine again. He is so austere and so fervent. And so full of simple devotion in his love letters to God. Truly those are the only love letters one ought to write: love letters to God. Is it very arrogant of me to say that I have too much love in me to give it all to just one person? The idea that one can love one person and one person only one's whole life long strikes me as quite childish. There is something mean and impoverishing about it. Will people never learn that love brings so much more happiness and reward than sex?

I fold my hands in a gesture that I have come to love, and in the dark I tell you silly and serious things and implore blessings upon your honest, sweet head. Yes, I pray for you. Goodnight, beloved.

*Saturday night.* I think that I can bear everything life and these times have in store for me.

And when the turmoil becomes too great and I am completely at my wits' end, then I still have my folded hands and bended knee. A posture that is not handed down from generation to generation with us Jews. I have had to learn it the hard way. It is my most precious inheritance from the man whose name I have almost forgotten but whose best part has become a constituent of my own life.

What a strange story it really is, my story: the girl who could not kneel. Or its variation: the girl who learned to pray. That is my most intimate gesture, more intimate even than being with a man. After all one can't pour the whole of one's love out over a single man, can one?

*12.10.42.* My impressions are scattered like glittering stars on the dark velvet of my memory.

The soul has a different age from that recorded in the register of births and deaths. At your birth, the soul already has an age that never changes. One can be born with a twelve-year-old soul. One can also be born with a thousand-year-old soul . . . I believe the soul is that part of man that he is least aware of, particularly the West European, for I think that Orientals "live" their souls much more fully. We Westerners do not really know what to do with them; indeed we are ashamed of our souls as if they were something immoral. "Soul" is quite different from what we call "heart." There are plenty of people who have a lot of "heart" but very little soul.

Yesterday I asked Maria[50] about somebody, "Is she intelligent?" "Yes," said Maria, "but only as far as her brains are concerned." S. always said of Tide, "She has an intelligent soul." Whenever S. and I spoke about the great difference in our ages, he always said, "Who can tell whether your soul is not much older than mine?"

Sometimes it bursts into full flame within me, as it has just done again: all the friendship and all the people I have known this past year rise up in overwhelming number and fill me with gratitude. And though I am sick and anemic and more or less bedridden, every minute seems so full and so precious—what will it be like when I am healthy once more? "I rejoice and exult time and again, oh God: I am grateful to You for having given me this life."

A soul is forged out of fire and rock crystal. Something rigorous, hard in an Old Testament sense, but also as gentle as the gesture with which his tender fingertips sometimes stroked my eyelashes.

*In the evening.* And then again there are moments when life is dauntingly difficult. Then I am agitated and restless and tired all at once. Powerfully creative moments this afternoon, though. And now utter exhaustion.

All I can do is to lie motionless under my blankets and be patient until I shed my dejection and the feeling that I'm cracking up. When I felt like that in the past, I used to do silly things: go out drinking with friends, contemplate suicide, or read right through the night, dozens of books at random.

One must also accept that one has "uncreative" moments. The more honestly one can accept that, the quicker these moments will pass. One must have the courage to call a halt, to feel empty and discouraged. Goodnight.

*Early next morning. Vorwegnehmen.* To anticipate. I know no real Dutch equivalent. Ever since last night, I have been lying here trying to assimilate just a little of the terrible suffering that has to be endured all over the world. To accommodate just a little of the great sorrow the coming winter has in store. It could not be done. Today will be a hard day. I shall lie quietly and try to anticipate something of all the hard days that are to come.

When I suffer for the vulnerable, is it not for my own vulnerability that I really suffer?

I have broken my body like bread and shared it out among men. And why not, they were hungry and had gone without for so long.

I always return to Rilke. It is strange to think that someone so frail, who did most of his writing within protective castle walls, would perhaps have been broken by the circumstances in which we now live. Is that not further testimony that life is finely balanced? Evidence that, in peaceful times and under favorable circumstances, sensitive artists may search for the purest and most fitting expression of their deepest insights so that, during more turbulent and debilitating times, others can turn to them for support and a ready response to their bewildered questions? A response they are unable to formulate for themselves, since all their energies are taken up in looking after the bare necessities? Sadly, in difficult times we tend to shrug off the spiritual heritage of artists from an "easier" age, with "What use is that sort of thing to us now?"

It is an understandable but shortsighted reaction. And utterly impoverishing.

We should be willing to act as a balm for all wounds.

*Letters from Westerbork*

# Westerbork

*Monday, 1:00 P.M., in the Mahlers' cubbyhole,*
*where Eichwald is at this moment making me*
*porridge.*[1]

My dear people,[2]

I really am going to send off a letter to you at last. This is the fifth time I've started. One experiences too much here and goes about with too many conflicting feelings to be able to write. Anyway, I can't. So I just send you my greetings. Besides, I think I'm going to have to come back to Amsterdam fairly quickly to have myself finished off in a high-class abattoir. I'm no good for anything, it's really very sad, there is so much to be done here. But there it is, something inside me has gone wrong, I am living on painkillers and will probably turn up without warning under your dearly loved noses. There is nothing I can do about it. Funny, I've been here nearly three days—it could be three weeks. It isn't as "idyllic" as in the summer, nothing like. I'll go and have a nap, and after that I'll start the endless march again through the barracks and the mud. What a pity I can't stay; I wish so much that I could.

Vleeschhouwer[3] is just coming in; I'll give him this letter. Good-bye for now, everyone, and please forgive this short, messy scribble.

Lots of love,
*Etty*

Father Han, Käthe, Hans, Sister Maria, greetings, that's all.

I find it impossible to write here, not for lack of time but because of all the different impressions that come bursting in. I'm sure I could talk for a year at a stretch about this one week. I am on the leave list for next Saturday. What a privilege to be able to get away from here and see you all again. I'm glad I didn't plunge into the thick of things during the first few days; once in a while I take to my bed for an hour, and then things are all right again. Suitcase, clothes, and blankets are ready. The Mahlers take wonderful care of me. It is now half past eight and I am sitting once more in their hospitable little nook, a real oasis. Next to me Vleeschhouwer is immersed in a book. Mahler and his wife and two friends are playing cards. Little Eichenwald, my faithful milk-provider, sits on the floor in a corner next to the dog Humpie, unpicking the seams of Mijnheer Speyer's coat, which he wants to turn into a lumber jacket. Sterzenbach's brother (this is for Hans) is writing letters and in a moment will tell us more about his prison experiences.[4] Auntie Leah's trusty little stove stands in the corner brewing all sorts of good things for the assembled company. Just now Witmondt[5] came in (I visited his wife a few times in Amsterdam; the people around me are all such close friends that I feel you know them well, too). He was wearing a voluminous cape, and we shouted in chorus, "Good God, Max, how did you come by that magnificent cape?" And Max—who looked like a skeleton when he was brought here from Amersfoort and has been carefully nursed by the Mahlers—said solemnly and dramatically, "This cape is still covered with blood from Amersfoort"—and there *were* some dark red spots on it. What a lurid story! I am sitting squashed into a corner, barely managing to write. Just now another young man came in, one from Kattenburg, who is due to go on transport in the morning. All this is happening in a little room measuring two meters by three.

The central heating is on—yes, really—and the men are sitting in their shirt sleeves. Everything here is full of paradox. In the big barracks, where so many people have to lie on metal springs without mattresses or blankets, they are dying of cold. In the little huts, where there is central heating, people can't sleep at night for the heat. I share one of these huts with five roommates. Two double bunks, so unsteady on their legs that when the fat Viennese woman above me turns over at night, the bed shakes like a ship in a storm. And mice nibble at our bedding and our food supplies, which can be somewhat disquieting.

And what do I actually do in this place? I'm back to juggling five miserable mugs to share out coffee among hundreds of people. Now and then I run away out of sheer frustration—like last time, when a little old woman fainted in a corner and there wasn't a single drop of water to be had in the whole camp, because the water supply had been cut off. And then the people from Ellecom[6] came. They were taken straight to the hospital. I sat by their beds stupefied. I still can't get it into my head that people can do such things to each other, and that some live to tell the tale.

I have started a small campaign to bring the library, which is stored in the cellar of a locked warehouse, out into the light of day. Everyone recognizes the need for books, but nothing gets done for lack of space. On Tuesday I'm going to have a talk with Paul Cronheim,[7] the Wagner man, and with the notary Spier.[8] I should so much like to help provide some spiritual nourishment; I'll see what chance there is of that.

It is certainly not very pretty here: a gypsy life, poverty, mud. This afternoon I went into a couple of the bigger barracks, where several children seemed to be dying before my eyes—

Dear children, I may not be writing with much inspiration, but I'm glad to be here. As for my health, I'm not completely fit yet. All sorts of little complaints haunt me, but never mind; I'll see to them later.

This is hardly a real letter, but I felt so guilty that I had sent you only one depressing little scrawl. Westerbork completely swallows me up. By the end of the week I'll have surfaced again. No, it is impossible to write from here; it would take the better part of a lifetime to digest it all. And how wonderful it will be to be with you again next week! Thanks for your letter, Papa Han. And lots and lots of love to all of you.

Till the weekend,
*Etty*

# Amsterdam

This time, as usual, I came back with various commissions from the heath. An ex-soubrette with gallstones asked for some hair dye. Then there was a girl who couldn't get out of bed because she had no shoes. And all sorts of other trifles. Not that the lack of shoes is a trifle, of course. And there was the commission from Dr. K. that I undertook with great pleasure, but I find that it weighs more and more heavily on me. The soubrette has long since dyed her hair again and the girl-without-shoes is able to get out of her bed again and brave the mud, but I have still not been able to fulfill Dr. K.'s request. To be honest, that's not just because I haven't been well for a few weeks.

A few evenings before I left Westerbork, I went to his austere little office, where he sometimes sits working deep into the night. He looked tired and thin and pale. He pushed a thick file aside for a moment, after first telling me some remarkable things about it, with appropriate humor. Then he looked around as if searching for something and with some difficulty found a few words: He had been feeling like an old man the last few months. The war would be over one day, surely . . . To start with, he would probably want to go and sit for a long time deep in a large forest and forget a good deal . . . then he might want to go and see Seville and Málaga, for where he should have memories of these cities, there are just a couple of gaps. He would also like to go back to work . . . there would surely be a League of Nations . . . How we suddenly got from the League of Nations to the two sisters in the Hague, one fair and one dark, I no longer remember. But, he said, once I was back in Amsterdam on leave, could I possibly write to them, something in my style, about life in Westerbork?

"Yes," said I, with much understanding, "it is certainly important to keep in touch with the outside world."

Your friend K. said almost indignantly, "Outside world? These two women mean much more to us here than just the outside world; they mean a whole part of our lives." And then, in that bare little office on that late evening, he spoke so movingly about you both that I gladly agreed to his request. But to be frank: now, sitting down to write, I'm not sure what exactly to tell you about life in Westerbork.

It was summer when I came here for the first time. Up till then, all I'd known about Drenthe was that it had a lot of megalithic tombs. And then suddenly there was a village of wooden barracks, set between heath and sky, with a glaringly yellow lupin field in the middle and barbed wire all around. And there were human lives as well, thick as flies. To be honest, I had never realized that refugees from Germany had already been held on Drenthe heath for four years, years in which I had been busy taking up collections for Spanish and Chinese children.[10]

During the first few days I walked around as if through the pages of a history book. I met people who had been in Buchenwald and Dachau at a time when to us these were only distant, threatening sounds. I met people who traveled all around the world on that ship without being allowed to disembark at any port.[11] You must have heard of that; the papers were full of it. I have seen snapshots of little children who are probably now growing up in some unknown corner of this earth. Who knows whether they will even recognize their parents—if they ever see them again?

In short, one had the feeling of seeing in tangible form a small part of the Jewish predicament of the last ten years. And we had thought there was nothing at Drenthe except megalithic tombs. It was enough to take your breath away.

In the summer of 1942—it seems years ago; so much more has happened in a few months than can be told in a few pages—this small settlement was turned upside down and shaken to the marrow. With horror, the old camp inmates witnessed the mass deportation of Jews from Holland to Eastern Europe. From the very beginning they had to make their own considerable contribution in terms of human lives when the quota of "voluntary workers" was not completely filled.

One summer evening I sat eating red cabbage at the edge of the yellow lupin field that stretched from our dining hut to the delousing station, and with sudden inspiration I said, "One ought to write a chronicle of Westerbork." An older man to my left—also eating red cabbage—answered, "Yes, but to do that you'd have to be a great poet."

He is right, it would take a great poet. Little journalistic pieces won't do. The whole of Europe is gradually being turned into one great prison camp. The whole of Europe will undergo this same bitter experience. To simply record the bare facts of families torn apart, of possessions plundered and liberties forfeited, would soon become monotonous. Nor is it possible to pen picturesque accounts of barbed wire and vegetable swill to show outsiders what it's like. Besides, I wonder how many outsiders will be left if history continues along the paths it has taken.

There you are—I could tell right away that nothing would come of my report on Westerbork. The first attempt has got me bogged down in generalities. On the whole, a person more or less contemplative by nature isn't really suited to describing a specific place or event. One discovers that the basic materials of life are the same everywhere, and that one can live one's life with meaning—or else one can die—in any spot on this earth. The Big Dipper looks down on some distant hamlet just as reliably as it does on a great city at the hub of a nation, or as it does on a coal mine in Silesia; so that all's right with the world . . .

All I really want to say is this: I am no poet. And I am rather at my wits' end to know how to honor my promise to K. For although the name Westerbork is highly charged for us, and will reverberate in our ears for the rest of our lives, I don't know precisely what I can say about it. Life there is so eventful, although many may consider it deadly boring.

But on the morning after I heard your friend K. speak the names of Seville and Málaga with such fanatical longing, I met him on the narrow paved path between barracks 14 and 15. He was wearing his usual trilby hat, which makes him seem so out of place among all the wooden planks and low doors. He was walking quickly because he was hungry, but he still found time when we passed to say pointedly, "Have you thought about what I asked you? You know, making the acquaintance of those two sisters will greatly enrich your life, too."

And so I find myself at an unheard-of late hour facing a blank piece of paper after all.

Yes—Westerbork.

If I understand it correctly, this place, now a focus of Jewish suffering, lay deserted and empty just four years ago. And the spirit of the Department of Justice hovered over the heath.

"There wasn't a butterfly to be seen here, not a flower, not even a worm," the very first German inmates told me emphatically. And now? Let me give you a rough idea from the inventory. We have an orphanage, a synagogue, a small mortuary, and a shoe-repair factory under construction. I have heard talk of a madhouse being built, and my latest information is that the expanding hospital barracks complex already has a thousand beds.

The two-person jail that stands like something out of an operetta in one corner of the camp is apparently no longer large enough, for they plan to build a bigger one. It must sound strange to you: a prison within a prison.

There are minor "cabinet crises," what with all the people who like to have a finger in every pie.

We have a Dutch commandant and a German one. The first is taller, but the second has more of a say. We are told, moreover, that he likes music and that he is a gentleman. I'm no judge, although I must say that for a gentleman he certainly has a somewhat peculiar job.

There is a hall with a stage where, in the glorious past when the word "transport" had not yet been heard, a rather faltering Shakespeare production was once put on. At the moment people sit at typewriters on the same stage.

There is mud, so much mud that somewhere between your ribs you need to have a great deal of inner sunshine if you don't want to become the psychological victim of it all. The physical effects, such as broken shoes and wet feet, you will certainly understand.

Although the camp buildings are all one story, you can hear as many accents as if the Tower of Babel had been erected in our midst: Bavaria and Groningen, Saxony and Limburg, The Hague and East Friesland; you can hear German with a Polish accent and German with a Russian accent; you find all sorts of dialects from Holland and Berlin—all in an area of half a kilometer square.

The barbed wire is more a question of attitude.

"*Us* behind barbed wire?" an indestructible old gentleman once said with a melancholy wave of his hand. "*They* are the ones who live behind barbed wire"—and he pointed to the tall villas that stand like sentries on the other side of the fence.

If the barbed wire just encircled the camp, then at least you would know where you were. But these twentieth-century wires meander about inside the camp, too, around the barracks and in between, in a labyrinthine and unfathomable network. Now and then you come across people with scratches on their faces or hands.

There are watchtowers at the four corners of our wooden village, each a windswept platform on four tall posts. A man with a helmet and a gun stands outlined against the changing skies. In the evening one sometimes hears a shot echo across the heath, as it did once when the blind man stumbled too close to the barbed wire.

Finding something to say about Westerbork is also difficult because of its ambiguous character. On the one hand it is a stable community in the making, a forced one to be sure, yet with all the characteristics of a human society. And on the other hand, it is a camp for a people in transit, great waves of human beings constantly washed in from the cities and provinces, from rest homes, prisons, and other prison camps, from all the nooks and crannies of the Netherlands—only to be deported a few days later to meet their unknown destiny.

You can imagine how dreadfully crowded it is in half a square kilometer. Naturally, few follow the example of the man who packed his rucksack and went on transport of his own accord. When asked why, he said that he wanted the freedom to decide to go when *he* wanted to go. It reminds me of the Roman judge who said to a martyr, "Do you know that I have the power to have you killed?" And the martyr answered, "Yes, but I have the power of letting myself be killed."

Anyway, it is terribly crowded in Westerbork, as when too

many drowning people cling to the last bit of flotsam after a ship has sunk. People would rather spend the winter behind barbed wire in Holland's poorest province than be dragged away to unknown parts and unknown destinies deep within Europe, from where only a few indistinct sounds have come back to the rest of us. But the quota must be filled; so must the train, which comes to fetch its load with mathematical regularity. You cannot keep everyone back as being indispensable to the camp, or too sick for transport, although you try it with a great many. You sometimes think it would be simpler to put yourself on transport than have to witness the fear and despair of the thousands upon thousands of men, women, children, infants, invalids, the feeble-minded, the sick, and the aged who pass through our helping hands in an almost uninterrupted flow.

My fountain pen cannot form words strong enough to convey even the remotest picture of these transports. From the outside the impression is of bleak monotony, yet every transport is different and has its own atmosphere.

When the first transport passed through our hands, there was a moment when I thought I would never again laugh and be happy, that I had changed suddenly into another, older person cut off from all former friends. But on walking through the crowded camp, I realized again that where there are people, there is life. Life in all its thousands of nuances—"with a smile and a tear," to put it in popular terms.

It made a great difference whether people arrived prepared, with well-filled rucksacks, or had been suddenly dragged out of their houses or swept up from the streets. In the end we saw only the last.

After the first of the police roundups, when people arrived in slippers and underclothes, the whole of Westerbork, in a single horrified and heroic gesture, stripped to the skin. And we have tried, with the close cooperation of people on the outside, to make sure that those who leave are equipped as well as possible.

But if we remember all those who went to face the winter in Eastern Europe without any clothes, if we remember the single thin blanket that was sometimes all we were able to dole out in the night, a few hours before departure . . .

The slum-dwellers arrived from the cities, displaying their poverty and neglect in the bare barracks. Aghast, many of us asked ourselves: what sort of democracy did we really have?

The people from Rotterdam were in a class by themselves, hardened by the bombing raids. "We don't frighten easily anymore," you often heard them say. "If we survived all that, we'll survive this, too." And a few days later they marched singing to the train. But it was midsummer then, and there were no old people yet, or invalids on stretchers bringing up the rear . . .

The Jews from Heerlen and Maastricht and thereabouts came telling stories that reverberated with the great send-off the province of Limburg had given them.[12] One felt that morally they could live on it for a long time. "The Catholics have promised to pray for us, and they're better at that than we are!" said one of them.

People came with all their rivalries. The Jews from Haarlem said somewhat loftily and acidly: "Those Amsterdammers have a grim sense of humor."

There were children who would not accept a sandwich before their parents had had one. There was a remarkable day when the Jewish Catholics or Catholic Jews—whichever you want to call them—arrived, nuns and priests wearing the yellow star on their habits.[13] I remember two young novices, twins, with identical beautiful, dark ghetto faces and serene, childish eyes peering out from under their skullcaps. They said with mild surprise that they had been fetched at half past four from morning mass, and that they had eaten red cabbage in Amersfoort.

There was a priest, still fairly young, who had not left his monastery for fifteen years. He was out in the "world" for the first time, and I stood next to him for a while, following his eyes

*Roundup: the Jews summoned for Westerbork gather in Amsterdam-South.*

*Official notification of Etty's new address in Westerbork.*

| BERICHT VAN ADRESWIJZIGING | |
|---|---|
| NAAM MET VOORLETTERS: | Etty Hillesum |
| BEROEP, KWALITEIT: | employee J.R. |
| **OUD ADRES** | |
| STRAAT EN HUISNUMMER: | |
| NAAM DER WOONPLAATS: | |
| **NIEUW ADRES** | |
| STRAAT EN HUISNUMMER: (ZOO NOODIG HUISGEDEELTE) | voor brieven ba. 41 |
| TELEF. & POSTBUSNR.: | J.R. Westerbork |
| POSTREKENING NR: | voor pakketten en pakjes ba. 34 |
| NAAM DER WOONPLAATS: (TOEVOEGEN, INDIER NOODIG: CENTRUM, NOORD, ZUID, OOST, ENZ. OF KANTOOR V. BESTELLING) | J.R. Westerbork |
| DATUM VAN INGANG EN HANDTEEKENING: | 16/7 Etty Hillesum |

*"A village of wooden barracks, set between heath and sky, a glaringly yellow lupin field in the middle and barbed wire all around."*

Facing page, top: *One of the 107 barracks in Westerbork: "those jam-packed hangars of drafty slats where, under a lowering sky made up of hundreds of people's drying laundry, the iron bunks are stacked in triple decks" [December 1942].*

Facing page, bottom: *Administration barracks in Westerbork. At night, the place was used as a theater.*

*Rebecca Hillesum.*

*Louis Hillesum.*

*Mischa Hillesum.*

*Christine van Nooten.*

Above left:
*Johanna ("Jopie") Smelik.*

Above right: *Osias Kormann.*

Left: *Philip Mechanicus,
author of* In Depôt, *a memoir of
Westerbork. He told Etty, "If I
survive this time, I shall emerge a
more mature and deeper person,
and if I die, then I shall die a more
mature and deeper one."*

Below: *Milli Ortmann.*

"*Slowly but surely six o'clock in the morning has arrived.
The train is due to depart at eleven, and they are starting to load
it with people and luggage. . . . The camp has been cut in two
halves since yesterday by the train: a depressing series of bare,
unpainted freight cars in the front, and a proper coach for the
guards at the back. Some of the cars have paper mattresses on the
floor. These are for the sick*" [August 24, 1943].

*"We left the camp singing . . ." Etty's last postcard, thrown from the train; it was found and mailed on September 15, 1943.*

as they wandered peacefully around the barracks where the newcomers were being received.

The others—shaven, beaten, maltreated—who poured in along with the Catholics that day stumbled about the wooden hut with movements that were still unsteady and stretched out their hands toward the bread, of which there was not enough.

A young Jew stood very still next to us. His jacket was much too loose, but a grin broke through his stubbly black beard when he said, "They tried to smash the wall of the prison with my head, but my head was harder than the wall!"

Among all the shaved heads, it was strange to see the white-turbaned women who had just been treated in the delousing barracks, and who went about now looking distressed and humiliated.

Children dozed off on the dusty plank floor; others played tag among the adults. Two little ones floundered helplessly around the heavy body of a woman lying unconscious in a corner. They didn't understand why their mother just lay there without answering them. A gray-haired old gentleman, straight as an arrow and with a clear-cut, aristocratic profile, stared at the whole infernal canvas and repeated over and over to himself: "A terrible day! A terrible day!"

And among all this, the unremitting clatter of a battery of typewriters: the machine-gun fire of bureaucracy.

Through the many little windowpanes one can see other wooden barracks, barbed wire, and a blasted heath.

I looked at the priest who was now back in the world again. "And what do you think of the world now?" I asked. But his gaze remained unwavering and friendly above the brown habit, as if everything he saw was known, familiar from long ago. That same evening, a man later told me, he saw some priests walking one behind the other in the dusk between two dark barracks. They were saying their rosaries as imperturbably as if they had just finished vespers at the monastery. And isn't it true that one can pray anywhere, in a wooden barracks just as well as in a stone monastery, or indeed, anywhere on this earth where God, in these troubled times, feels like casting his likeness?

For those who have been granted the nerve-shattering privilege of being allowed to stay in Westerbork "until further notice," there is the great moral danger of becoming blunted and hardened.

The human suffering that we have seen during the last six months, and still see daily, is more than anyone can be expected to comprehend in half a year. No wonder we hear on all sides every day, in every pitch of voice, "We don't want to think, we don't want to feel, we want to forget as soon as possible." It seems to me that this is a very great danger.

True, things happen here that in the past our reason would not have judged possible. But perhaps we have faculties other than reason in us, faculties that in the past we didn't know we had but that possess the ability to grapple with the incomprehensible. I believe that for every event, man has a faculty that helps him deal with it.

If we were to save only our bodies and nothing more from the camps all over the world, that would not be enough. What matters is not whether we preserve our lives at any cost, but *how* we preserve them. I sometimes think that every new situation, good or bad, can enrich us with new insights. But if we abandon the hard facts that we are forced to face, if we give them no shelter in our heads and hearts, do not allow them to settle and change into impulses through which we can grow and from which we can draw meaning—then we are not a viable generation. It is not easy—and no doubt less easy for us Jews than for anyone else—yet if we have nothing to offer a desolate postwar world but our bodies saved at any cost, if we fail to draw new meaning from the deep wells of our distress and despair, then it will not be enough. New thoughts will have to radiate outward from the camps themselves, new insights, spreading lucidity, will have to cross the barbed wire enclosing us and join with the insights that people outside will have to earn just as bloodily, in circumstances that are slowly becoming almost as difficult. And perhaps, on the common basis of an honest search for some way to understand these dark events, wrecked lives may yet take a tentative step forward.

That's why it seemed such a great danger to me when all around one could hear, "We don't want to think, we don't want to feel, it's best to shut your eyes to all this misery." As if suffering—in whatever form and however it may come to us— were not also part of human existence.

I see that I have strayed far beyond your friend K.'s innocuous request. After all, I was to tell you something about life in Westerbork, not about my own views. I couldn't help it, they just slipped out.

But what about the old people? All those aged, infirm people? What use is my philosophy when I have to face them? In the history of Westerbork, surely the saddest chapter will be the one that deals with the old. Probably even sadder than the story of the people from Ellecom, who arrived mutilated, sending a shudder of horror throughout the camp.

To the young and healthy, you can say something that you believe in and can act upon in your own life: that history has indeed laid a heavy destiny on our shoulders, and that we must try and attain the grandeur we need to bear it. You can even say that we should consider ourselves front-line soldiers, although we are sent to very peculiar fronts. It may seem as if we are doomed to complete passivity, but no one can prevent us from mobilizing our inner forces. No one. But have you ever heard of front-line soldiers aged eighty, bearing the red-and-white canes of the blind as their weapons?

One summer morning I came upon a man mumbling to himself, "For heaven's sake, look at the kind of labor forces for

Germany they've sent us now!" And when I hurried around to the entrance, masses of old people were just being unloaded from dilapidated trucks onto our heath. There we stood, almost beyond speech. That was really going too far, we thought. But later on we knew better and would ask each other with every new transport: "And—how many old people and invalids this time?"

There was a little old woman who had left her spectacles and her medicine bottle at home on the mantel—could she go and get them now, and where exactly was she, and where would she be going?

A woman of eighty-seven clung to my hand with so much strength that I thought she would never let go. She told me how the steps in front of her little house had always gleamed and how she had never in her life thrown her clothes under the bed when she went to sleep.

And the bowed little gentleman of seventy-nine: he had been married for more than fifty years, he told me; his wife was in the hospital in Utrecht, and he was about to be taken out of Holland the next day . . .

Even if I went on for pages, I still couldn't convey any idea of the shuffling and the stumbling and the falling down, the need for help along with the childish questions. You can't do much with words. A helping hand on the shoulder is sometimes too heavy. Oh no, these old people, they need a chapter to themselves. Their helpless gestures and exhausted faces crowd many a sleepless night . . .

In a few months the population has swelled from a thousand to roughly ten thousand.[14] The greatest influx dates from the awful days of October, when after a massive Jew hunt throughout the Netherlands, Westerbork was swept by a human flood that threatened to engulf it.

Hence this is not exactly an organically evolved community, with its own even rhythms. Yet—and this is what takes the breath away—you can find every attitude here, every class, ism, conflict, and current of society. And the area still remains only half a kilometer square.

In retrospect is that really so surprising, since every individual carries deep in his inner being the trend, the part of society, the cultural level he represents? But what always strikes one anew is that even at a time of shared distress these distinctions are maintained.

One day in the mud between two big barracks I met a girl who told me she had ended up in Westerbork by chance. This is a typical phenomenon: everyone views his *own* case as an unfortunate accident. We have not yet gained a common sense of history. But to come back to the girl: she told me a pathetic tale of little packages that failed to arrive and of a pair of lost shoes. And then her face brightened, and she said: "But we have been lucky with people; our barracks is full of the best people. Do you know what they call it? The bocht van de Herengracht!"[15] Confounded, I looked from her worn-out shoes to her made-up face and did not know whether to laugh or cry.

Of all the shortages in Westerbork concentration camp, the shortage of space is surely the worst.

About two and a half thousand of the more than ten thousand people are housed in 215 small huts, which used to be the main part of the camp and which held one family each in pre-transport times.

Every little hut has two small rooms, sometimes three, and a little kitchen with a faucet and a WC. There is no doorbell, which makes entering a quick and unceremonious business. As soon as you open the front door, you're standing in the middle of the kitchen. If you're there to visit friends who live in the little back room, then with your newly acquired informality you rush straight through the front room, where another family may be sitting at the table or having a fight or getting ready for bed.

And for some time now, these little rooms have usually been crammed with visitors eager to escape for a while from the big barracks. The hut dwellers are housed like princes by comparison, envied and constantly besieged by all Westerbork.

The scandalous shortage of space in Westerbork is really clear in the colossal, hastily built barracks, those jam-packed hangars of drafty slats where, under a lowering sky made up of hundreds of people's drying laundry, the iron bunks are stacked in triple decks.

The poor French would never have suspected that Jews, exiled to one Drenthe heath or another, would someday dream their fearful dreams on beds built for the Maginot Line. I'm told that's where these bunks come from.

On these iron beds people live and die, eat, fall ill, or lie awake through the night, because so many children cry, or because they cannot help wondering why so little news comes from the thousands who have already set out from this place.

The beds provide the only storage space there is: suitcases lie under them, and rucksacks hang over the iron bars. The other furniture consists of rough wooden tables and narrow wooden benches. Matters of hygiene I shall not mention in this modest account, lest I cause you some unappetizing moments.

Scattered through this vast space are a few stoves, which don't even give enough heat for the old ladies crowded around them. How people are expected to live through the winter in these barracks has not yet been made clear.

All these great human warehouses have been put up in precisely the same manner in the middle of the mud and have been furnished in the same, let us say austere, style. But the remarkable thing is that while a trip through one barracks may make you feel you are in a squalid slum, another will give the impression of a solid middle-class district. In fact, every bunk and every rough wooden table seems to radiate its own atmosphere.

I know of a table in one of the barracks where a candle burns in a glass lantern every evening. Some eight people usually sit around it, and it's called the "bohemian corner." When you go on a few steps to the next table, also with eight people sitting around it, the only difference may be that it holds a couple of dirty pans instead of a candle, but it is an entirely different world.

Like circumstances do not yet seem to produce like people.

Leading lights from cultural and political circles in the big cities have also been stranded on this barren stretch of heath five hundred by six hundred meters. With one mighty convulsion all their scenery has collapsed about them, and now they stand around a little hesitantly and awkwardly on this drafty, open stage called Westerbork. These figures wrenched from their context still carry with them the restless atmosphere of a society more complicated than the one we have here. They walk along the thin barbed-wire fence. Their silhouettes move, life-size and exposed, across the great stretch of sky. You cannot imagine it . . . Their armor of position, esteem, and property has collapsed, and now they stand in the last shreds of their humanity. They exist in an empty space, bounded by earth and sky, which they must fill with whatever they can find within them—there is nothing else.

One suddenly realizes that it is not enough to be an able politician or a talented artist. In the most extreme distress, life demands quite other things.

Yes, it is true, our ultimate human values are being put to the test.

Perhaps I have persuaded you, with my chatter, that I have now told you something about Westerbork. But when I let Westerbork rise up in my mind's eye, in all its facets and with all its spiritual and material needs, I can see that success has eluded me. Furthermore, this is a very one-sided story. I could have told quite another, filled with hatred and bitterness and rebellion.

But rebellion born only when distress begins to affect one

personally is no real rebellion and can never bear fruit. And the absence of hatred in no way implies the absence of moral indignation.

I know that those who hate have good reason to do so. But why should we always have to choose the cheapest and easiest way? It has been brought home forcibly to me here how every atom of hatred added to the world makes it an even more inhospitable place. And I also believe, childishly perhaps but stubbornly, that the earth will become more habitable again only through the love that the Jew Paul described to the citizens of Corinth in the thirteenth chapter of his first letter.

The more I think about it, the worse it seems that I have left you without news for so long. I wanted to write as soon as I got back here, to you and to Rosenberg and Haussmann: you were always so kind and hospitable, I felt so much at home with you. Haussmann's potato soup certainly lives as a culinary high point in my memory, and the Hanukkah lights in the big barracks are an even more precious memory because I was there with you.

The reason I haven't managed to write is probably that I felt rather ill, quite apart from being downcast when the doctor told me I would have to rest for another five weeks. But my good humor is gradually creeping back.

I am so glad that I spent those weeks in Westerbork and that among other things I know how and where you live. Dear Osias, I promise that there won't be any more long pauses from now on. Please remember me to Rosenberg of course, and to your comrades Haussmann ("niece" and all) and Frank and Grüneberg, won't you? And lots and lots of love to you, from

*Etty*

Now look, Osias,[16] this is terrible: have you really not received any letters at all from me up to now? That's the impression Vleesch- houwer gave me. How treacherous you must think I am! But I must be honest and confess: I have written you only once so far, though at some length, in the middle of the night, with a promise to write again soon. But the "soon" stretched into a few weeks.

You know, Osias, I have many friends. Some come to me with their spiritual needs, and those I must talk to for a long time. Then there are others to whom I write regularly and in detail because I know that they need it and also because I want to help them. But with you it's quite different: you are there in my life, your absence from it is unimaginable. I often have conversations with you, but feel no need to write them down; I always believe you'll sense them without letters. So if you don't hear from me for some time you mustn't be disappointed or even unhappy; I still have the same strong, good feelings about you. This morning as I lay thinking of you, I was suddenly overwhelmed with the need to tell you again that I should be terribly sorry if you thought I cared less for you than before. Everything decent and beautiful that I have shared with you has become part of my emotional life, and will always be there.

I hope my first letter has arrived by now. There were a few bits and pieces in it I very much wanted you to see. Are you very busy? Would it be possible sometime to have a few words from you? And are you still living with good old Rosenberg[17] in the quiet back room? How I would love to be fit again and surprise you by just turning up. Meanwhile my orders are: rest, rest, and more rest. But even in bed one can live one's life, or at least try to.

Until another time, Osias Kormann!

In friendship,
*Etty*

Regards to Rosenberg.

Greetings from a girl with an excruciating big toe, Osias. You may recall that this girl is a good friend of yours or you may have forgotten, since so much goes on where you are—too much.

As for me, the same contradiction still applies: the spirit is livelier and more creative than ever, but the flesh cannot form a structure solid enough to support so ardent a spirit.

However, I am patient—not always, of course—and live sensibly so as to be well again as soon as possible. And then I'll turn up again. You must have some work for me by now in the "V," or are there already too many people and not enough room?[18]

Your village has been suddenly turned into a city, without doubt a very sad and strange one.

I have the uneasy suspicion that you don't sleep at all anymore. You ought to now and then. You will, won't you please?

So Rosenberg's mother has arrived. How is he coping? Is he able to make her life a little easier? My very best wishes to them, please. And to Unger as well.

These days many people think: life is coming to an end, this is a great eclipse. Perhaps much later it will be seen as a new beginning as well. Why don't I keep my feet on the ground? Am I a dreamer? Oh please let me be, there have to be people like me, too. My realities may be different from what most people call reality, but still they *are* realities.

Osias Kormann, dear friend on the Drenthe heath—what a bizarre business life really is—I send you my love, I'm very fond of you.

*Etty*

Is it a long time since I last wrote you, Osias? It feels like just a few days, but that goes to show how quickly time passes for me.

Anyway, may I smile on you again from afar? I have a doctor who gets furious when I come into his office beaming. He says it's unforgivable to smile at all times like these. I think he's wrong; what do you say? Hello, Osias, how are you, what are you up to? Are you very busy?[19] Are you in a good mood? Will you need an assistant in the near future? I don't ask for high wages, just friendly treatment. For now I am still going in for morning exercises, the sun, the Bible, Russian, potato peeling, literature, and conversations with much-too-optimistic or much-too-pessimistic, polemical, suicidal, angry, sad, or what-have-you people. A varied program, you can see. And for the rest, I still have a young heart and old bones; the balance between them could be a bit better. My doctor is unable to come up with anything wiser at the moment. He says that most people in these unbearable times suffer in the soul and the mind, but with me the sufferer is the body. Though I swallow bitter, sweet, sour, solid, and liquid things in turn, I'm sure it's a lot of nonsense and we should look to nature for restoration. All in all, however, I think I will be a useful person again one day, and you'll make fabulous coffee when I come back, won't you?

Lots of love, Osias, and think kindly now and then of

*Etty*

And best wishes to Rosenberg.

It seems that the good Lord and the Zentralstelle[20] don't want me to have coffee with you this week; we shall have to wait and see whether next week brings my travel permit. I hope you are especially well in all respects, my dear Osias; it would be nice if I could come and see for myself.

How are the yellow lupins—are they out again? And are you having spring now and then, despite everything? And give my regards to Rosenberg. And accept a harmless but nonetheless heartfelt hug from

*Etty*

Until next week, then. And regards from my father, who was glad to receive your greetings. And don't spoil your nice eyes, please, with these awful hieroglyphics. (I used to write everything on the typewriter, but lately I've had to get used to writing by hand again.)

'Bye,
*E.*

My watch has broken, Osias. Now I absolutely must come back to Westerbork, since there isn't a single person left in Amsterdam with time to mend a watch. You know that my needs are few, but one thing I cannot do without is a watch. As you can probably guess, there are a few other reasons, too, why I want to be back among you all. And I look forward to seeing you yourself just a tiny bit!

I have more glad tidings, especially for you: my wisdom tooth has emerged, not without severe labor pains, but in the end it proved to be there. So you can still entertain hopes that I will be wise one day. What does wise mean to you: egoistic? All this egoism is getting so boring. Since people have been telling each other for centuries that man is basically an egoist, one begins to believe it and actually becomes egoistic. There are so many sides to a human being that it would be nice to try something else, just for a change from boring and unproductive egoism. Anyhow, we'll argue about that when we see each other, won't we? Your letter was nice; you're an old cynic but a very dear person.

In Westerbork I'll have to look out for hundreds of people—not only friends but the children, the parents, and the grandparents of friends. That will be a labor in itself, and other labor will surely turn up without my looking for it.

My dear friend, I look forward to seeing you—but I've said that already.

Until next week.

'Bye!
*Etty*

*Amsterdam, 5 May 1943*

Osias my dear,

Again it must look as if I've been faithless, but the real reason why I haven't written is just human inertia. Your coffee must have grown cold by now, but it's not my fault. I feel almost like a soldier awaiting his next orders. On the one hand I am grateful for every day I can spend here at my desk immersed in things that are close to me. On the other, I want nothing more than to be back with you all as soon as possible. When I stop to add it up, I see that I have already been away from your Heath Metropolis for five months, though oddly it feels like only a week—rather, it feels as if I've never been away at all. One could go on living in several places at once this way, couldn't one?

Osias, you know the Skating Club, next to the Concert-gebouw? I sometimes go walking there with you along the railings, and we have such a lovely time together. Usually you arrive quite out of the blue. I take my customary turn around the club grounds, and suddenly you are at my side, and I delight in your closeness all over again.

As far as my health goes, I don't have much to complain about. I have admittedly become a shade less productive than I was before my illness, but that must be true of many people in this blessed Europe of ours.

Osias my dear, this must be enough for today. I am waiting anxiously to find out when we will see each other again at last—

Please give my special regards to Petzal. I mean so often to write to him, but—laziness, etc., as you well know. And best wishes again, of course, to Rosenberg.

And to yourself: most definitely *auf Wiedersehen!*

'Bye!
*Etty*

My dear Osias,

Every evening for the past few days I have meant to send you another bulletin, but each day is so unsettled now. My blankets will have to wait up on your wooden gallery a little longer than I thought, until they can cover me again.

On the morning of April twenty-fourth my call-up came: I was to report on the twenty-fifth. I started getting my rucksack ready right away, but was told in the afternoon that my call-up had been an "error." That seems a curious expression, as if it wasn't an "error" for everyone else. Oh well, I shan't start philosophizing on this unpleasant subject now; we can talk to each other soon enough.

Today I heard that fifteen colleagues from the Jewish Council in Westerbork will get leave and fifteen volunteers here will be needed as replacements. I shall volunteer, of course, and then just wait and see whether they can use me, since I represent a somewhat peculiar, nihilistic faction. But I think we shall soon see each other in any case now that the "liquidation" of "Jewish remnants" has taken on a faster tempo.

To think that ten months have already passed since I met a small man with a gray cap and heavy spectacles in the school in Westerbork, and since that man told me fantastic stories about the camp and said afterward, "You are definitely no Dutchwoman; you have too much warmth." Yes, Osias, and all the rest.

This is not really a letter, only a hasty greeting. I expect your work is sad again right now. *Auf Wiedersehen,* in a few days or in a few weeks, but anyway *auf Wiedersehen!*

*Etty*

*Saturday evening, 5 June 1943*

Little Maria,

Don't let's be too materialistic: a few days more or less, and whether or not we managed to see each other doesn't really matter to us, does it? It's a pity, I would so much have liked to see you, but that will happen again, I'm absolutely certain.

It is late; I can't tell you how tired I am. I had hoped to reach you by telephone in Wageningen, because I stayed a day longer, but I didn't manage it.

You ask for a diary. Because it's you, I'm leaving a silly piece of writing behind. There's a lot of rubbish in it, indiscreet woman that I am!

If you ever have a hard time, pour your soul out on a scrap of paper and send it to Etty; she'll be sure to answer you.

Look after Father Han—but you do that anyway. He'll tell you all sorts of thrilling stories about the last two days. I can hardly keep my eyes open; what hard work carrying a rucksack is! I am not saying good-bye; we are not really leaving each other, are we?

May all go very well with you, dear child.

*Etty*

# Westerbork

My very dear people,

Did you go on waving to my two rosebuds for a long time? You are all so dear to me; I held onto that thought during the whole train trip, and now the camp with its large-scale misery of transports coming and going has swallowed me whole again. I have been here a hundred years already. The journey was pleasant enough. There is a nice spirit of comradeship among our people. They told me some tall tales, starting with the news that we had to walk the whole way from Assen to the camp, luggage and all. I wasn't too pleased to hear that. But when they announced that a shop selling nougat had opened in the camp, that the orphanage had held a flower show, and that polo was the latest craze, my eyes were opened.

In Assen it was pouring rain, and a leaky truck was waiting for us. We all were a bit wet when we arrived. Together with our dripping luggage we were ushered into a hall (which isn't what used to happen), where our rucksacks and suitcases were searched by the police. I readily opened the little bag with the

Koran and the Talmud in it; they didn't bother with my ruck-sack, which is as big as a house, and I certainly didn't mind.

The hut where I have been put this time is something be-tween a small storehouse and a boudoir. Beds, two or three tiers high, suitcases and boxes everywhere, flowers on the table and in the window, and a couple of languid females in long silk pei-gnoirs. Most astonishing. I share my place with a former beauty queen from Het Leven.[21] At ten o'clock she propped a mirror against my butter dish and busied herself for half an hour with her eyebrows. There was no bed for me; but we had to work anyhow that night, because a transport from Vught had ar-rived.[22] We were due to report at 4:00 A.M., so at eleven I rolled myself in a blanket, clothes and all (the sleeping bag was wet and had been hung up to dry), on a bed whose regular occupant was said to be working through the night. When I had been lying down for an hour, greatly enjoying the musical gnawings of the mice (which seem to have multiplied since I was last here), along came the bed's real tenant, a nearsighted lady with a pitch-black mustache from Lijnbaansgracht, a place I have never much liked. So then we lay side by side together on her narrow bunk—what you might call a piquant situation.

I woke up fairly stiff at about four o'clock. I fortified myself with your delicious wheaten creation, darling Käthe, and then walked again through the nocturnal Westerbork landscape. First of all we underwent a Lysol treatment, because so many lice always arrive from Vught. From four to nine I dragged screaming children around and carried luggage for exhausted women. It was hard going, and heart-rending. Women with small children, 1,600 (tonight another 1,600 will arrive); the men had been deliberately kept back in Vught. The morning trans-port is ready, Jopie and I have just been walking along it. Large, empty cattle cars. In Vught two or three children die every day. An old woman asked me helplessly, "Could you tell me, please could you tell me, why we Jews have to suffer so much?" I couldn't answer. There was a woman who had had to feed her four-month-old child on cabbage soup for days. She said, "I keep calling, 'Oh God, oh God'—but does He really still exist?" Among the prisoners I met an ex-assistant of Professor Scholten, who taught me procedural law once upon a time. I hardly recognized him because of his emaciation, beard, and staring eyes. I also met my internist, Schaap. When I was in the NIZ,[23] Schaap stood by my bed wearing an expression that implied my nonexistence and explained to the other doctors gathered around: "Here lies a young lady who positively wants to go back to Westerbork," as if I were an incomprehensible case. Now he looked fit and cheerful (he has already been here for some time). This evening's delivery from Vught included his wife and children, who also looked quite good (tell Tide this). On my journey through the camp this morning I met many old friends—friends of my parents, too. People whom I used to know as decent citizens, living in peaceful and comfortable circumstances, I now find inhabiting the big barracks as regular members of the proletariat. It is very moving, the state some of them are in. I'd rather not have my parents here. At the moment I am sitting in Jopie's little house, and he is sitting opposite me in soldier's trousers and a dirty gray jacket. He sends you his kind regards. One of his best friends died a few hours ago. The friend's wife and child were sent through some time past; the man was in an advanced stage of TB and couldn't go with them. Jopie told me that theirs was one of the few good marriages he had known. Several days ago another good friend of his died.

This afternoon I shall try and get a little sleep; I now have a bed—someone went on leave today. At four in the morning another transport comes from Vught. Last night I was able to piece together a picture of Vught, a truly horrible picture.

I am glad I've come back to Westerbork. I am greeted warmly on all sides. I went to see Hedwig Mahler, who is being allowed to stay here for the time being, and met a woman who was once the headmistress at Father's school.[24] They gave me a bowl of semolina. Then I went to see Kormann, who almost killed me with pleasure and gave me another bowl of semolina. Later I went to visit someone else and was given more semolina. I let the rest of them have the cabbage. One and all seem to be well.

With everything I've been doing, it is now half past twelve. I have just fetched my bread ration and ten grams of butter from the kitchen, as well as a small vitamin C tablet, which was a surprise. Now I'll stop this muddled tale. Tonight at seven I'll go and see Herman B. in the hospital; I couldn't make it last night.[25] I can't do the night work the way I used to; I collapse in the middle. But don't worry—I'm not rushing at things head-long anymore. At the moment I itch all over despite the Lysol.

A hasty farewell to you all, too many to mention by name. You are all of you so very dear to me.

More later, dear people.
*Etty*

My little Maria,

Why don't you write Etty to say how you are? Are you happy, are you sad, do you rush around, do you sit quietly at home, what does Ernst have to say, what does Amsterdam have to say, what does Father Han do, does Käthe go to bed on time? As I walk through the mud between the wooden barracks, I feel as if I am walking at the same time along the corridors of my six-year home, or sitting at a shaky table in the noisy little parlor, or working at my beloved, untidy desk. I talk to many people here who say, "We don't want to remember anything from before; otherwise we couldn't manage to live here." But I can live here as well as I do just *because* I remember everything from "before" (it's not really a "before" for me), and I go on living.

*Noon*

My soul is content, Maria. I was given four hospital barracks today, one large and three small; I have to check whether the people there need any food or luggage from the outside. The wonderful thing about it is that I now have free access to the whole complex of hospital barracks at almost any time of day.

*Later*

Take these few words just as they come, little one. There isn't much time for writing here—but the letters I send you in my thoughts are much longer.

I am fine, and content. I live just as I did in Amsterdam, really; sometimes I don't even notice that I'm in a camp, which is very strange. And all of you are so close to me that I don't even miss you. Jopie is a cherished companion. In the evenings we go and watch the sun setting over the purple lupins behind the barbed wire. And if I get leave I'll probably be back.

Do write.

'Bye!
*Etty*

My dear people,

Not much heath is left now inside the barbed wire; more barracks are always being added. Only a little piece remains in the farthest corner of the camp, and that's where I'm sitting now, in the sun under a glorious blue sky, among some low shrubbery. Right across from me only a few meters away, a blue uniform with a helmet stands in the watchtower. A guard with an enraptured expression is picking purple lupins, his gun dangling on his back. When I look to the left I see billowing white smoke and hear the puffing of a locomotive. The people have already been loaded onto the freight cars; the doors are closed. There are many green police,[26] who sang this morning as they marched by the side of the train, and the Dutch military police are out as well. The quota of people who must go is not yet filled. Just now I met the matron of the orphanage, carrying a small child in her arms who also has to go, alone. And a number of people have been taken out of the hospital barracks. They are doing a thorough job here today; big shots from The Hague have come on a visit. It's very strange watching these gentlemen at work from close quarters. I've been up since four this morning dealing with the babies and carrying luggage. In a few hours you can accumulate enough gloom here to last a lifetime. The nature-loving policeman has gathered his purple bouquet now, perhaps he's off to court some farmer's daughter in the neighborhood. The engine gives a piercing shriek. The whole camp holds its breath; another three thousand Jews are about to leave. There are babies with pneumonia lying in the freight cars. Sometimes what goes on here seems totally unreal. I haven't been given any particular job, which suits me very well. I just wander about and find my own work. This morning I had a brief talk with a woman who had come from Vught, who told me her latest experiences in three minutes. How much can you really tell in a few minutes? When we came to a door, and I wasn't allowed to go any farther, she embraced me and said, "Thank you for being such a help."

Just now I climbed up on a box lying among the bushes here to count the freight cars. There were thirty-five, with some second-class cars at the front for the escorts. The freight cars had been completely sealed, but a plank had been left out here and there, and people put their hands through the gaps and waved as if they were drowning.

The sky is full of birds, the purple lupins stand up so regally and peacefully, two little old women have sat down on the box for a chat, the sun is shining on my face—and right before our eyes, mass murder. The whole thing is simply beyond comprehension.

Love
*Etty*

[21 June 1943]

Dear Milli,[27]

Later on I'll write you a longer letter about this, the hardest day of my life. My parents and Mischa are being tremendous; I am amazed. The jam-packed freight train drew into the camp this morning. I stood beside it in the rain. The cars were shut tight, but there were a few small openings here and there high up, where the planks had been broken. Through one of these I suddenly spotted Mother's hat and Father's glasses and Mischa's peaky face. I started to shout, and they saw me.

Now I shall have to share the same torture with them that I went through last night with the Levies and the two small children: registration, hours and hours of waiting, more registration outside in the rain, quarantine. Thanks to the many friends I have here, it'll be possible to make life easier for them in all sorts of small ways. Soon I'll have to take them to the large barracks, where all hell has been let loose. I don't think there are even enough beds for everyone, and there are no mattresses for the men. Still, my threesome is remarkably fit and cheerful and good-humored.

Now down to business. The Jewish Council thinks it imperative that you pursue the Barneveld option strenuously with the Zentralstelle on behalf of Mischa and the family (remember: not me!), and urges you to do so.[28] Perhaps you will still be able to get Mengelberg to intervene personally with Rauter.

Suddenly it's all coming to an end.

*Etty*

Christine,[29]

They are so indescribably efficient in this utter hell. In the early
morning a line of freight cars pulled into the muddy camp. As I
stood next to them I spotted my father's crumpled hat and
glasses, my mother's hat, and Mischa's narrow face in a small
opening high in one of the cars. And now that I am sharing
their martyrdom, I am thankful I can take care of all sorts of
minor details for them. Although at the moment there is nothing to take care of: what we have now is a complete catastrophe.
During the last twenty-four hours the camp has been engulfed
by successive tidal waves of Jews. I must tell you: I was shocked
by Father and Mother today, and Mischa, too. Father is completely helpless, and his collar has grown a lot too big for him
over the last twenty-four hours, and the gray stubble of his beard
is pathetic. But he waved a small Bible about this morning while
we waited for hours and hours in the rain, and found a marvelous quotation from Joshua. They are in a big barracks now, a
jam-packed human warehouse: people sleeping three to a bed on
narrow iron bunks, no mattresses for the men, nowhere at all to
store anything, children terrified and screaming, the greatest
possible wretchedness. I shall try to get through it as best I can, I
even feel quite strong and brave, although sometimes I can see
nothing but blackness and nothing makes any sense at all.

Now for something practical. We must try to get Father some
bread, since he doesn't eat hot food. You can still send registered
"letter-parcels" from the provinces weighing up to two kilos.
Please see if you can get one of them through to us. You won't
think it impertinent of me to ask you straight out like this; needs
must. Rye bread would be very welcome, too. Don't send coupons here, we can't do anything with them. Mail them to Jacobs,
Retiefstraat 11, and tell him that from Amsterdam he can still

send parcels weighing up to five kilos, preferably registered. It's safest to address them to me: Dr. E. Hillesum, Assistant, Jewish Council, Westerbork Camp, Post Hoog-Halen, O, Drenthe. Top left: Barracks 34. Write us a postcard if you do send us something, then I can look out for it—

I hope I'll find a bed tonight, every square millimeter is taken. More later. Please pray a little for us.

Love,
*Etty*

Well, children, here I am again. The letter I started is back under my orange checked sleeping bag, and now I'm sitting in another corner of the camp carrying on this chat with you on a bit of paper that's turned up. I have just been with my papa. This is a historic moment for him—he ate a plateful of cabbage, and this morning he even drank some milk, although he always swore that he'd rather go to Poland than drink milk. An angel of a stalwart Russian in the bed next to him guides him through every clumsy movement and whistles at night when he snores too loudly. Four hundred people from the hospital will apparently have to go on the next transport. Walking through the barracks, particularly the one with most of the old women, is an act of despair. One after another they clutch at you and implore, "I don't really have to go on this transport, do I?" and "Surely they won't take us away from here," and then always the same thing over and over—"Isn't there anything you can do for me?" Yesterday a very old woman, sick, nothing but skin and bones, asked me, "Do you think there will be medical assistance in Poland?" In the face of something like that, I feel like running away. It is almost beyond comprehension, the strength with which people whose lives are almost entirely behind them hang on to the wretched bits of carcass that are left. But they all want to live to see peace and see their children and families again, which is perfectly understandable, really—

Just when I was about to descend from my third-story heaven to solid ground this morning, Anne-Marie climbed up to me; she looked like an aviator in her beret and goggles.[30] She's on indoor duty in the barracks where I was assigned last year. She's doing extremely well; tell Swiep in particular.[31] She sleeps well, eats well, doesn't have any hard work, and is here on her own. That's very important; I can see in myself the effects of worry about the family. It gnaws at you worse than anything else. I haven't seen Mischa and Mother today; I've been in bed, and Mother's been laid up with a bit of an upset stomach. I always have a strong inner resistance to overcome, a kind of fear, before I can go inside their barracks, where the sour, fetid human reek hits you in the face. Sam de Wolff is in the same barracks as Mischa; I run across him now and then pottering about between the iron bunks.[32]

We are expecting a transport from the Hollandsche Schouwburg any day now.[33] Everyone thinks it will be sent straight through to Poland. All we know about Jaap is that he is in the Schouwburg, nothing more.[34] I shall do whatever I possibly can to hold onto him here, but there's no way of forcing things to happen. Everyone has to accept the fate allotted to him; there's nothing else for it. Just now a woman who cleans for Kormann said to me, "You always look so radiant." But I feel just as I always have, wherever I've been. Of course I'm a little weary and worn down, and giddy with worry now and then. But everyone has worries here, so why shouldn't we share them and bear them together honestly? I am experiencing much that is good here. Each day Mechanicus, with whom I go for walks along the narrow, barren strip of earth between the ditch and the barbed wire, reads me what he has just written.[35] You develop friendships here that are enough for several lives at once. I still find time every day for a short philosophical conversation with Weinreb, a man who is a private world to himself with an atmosphere all his own that he manages to preserve no matter what happens.[36]

It's a shame I have so little time to write, there is so much I want to tell you. I'll save it up for later, I promise. But now we must concern ourselves with cabbage, a favorite dish in these parts.

The cooking is good here; I won't hear a word against it. Children, I would so much like to know how you all are. Why don't I hear anything from Maria? Is it true, Maria, that Ernst is coming to visit us here? So Renate told me.[37] I meet Paul's mother now and then on some muddy little path or other, and we gossip for a few minutes. There is no time for real "visits," nor is there a quiet place anywhere to sit down together. People talk to each other in passing, outdoors. Really, one keeps walking about all day long—

Oh yes, there is something else, something the whole Jewish Council here is so full of that I put it completely out of my mind. The latest news (although it's sure to change again a few times): sixty of us may stay here, the other sixty must go back to Amsterdam, where they will get special "exemptions." Because my parents are here, naturally I am one of those who want to stay on, come what may. Most of us do, actually, since almost everyone has family here whom he can still protect a little by his presence. So you have a paradoxical situation: while each of us would give anything to get away from W., many of us would have to be thrown out before we'd go. People are terribly wound up. Debates, computations, laws of probability, are the order of the day. I keep well out of it. All this talking takes up energy, and nothing comes of it in the end. Improbable though it may sound to you, I am really and truly the most taciturn person in the whole JC. People here fritter their energy away on the thousand irksome details that grind us down every day; they lose themselves in detail and drown. That's why they get driven off course and find existence pointless. The few big things that matter in life are what we have to keep in mind; the rest can be quietly abandoned. And you can find those few big things anywhere, you have to keep rediscovering them in yourself so that you can be renewed. And in spite of everything you always end up with the same conviction: life is good after all, it's not God's fault that things go awry sometimes, the cause lies in ourselves. And that's what stays with me, even now, even when I'm about to be packed off to Poland with my whole family.

And now I'm going to look for Mother and Mischa. 'Bye for now.

*Last stage*

I am sitting on my suitcase in our little kitchen, it's so full in here that not another mortal can enter. Now for a few practical details . . . Intermezzo: A nice man just came in who used to be one of Spier's subjects; he sat on another suitcase and suddenly we were right in the middle of chirology. I meet quite a few of Spier's clients and pupils here. And we always say the same thing: What a mercy it is that he is no longer with us. Now for some business. I am enclosing a few more bread coupons. Would Frans take it badly if you telephoned and asked him to send us some more Sanovite biscuits? Is Frans still there, anyway? Mother eats hardly anything anymore, she cannot stand the bread here, and I should like to be able to give her a little Sanovite now and then. Is it a great bore for you, my making such a nuisance of myself? I hope the soap coupons haven't been used up yet; I always forget to send them. I do the washing here myself in a bucket outside the house, and we hang it up on a piece of string. A little primitive, but it does the job.

This letter is also for Mien Kuyper; I won't have a chance to write her today. Would you be kind enough to tell her that up to now, Sunday, none of her parcels have arrived? Her letters have come, so she knows the address. It would be a pity if anything of hers went astray; she also wrote that she has sent things twice. Please ask if she'd be kind enough to send tomatoes and other fresh things. Since there is a continuous sandstorm here, people are full of dust and completely dried up, so that they need fresh things even more than bread. I don't myself have any such craving. That's to be expected; ever since that police-raid transport I haven't been hungry, have had no sleep or anything. But I feel very well, all the same. One concentrates so much on others that one forgets oneself, and that's just as well. Ask Mien to give our best regards to Milli Ortmann; as soon as I can I'll write her, too. Let's hope that Mischa gets out of Westerbork; being here won't do him any good in the long run, but I can't do anything with him while our parents are still at risk here. I shall now break off before I ruin my eyes permanently. Love to everyone dear to me—you know who they are well enough.

'Bye,
*Etty*

Would you be kind enough to send some postage stamps next time?

Christine,

We are sitting just now, Father and I, on a kind of stone drain.
A glorious fresh breeze is blowing. In front of us, people with
yellow stars are digging a moat to stop us from running away,
and beyond that stretches the barbed wire. To the left, in the
corner of the camp, the military policeman stands high up in his
little hut on posts. We are black with sand; the breeze is a real
sirocco. I have just lifted Father down from his second-tier
bunk, and we are airing it a bit. I am very grateful that he has a
bed to himself now; in the big barracks he would have gone to
pieces within a week. We shall try somehow to pull each other
through. Mother is admirable. It's almost unbelievable—she
goes about just as spryly and neatly turned out as always. Today,
for instance, she did a big wash in a bucket and hung the clothes
out on a piece of string. Mischa's attachment to them both is
touching. He lives in constant fear that they will have to go to
Poland, and says there's no question but that he'll go with them.
However, everything will work out. Until further notice I'm
keeping them here for certain. Our greatest worries are for
Mischa; we are afraid that things will soon get too much for
him. It is really beyond comprehension why people don't all go
mad here.

Anyway. Now to come to the point. This morning a very
welcome parcel arrived from Simon.[38] Nothing from you; we'll
just have to wait a little longer. Perhaps it's as well that everything is being sent via the Jewish Council. Mother is looking
forward to your shrimp pies. How do you like that? We're
going in for special orders now. This morning she said how
wonderful it would be if we could have something spicy to eat
for once, and immediately Mevrouw de Groot from Ceintuur-
baan said that she still had lots of spicy things left. Oh well, I am

noting it all down like a dutiful secretary. And do you know, we can again change bread and butter coupons in the canteen here. If you have any left over, you might be kind enough to send a few. Half the camp has lectured Father about eating something hot, but so far he hasn't managed to.

Now we are right in the middle of a sandstorm; can you read my writing? Everything here is mad and incredible and desperate and comical, all at the same time. Everything I write is all mixed up, too, but that's the way things are. Oh yes: it's quite possible that I will shortly be stripped of my privileged position, because the Jewish Council here is about to be dissolved. Then I won't be able to write as often as I would like. But we'll still have a writing day once every two weeks, so you'll go on hearing from us. And now we must leave our nice stone seat; otherwise we'll develop galloping consumption. Let us hope that a time will come when we'll be able to tell you everything in person, let us truly hope for that. And yes, please pray for us a little. And thank you for everything.

Much love,
*Etty*

Very dearest Milli,

First for something absolutely crucial: the Zentralstelle must tell our camp commandant through official channels that my parents and Mischa are to be kept on here. Otherwise it won't be any use at all.

We have managed to survive the latest transport night: Mischa has been "deferred" temporarily, and we've hung on to my parents, too, because they are on the "parents' list" of Westerbork staff. But the list is not something you can rely on. Next week the battle starts all over again. If they go on sending out one transport a week, it will be impossible to hold my parents back without some intervention from outside. Last night the Hollandsche Schouwburg lot arrived, and I stood guard all night because we were expecting Jaap. To our utter delight he didn't turn up. We heard a vague report that he had been kept back because he was on the Meijer list (what sort of list is that, for heaven's sake?). At five o'clock in the morning I forced my way into the hospital to make sure they weren't going to drag Father off by accident and to tell him the joyful news about Jaap. Lots of the sick who were due to leave were being dressed by the male nurses. The long train of dilapidated boxcars had stood waiting the whole day. Empty cattle cars, each with a bucket in the middle. Paper mattresses on the floor for the sick. After I'd been to see Father I walked right across the camp to Mother's large barracks, where almost everyone was getting ready to leave. The people were dignified, calm, and disciplined. I saw off a great many good friends. Just now I went back again to Mother's. She was lying on her narrow iron soldier's bed in a state of exhaustion. After a transport night like that, we all feel sick and and ready to drop. Then we take a deep breath and go on with life until the next transport. I keep hoping and hoping that there will be some message from the Zentralstelle. My parents are really bearing up splendidly. Inwardly they are preparing for Poland. They make few demands and do not complain; I am terribly proud of them. Mischa is the same as ever. He is a bit grubby and now and then gets very worked up, and he never turns up on time for the roll calls. But his wonderful sense of humor hasn't deserted him even here.

I got your letter and the one from Grete and Cor as well. You are all being terribly kind. Many thanks for the parcels. What a nuisance we must be to you, it often weighs on my mind. Anyway, 'bye for now.

Love,
*Etty*

Little Father Han, Käthe, Maria, Hans,

Just a telegram-style message for you out of the blue. Stood guard last night to watch out for Jaap. He wasn't in the Schouwburg transport; we were delirious with joy. In the morning another big transport left. I even went to the hospital at five o'clock to make sure they hadn't taken Father along by mistake—there are plenty of mistakes. Then to Mother's big barracks, where she was lying on her cramped soldier's bed. She was delighted by the news about Jaap. My parents are taking things nobly, I am very proud of them. They don't even dread Poland anymore—they say. I hope I can keep them here, but nothing is certain. In a few days you can drift far from your former moorings. New and powerful forces enter into you. Accepting your own doom needs inner strength.

I got a letter from Leguit that touched me very much. He is another one of those people who make you want to survive just so you can see them again later on. He enclosed a quotation from Dr. Korff: "And yet God is love." I completely agree, and it is truer now than ever. Leguit also wrote: "It would surprise me if you had enough resilience of spirit left to spare even half an ear for those who have stayed behind." I have all my ears and all my attention to spare for you. I go on living with you just as before, and pause with you now and then to rest from all that overwhelms me here. It is more difficult for you to digest the events at Westerbork than for us. I have noticed that in every situation, even the most difficult, man generates new faculties that help him go on living. As far as that is concerned, God is merciful enough. And for the rest: several suicides last night before the transport, with razors and so on. This morning, while I stood at the tub with a colleague, I said with great emotion something like this: "The realms of the soul and the spirit are so spacious and unending that this little bit of physical discomfort and suffering really doesn't matter all that much. I do not feel I have been robbed of my freedom; essentially no one can do me any harm at all." Yes, children, that's how it is, I am in a strange state of mournful contentment. If I once wrote you a desperate letter, don't take it too much to heart; it expressed only a brief moment. It's true you can suffer, but that need not make you desperate. And now I'm going to jump in at the deep end again; I'm off to the hospital with a little tin box for my beloved father under one arm and my official folder under the other. I shall find many empty beds there after this transport. Be of good cheer, my dear good friends. How is Cousin Wegerif? And Käthe, are you being good? And isn't Father Han being silent to a fault? Hannes's mother did *not* go to Theresienstadt. Regards to Adri from Ilse B.

'Bye!

Christine, my dear,

I am stealing a few moments in the sun to scribble to various friends. It is a glorious day—how different life suddenly looks! I am so glad my work is in the hospital area; it means I can drop in on Father whenever I like. And when I can't go inside his barracks, we can have a little chat through his open window, since his bed is right next to it. I have just taken him your letters; he was very pleased. Now I have your note in front of me. I gave an Indian whoop of joy over the goggles; without them our eyes are completely ruined here. How nice of you to send them on your own initiative! It's so sweet, the way you look after us. I'm sure you people in the outside world have enough troubles of your own without adding all of ours. Your letter to Mischa was lovely. Father has it now and will hand it on when Mischa visits him today.

(Half an hour later. Just now a picturesque interlude: A good friend of mine from Amsterdam, a talented young musician, came past in filthy overalls with a barrowful of sand. Between the barbed wire and the little pieces of string on which the dingy washing has been hung out to dry, we delivered ourselves of philosophical observations concerning the marvels and mysteries of this earthly existence. Let's hope that not too many more friends come past with barrows, since I have a lot more to write you.)

An end will come soon enough to all the scribbling. I am only too grateful that I'm allowed to stay on. Have I already told you that of the hundred and twenty people working for the Jewish Council, sixty *must* go home? Luckily I am not one of the sixty, so I can keep on protecting my parents as best I can. You see, there is always new cause for satisfaction. In Amsterdam the fight for Barneveld continues. I hope and pray that it will work out. I myself would ten times rather go to Poland or wherever, if only I am able to get my dear ones away from this place first. Well, we must simply have patience—which, indeed, we already do have in plenty.

When I am not allowed to write anymore, I'll still be able to send a postcard following the arrival of a parcel, with the words "Parcel received"—nothing else. So if a meaningless card like that comes, you'll know why. And something else: we are permitted to send telegrams to the Jewish Council to ask for things we need—also without further comment.

But we are forbidden to be specific; we can only put something like "food" in the telegram. So let's agree now on, for example: book = butter, writing = jam, ink = rye bread, shoelaces = fruit. (If it comes to the point where I have to send telegrams like that, then you will get in touch with Simon, won't you?)

Do you know, we can utter a lot of "important words" here without turning a hair. I can name fruit, tomatoes, and things like that with no difficulty at all. Yet I don't even know if you in the outside world have any of these. You must not think it presumptuous if we ask for impossible things; please remember it is due to ignorance. What Father, for instance, badly needs is fruit and green vegetables. We get so dried up here because of the continuous sandstorms. The water is not very good either; we are advised not to drink too much of it because of the "camp sicknesses," and everything else available to drink is awful. I am pretty sure that Mother has lots of different bottled drinks in the Deventer house, but it would probably be quite a business to get them over here. I have the feeling that we are giving you a lot of trouble, but it's all to keep each other alive. Oh Christine, just imagine, a time may come once more when we can tell each other everything. And if we survive, we will surely be grateful that we were present at one of the many fronts in Europe, where we could share some part of all the suffering. Yesterday the man who regularly cuts Father's hair said to me, "You're the sort of person who makes something of her life in any circumstances."

Father is marvelous, and wonderfully resigned. Yesterday morning all the beds were standing outside his barracks, in the sand blowing about between two great empty hospital buildings. It looked like an open-air sanatorium. Walking past, I heard Father's hearty laughter ringing out over the entire area. He has nice people around him who search over and over for all the little things that, with some *grandezza* and a certain nonchalance, he loses daily. There is a journalist, Philip Mechanicus, a stylish, strong-minded character, who regularly drops by and chats with him. Father has also come across many old student friends here. He studies the Bible with great concentration, comparing the French, Greek, and Dutch versions. I brought him the writings of Meister Eckhart and another couple of books I had here. He doesn't eat all that much; we are able to share out quite a lot of his bread. It's a good thing, since we are all beginning to feel the pinch badly now that the outside world, which used to send supplies regularly, has shrunk so much. For all the families and acquaintances of most Jews are here now.

I'm going to abandon my sunny, windy little corner and the well I'm sitting on. I shall walk past Father's window and then go to take pot luck in my barracks. We are very, very happy Jaap isn't here yet; it's nice that you went to look him up. When the transport from the Hollandsche Schouwburg arrived a few nights ago, I stood watch all night to catch him. Thank God it wasn't necessary. I'll write more later; I won't send this letter off until your parcel arrives. Good-bye for now.

*5:30 P.M.*

If you only knew what it means here just to be able to be in a little room all by yourself. I am sitting in such a room now and will finally be able to finish answering your letter. Are you still interested in special requests? It would make me radiantly happy if you could send paper handkerchiefs. People here have chronic colds, aggravated by the climate, and regular handker-chiefs get filthier rather than cleaner when you wash them. The hygiene problem is really the most desperate of all. Father com-plains bitterly that he is the biggest gypsy in Westerbork; he doesn't see that everyone else is in the same boat. Can you still get sanitary napkins? And ordinary rolls of bandages? An obsti-nate eczema that I once had for a few years on my right hand has flared up again, and I keep it bandaged because of the dust. I ask you for all these things with a heavy heart; for I know they're not easy to come by, are they? And oh yes, if there's still one of our little pots of jam there, perhaps it also could make the trip here in the course of time. One should avoid having too many special requests these days, I think. But that's the difficult part, you see. I wouldn't beg favors for myself, but I would turn the world upside down to get my parents something to lighten their lives a little. There you are. We wish you all a very nice holiday. Father's writing day is tomorrow; I think he plans a letter to you. It will take a week to arrive; it's got to pass a special censor. Forgive my saying everything in such a muddle, that's what these surroundings do to one. I hope I can still write you often, but it looks as if that won't be possible much longer. I don't need writing paper yet.

Lots of love, and thanks for everything,
*Etty*

P.S. from Mother: Perhaps you would be kind enough some time to get in touch with Gantvoort, the baker, private address c/o Larese, 23 Sweelinckstraat. He once said that he would like to bake something. Sorry and all that, but it isn't for myself.

Jopie, Klaas, my dear friends,[39]

Here I am on the third tier of this bunk hurrying to unleash a veritable riot of writing, for in a few days' time it'll be the end of the line for my scribblings. I'll have become a "camp inmate," allowed to write just one letter a fortnight, and unsealed at that. And there are still a couple of little things I must talk to you about. Did I really send a letter that made it look as if all my courage had gone? I can hardly believe it. There are moments, it's true, when I feel things can't go on. But they do go on, you gradually learn that as well. Though the landscape around you may appear different: there is a lowering black sky overhead and a great shift in your outlook on life, and your heart feels gray and a thousand years old. But it is not always like that. A human being is a remarkable thing. The misery here is really indescribable. People live in those big barracks like so many rats in a sewer. There are many dying children. But there are many healthy ones, too.

One night last week a transport of prisoners passed through here. Thin, waxen faces. I have never seen so much exhaustion and fatigue as I did that night. They were being "processed": registration, more registration, frisking by half-grown NSB men, quarantine, a foretaste of martyrdom lasting hours and hours.[40] Early in the morning they were crammed into empty freight cars. Then another long wait while the train was boarded up. And then three days' travel eastward. Paper "mattresses" on the floor for the sick. For the rest, bare boards with a bucket in the middle and roughly seventy people to a sealed car. A rucksack each was all they were allowed to take. How many, I wondered, would reach their destination alive? And my parents are preparing themselves for just such a journey unless something comes of Barneveld after all.

Last time I saw my father, we went for a walk in the dusty, sandy wasteland. He is so sweet, and wonderfully resigned. Very pleasantly, calmly, and quite casually, he said, "You know, I would like to get to Poland as quickly as possible. Then it will all be over and done with and I won't have to continue with this undignified existence. After all, why should I be spared from what has happened to thousands of others?" Later we joked about our surroundings. Westerbork really is nothing but desert, despite a few lupins and campions and decorative birds that look like seagulls. "Jews in a desert, we know that sort of landscape from before." It really gets you down, having such a nice little father, you sometimes feel there is no hope at all.

But these are passing moods. There are other sorts, too, when a few of us laugh together and marvel at all sorts of things. And then we keep meeting lots of relatives whom we haven't seen for years—lawyers, a librarian, and so on—pushing wheelbarrows full of sand, in untidy, ill-fitting overalls, and we just look at each other and don't say much. A young, sad Dutch police officer told me one transport night, "I lose two kilos during a night like this, and all *I* have to do is to listen, look, and keep my mouth shut." And that's why I don't like to write about it, either. But I am digressing. All I wanted to say is this: The misery here is quite terrible; and yet, late at night when the day has slunk away into the depths behind me, I often walk with a spring in my step along the barbed wire. And then time and again, it soars straight from my heart—I can't help it, that's just the way it is, like some elementary force—the feeling that life is glorious and magnificent, and that one day we shall be building a whole new world. Against every new outrage and every fresh horror, we shall put up one more piece of love and goodness, drawing strength from within ourselves. We may suffer, but we must not succumb. And if we should survive unhurt in body and soul, but above all in soul, without bitterness and without hatred, then we shall have a right to a say after the war. Maybe I am an ambitious woman: I would like to have just a tiny little bit of a say.

You speak about suicide, and about mothers and children. Yes, I know what you mean, but I find it a morbid subject. There is a limit to suffering; perhaps no human being is given more to bear than he can shoulder; beyond a certain point we just die. People are dying here even now of a broken spirit, because they can no longer find any meaning in life, young people. The old ones are rooted in firmer soil and accept their fate with dignity and calm. You see so many different sorts of people here, and so many different attitudes to the hardest, the ultimate questions . . .

I shall try to convey to you how I feel, but am not sure if my metaphor is right. When a spider spins its web, does it not cast the main threads ahead of itself, and then follow along them from behind? The main path of my life stretches like a long journey before me and already reaches into another world. It is just as if everything that happens here and that is still to happen were somehow discounted inside me. As if I had been through it already, and was now helping to build a new and different society. Life here hardly touches my deepest resources—physically, perhaps, you do decline a little, and sometimes you are infinitely sad—but fundamentally you keep growing stronger. I just hope that it can be the same for you and all my friends. We need it, for we still have so much to experience together and so much work to do. And so I call upon you: stay at your inner post, and please do not feel sorry or sad for me, there is no reason to. The Levies[41] are having a hard time, but they have enough inner reserves to pull them through despite their poor physical state. Many of the children here are very dirty. That is one of our biggest problems—hygiene. I'll write again and tell you more about them. I enclose a scribbled note I began to write to Father and Mother, but didn't have to send; you might find some of it interesting.

I have one request, if you don't think it too immodest: a pillow or some old cushion; the straw gets a little hard in the end. But you are not allowed to send parcels weighing more than two kilos from the provinces, and a pillow probably weighs more than that. So if you happen to be in Amsterdam and should call at Pa Han's (please don't abandon him, and do show him this letter), you might perhaps send it from some post office there. Otherwise, my only wish is that you are all well and in good spirits, and send me a few kind words from time to time.

Lots and lots of love,
*Etty*

[To Father Han and others]

*Westerbork, [Monday], 5 July [1943]*

I must try to conjure up a letter in haste, for if tomorrow or the day after I am not allowed to write anymore, I shall regret not doing it now. It's a difficult day. A transport leaves tomorrow morning, and last night I heard that my parents were on the list.[42] Herman B. whispered it in my ear as I sat on the edge of Father's bed having a cozy chat—Father all unsuspecting. I didn't say anything and immediately went to see the various authorities. I was told that my parents are still safe, but you can't be certain until the last minute. I shall keep as close a watch as I can until tomorrow morning. Tonight another transport is coming in from Amsterdam, so I'll be up then in any case. Mechanicus, with whom I have struck up a firm friendship in a short time, is also on the list; we are still trying everything we can. Weinreb was taken away some time ago—by car to The Hague in the care of a couple of VIPs. You mustn't become too attached to people here.

This morning I worked in the punishment barracks, where people are in special custody, and took news back from the detainees to their relatives in the camp. I have just been to see Father again. He was lying down, reasonably content, reading a French novel and unaware that his name still has to be taken off the list. The hardest labor camp is better than this suspense every week. It didn't bother me so much before, because I had accepted the fact that I would be going to Poland. But living in fear for your loved ones, knowing that an infinitely long martyrdom is in store for them while your own life here stays relatively idyllic, is something few can bear. I sometimes feel like quietly packing my rucksack and getting onto the next transport to the east. But enough; it's not right for a human being to take the easy way out.

It is ten o'clock. I am sitting in our empty workroom; it is wonderfully peaceful; most of my colleagues are asleep in their barracks. A couple of boys are leaning on the windowsill gazing gloomily at the locomotive, which is belching clouds of smoke again. The rest of the train is hidden from view behind a low barracks. People have been busy loading the freight cars since six o'clock this morning; the train is ready to pull out. I feel as if I've just gone through labor on my parents' behalf; this time we managed once again to keep them off the train. Otherwise I find it difficult to say honestly how I feel.

Yesterday was a day like no other. Never before have I taken a hand in "fixing" it to keep someone off the transport. I lack all talent for diplomacy, but yesterday I did my bit for Mechanicus. What exactly it was that I did, I'm not sure. I went to all sorts of officials. Suddenly I found myself walking around with a mysterious gentleman I've never seen before who looked like a white slave trafficker in a French film. With this gentleman I went to all sorts of camp VIPs who are usually not available, especially before a transport. But this time invisible doors opened: one moment I had an interview with the Registrator, and the next I was appearing before a senile little man who presumably holds a mysterious position of power and can get people off the transport even when all seems lost. There is a sort of "underworld" here in Westerbork; yesterday I sensed something of it, I don't know how it all fits together, I don't think it's a savory story— Anyway, I trudged around the whole day, while my parents were entrusted to Kormann's watchful eye and to the staff of the Jewish Council, who assured me that everything would be all right this time.

As far as Mechanicus was concerned, things were in doubt until the very last moment. I helped him pack his bags, sewed a few buttons on his suit. He said, "I've grown softer here in this camp, everyone has become the same for me, they are all like blades of grass, bending to the storm, lying flat under the hurricane." He also said, "If I survive this time, I shall emerge a more mature and deeper person, and if I die, then I shall die a more mature and deeper one." Later my father said as I patted the top of his head, now almost white, "If I get my call-up tonight, truly I won't be upset, I'll leave quite peacefully." (People usually get their call-up in the night, a few hours before the transport leaves.)

At eight o'clock I walked about with Mother, said good-bye to various friends who had to go, then went for a walk with Liesl and Werner. At about ten o'clock I sat down with Jopie, who looks gray with fatigue. And after that I really couldn't stand up any longer. I excused myself from night work and let things take their course. This morning at eight o'clock Jopie came by and told me through the window that my parents were still here, that Jaap didn't arrive last night (we were expecting people from the NIZ), and that Mechanicus is *not* on transport.[43] And now it is eleven o'clock and I am going to the hospital, where I shall find a lot of empty beds. A day like yesterday is a killer, and next week the same thing starts all over again.

### Late afternoon

Well, children, here I am again on the top bunk, three tiers up. This afternoon, for a change, I fainted in the middle of a large, stuffy barracks. It serves as a reminder that there are limits to one's physical strength. In addition to the hospital barracks, I have now been assigned the punishment barracks as well. Since half our colleagues have gone back to Amsterdam, there are many jobs to cover. Then Kormann told me that my parents must still expect to be put on transport next week. It will become more and more difficult to keep people back—but you never know in advance, and that is precisely what saps you, the uncertainty until the last minute. Then I went to see Mother, who was feeling dizzy and sick herself; and then I felt I had reached the end of my tether and fainted. Tomorrow, things will be better. I suddenly remember that it's the "summer holidays" in the outside world. Do you have any plans? You will tell me everything, won't you? Maria, thank you for your letter! It was exactly what a letter from you ought to be. If I am allowed to write tomorrow, I'll send you another scrawl; otherwise I shall keep quiet for the time being—

We learn everything from the doctors here. What a desperate state of affairs. We have a surfeit of doctors, who are unable to do anything useful. Jan Zeeman's father is here, too!

Good-bye! Be strong!
*Etty*

Milli darling,

Just a brief cry of distress. I did start a letter to you and Mien, but a letter gets out of date here even as you write it. Today my strength failed me for the first time, and I fainted right in the middle of a big barracks. This morning yet another transport of 2,500 left. I managed with difficulty to keep my parents off it, but things are getting quite desperate. Good friends of mine here, who have what is called influence, told me in confidence this morning that my parents must make ready for next week's transport. Slowly but steadily the camp is being sucked dry. Without some miracle from outside, it will all be over in a week or two. What we really want is to get Mischa, who is determined to stick with his parents and face certain doom, away from here. Is it really true that he could have gone to Barneveld by himself? And wouldn't it still be possible, even if our parents don't go to B., for him to get an order telling him that he *must* go? Even though, to be honest, I know quite well that nothing will make him go without his parents. "If they are sent on transport, that'll be the end of me, too," he keeps saying. Between ourselves, it's all a long tale of woe. And the worst part is that you are able to do so much less for your people than they expect. Six months ago it would probably still have been fairly simple to keep them back here and make them feel quite at home, but I am becoming more helpless all the time. You yourselves know very well what sort of feeling that is. I won't write more now, for I can see this is not going to be a sunny letter.

You are such dears; all the trouble and effort and worry we are causing you weigh heavily on my conscience. I have just read Cor's letter to Mischa. A Kuyper-Glassner parcel has arrived, but no Kuyper-Ortmann parcel. It's sad when parcels you have prepared with so much care and love don't get through, but I think that everything else has arrived. It's all so welcome, and I often wonder how you manage to bring it off, since things can't be that easy with you either. We have also received a large box of tomatoes and cucumbers without the sender's name. So I don't know who it was, but report arrival in any case.

I must cut this short, dearest friend. I am feeling a bit downhearted, but things are bound to be better tomorrow. Regards to Grete and Cor.

Love,
*Etty*

Sooner or later I won't be allowed to write more than once every two weeks, so if you suddenly stop getting any signs of life from me, you'll know there was nothing I could do about it.

[To Father Han and others]

*Thursday afternoon, [8 July 1943]*

Hello! I've been telling myself for the past half hour, half asleep, to write some more to you. Every writing day is an event: there's been nothing definite said yet about having to stop writing. And so I scribble on.

A few things before I forget them. Leo Krijn[44] has been sent through; leaving won't matter very much to him. His brother, who is still here, said to me yesterday, "He has the naive hope that he will find his wife and son again over there."

Herman B. is worried; for a whole week he has heard nothing from Wiep[45] and his mother. Is anything the matter? He is as well as always. He doggedly feeds my father cucumbers and tomatoes all day long. I pity Father sometimes because he's not allowed out of the barracks, but it doesn't seem to bother him very much, the clouds of dust outside hold no attraction for him.

I took Swiep's parcel to Anne-Marie. She was so nice that I've arranged to meet her one evening; she wants to introduce me to a sociable Russian professor so we can have a bit of a chat.

My right hand is bandaged up because of the eczema, and that's why I am writing even less legibly than usual. Now you'll have to retouch even more letters, dear Father Han. Thank you for your lovely letter. I would find it hard to bear if Käthe really went away. Is it irrevocable? Please don't let it be!

At the moment I am lying in the middle of a battlefield of sick women. The wrong kind of bacillus is raging through our barracks, we have all got the "runs," as it is poetically termed. I am quite pleased to be immobilized; it gives me a chance to write to you. I gather from Grete Wendelsgelst's latest report,[46] which I got this morning, that my family will be able to stay here after all. Yesterday it appeared that they had to go.

After I had fainted twice on the same day, I made up my

mind to start a new life without all these tensions. I was also beginning to suffer from "stampitis": they stamp your papers with red, green, and blue identification marks; you can talk about them for twenty-four hours at a stretch—it is an inexhaustible subject. Jopie is really sick of stampitis—when he hears the word *stamp,* he wants to vomit. At the moment feelings are at fever pitch: all stamps, all colors, have been suspended; there is to be a regrouping. What the next transport will look like no one knows—the lists still have to be made up, and in the process all kinds of things are bound to go on behind the scenes. They are playing a game with us, but we allow them to do so, and that will be our shame for generations to come. I told you a few days ago something about a senile little man for whom closed doors mysteriously opened. He's really a pleasant little man; he served as a courier in the Great War and among other things was a friend of Archbishop Söderblom.[47] He is the only person allowed to call unannounced on the commandant—who even returns his visits, which is a very great honor here, God help us. Yesterday I walked with him and Mechanicus for a couple of hours, and he came up with reminiscences about Poincaré and the queen; no lesser person would do for him. But he also said something very much to the point: "In Westerbork there is only one service that's equitable: the water supply. It provides water for 10,000 Jews, and each one gets the same amount."

You don't mind my writing everything a bit mixed up, do you? It's because I am so sleepy. You see, I keep striking the same chords even here. Experience has shown me forcibly: if you allow yourself to get involved in all the tensions here each week, then in three weeks you're done for, absolutely done for. And when it's finally your turn to go off in the Moscow direction, you're just not able to make it anymore. So I am trying to live my life away from all the green, red, and blue stamps and transport lists.

Now and then I join the gulls. In their movements through

the great cloudy skies one suspects laws, eternal laws of another order than the laws we humans make. This afternoon Jopie, who feels thoroughly sick and all in, stood together with his sister-in-arms Etty for at least a quarter of an hour looking up at one of these black-and-silver birds as it moved among the massive deep-blue rain clouds. We suddenly felt a lot less oppressed.

One should be able to write fairy stories here. It sounds strange, but if you wanted to convey something of Westerbork life you could do it best in that form. The misery here is so beyond all bounds of reality that it has become unreal. Sometimes I walk through the camp laughing secretly to myself because of the completely grotesque circumstances. One would have to be a very great poet indeed to describe them; perhaps in about ten years I might get somewhere near it.

*In the evening*

I have to stop right in the middle of the fairy tales—

*Next morning*

People live an episodic life here; I have a quarter of an hour to spare, so another few words. Yes, really, it's true, there are compassionate laws in nature, if only we can keep a feeling for their rhythm. I notice that afresh each time in myself: when I am at the limits of despair, unable, I am sure, to go on, suddenly the balance shifts over to the other side, and I can laugh and take life as it comes. After feeling really low for ages, you can suddenly rise so high above earthly misery that you feel lighter and more liberated than ever before in your life. I am now very well again, but for a few days I was quite desperate. Equilibrium is restored time and again. Ah, children, we live in a strange world—

It is a complete madhouse here; we shall have to feel ashamed of it for three hundred years. The *Dienstleiters* themselves now have to draw up the transport lists.[48] Meetings, panics—it's all horrible. In the middle of this game with human lives, an order suddenly from the commandant: the *Dienstleiters* must present themselves that evening at the first night of a cabaret that is being put on here. They stared openmouthed, but they had to go home and dress in their best clothes. And then in the evening they sit in the registration hall, where Max Ehrlich, Chaya Goldstein, Willy Rosen, and others give a performance.[49] In the first row, the commandant with his guests. Behind him, Professor Cohen.[50] The rest of the hall full. People laughing until they cried—oh yes, cried. On days when the people from Amsterdam pour into the camp, we put up a kind of wooden barrier in the big reception hall to hold them back if the crush becomes too great. During the cabaret this same barrier served as a piece of decor on the stage; Max Ehrlich leaned over it to sing his little songs. I wasn't there myself, but Kormann just told me about it, adding, "This whole business is slowly driving me to the edge of despair."

I will have to put an end to this letter, otherwise I won't be able to send it off. I must just think what else I should add. I received a cigar box full of tomatoes from Gera;[51] please thank her if you see her; I can't write as many letters as before. Mevrouw Nethe's Jim is also here from Mien's house, so I know the latest news.[52] Oh yes, Father Han, please send me ten guilders in a letter; even now money can sometimes come in very useful, however silly that may sound. They are still working on getting a short leave for us in order "finally" to settle our affairs. If it comes off, it will be a lovely extra gift, but I don't count on it any longer. If I am allowed to write tomorrow, I'll send another scribble; otherwise you must have a little patience—

However improbable it may sound: I am more saddened by what happens in the outside world than by events on the battlefield here. I remember a lunch with Johannes Brouwer; he was a sensitive man[53] . . . now they're making me move from here, too.

Good-bye!
*Etty*

*Westerbork, Thursday night, 8 July [1943]*

Dearest Christine,

I am on night duty now, so if no great panic occurs at my little table, I can scribble one or two words between business. In any case I want to send off a letter this evening so that your sister gets it in time. Do forgive me if this is all somewhat incoherent.

Christine, that Groningen cake! It was princely. Altogether it was such a magnificent parcel. I immediately gave Father a few small slices and half a bar of chocolate. It's marvelous, I just run over to him, five minutes from my barracks, pass him something through the window, and run back again. By holding on to one's people here, you can look after them and keep them going—with the help of the outside world. Mischa was there when I unpacked the parcel; he beamed. You had prepared it with such care and love, it sustains us—not just the contents, but also the thought that there are people who so much want to help us. Meanwhile another parcel has arrived from the Jewish Council in Deventer with glorious rye bread from Gantvoort. I always give half to Mother, who shares it with Mischa, and keep the other half for Father.

Tense and stirring days behind us. Father was on the transport list. We were able to get him off once again. I must explain that the call-ups for the transport come in the middle of the night, a few hours before the train leaves. If people are still needed at the last minute to fill the quotas, then Jews are seized here and there at random from the barracks. And that's why the days before the transport are so nerve-racking. The day afterward I fainted twice, but I'm fine again now—until the next transport. Sunday evening while I was sitting talking on the edge of Father's bed, an acquaintance suddenly whispered in my ear: "Your father is on the list." People are afraid on such occasions to tell you the truth. And all Monday that long row of unpainted freight cars stood there, about seventy people—men, women, invalids, babies—squashed into each one, the doors slammed shut, a little air coming through the air holes and the broken planks, paper mattresses on the floor for the sick; for the rest only a hard floor, a bucket in the middle, and a three-day journey ahead. Can you imagine what that means? I have got used to the idea that I'll have to go myself one day. Above all else in the world I wish I could spare my parents and my brothers. But you can't play the ostrich here; a transport leaves every week, and the quota must be filled. Just a little while longer, and all our turns will come. My father takes it very quietly. "What all those thousands before us have borne, we can also bear," he says. I am grateful to have him here still, but on Monday the misery starts all over again. However—according to a report I received today from a good friend who is working on our behalf—it seems that something is being done for us from The Hague after all.

Father and Mother give me a great deal of pleasure, for they are coping in their own ways; I admire them tremendously. Father now has two pupils in his hospital barracks, one boy who is not too ill and one who is very sick. Both want to learn a little Greek and Latin as a distraction, and he takes pleasure in giving them lessons for two hours a day, going through Homer, Ovid, and Sallust. For the rest, he reads a great deal, philosophizes with ancient rabbis and old student friends, and now and then strolls with his daughter through the dusty sand of the hospital grounds. Oh Christine, if only they could stay here in case nothing comes of Barneveld. There might be a chance of getting through here with the help of the outside world, however difficult everything may be. But once they're on the train, then I expect nothing but an endless martyrdom—We shall just have to wait and see—

Oh yes, the soap powder—I'd love it. Something like that is almost more important than food, the crowding has compelled such a poor state of hygiene. We wash our clothes often enough, in a variety of buckets obtained with difficulty. The clothes don't get much cleaner, it's true, but the idea that you have done a wash makes you feel a bit better—

I don't answer your letters as regularly as you answer mine because it's almost impossible here. Mischa's barracks is number 62.

The end of my duty; I shall rush over to my barracks. I have a fever and something poetically termed the runs; half the camp has got it at the moment, but I never like staying in bed, I prefer making myself useful.

What did I tell you? A messy, incoherent letter. Writing will really be coming to an end soon. I've heard that we're no longer allowed to acknowledge private parcels from the provinces with a postcard. If I write "Parcel received" to Simon, then I mean a parcel from the Jewish Council, but if I write "Little parcel," then I mean it's from you—although it would be more appropriate the other way around, as far as the size is concerned.

Much, much love from us all. We got a nice letter from van Kuyk.

Have a good holiday.

'Bye!
*Etty*

Milli, my priceless Milli,

I could fling my arms around your neck! Poor lamb, I keep sending you such terrible letters. Today the report from Grete, in which she says that the papers are on their way. We had heard nothing about it. Now there are high hopes that we'll be able to keep my parents here. All stamps have been declared invalid, everyone is due for transport except those whose affairs are still being considered in The Hague. And oh, Milli, I'd much sooner not see them in the freight cars, though I don't mind for myself. Well, we'll have to wait and see. In great haste. At the moment I'm not all that well: temperature, diarrhea—but half the camp has it. I'll send Wegerif a fuller letter tonight meant for you all. Hug Grete for her lovely letter. All of you are so kind even though you have worries enough yourselves. I am on the trail of your Aunt Hermine; I'll call on her tomorrow. It's all very well, but they ought to have left the old people in peace. How are all of you? Just think, Cor now lives so close to you! No, there's no chance that you might be able to come here. Thanks for everything. Won't you please ask Wegerif to reimburse you for all the expenses you have had? Although what you have done for us is really beyond price! In haste. More later, if it's still allowed.

'Bye,
*Etty*

Poor Milli,

I am so sorry for you, you have done so much running about
and worked so hard. Barneveld is off, and off for Mischa, too.
Father and Mother are on transport; Mischa has permission to
stay but doesn't want to. It's getting very difficult to keep him
quiet. He says: "I'm going to go and tell the commandant he is a
murderer." We have to watch out that he doesn't do anything
dangerous. Rauter's secretary is here in the camp at the moment,
and Mother was specially summoned to be given the news. She
was told expressly that they are now due for transport on Tuesday. Whether anything can still be done from here, I don't
know, I'll have to see. Our "parents' list" is unreliable right now;
I don't even know whether my parents still come under that
heading after the orders from The Hague. I just hope that some
luggage will reach us from Amsterdam in time, although—we
are more and more certain of this—everything is taken away
from you anyway.

Let me arrange with you now something I've already written
to Nethe. If Mother and Father leave next Tuesday and I am no
longer allowed to write, then I shall wire Nethe. (We can still
send certain specified telegrams to Jews in mixed marriages;
they are delivered by courier.) My message will say, "Send two
winter coats." If Mischa has gone as well, then I'll wire, "Send
three winter coats." In the same way that Mischa wants to go out
of love for his parents, I won't be going—out of a different kind
of love. Perhaps it is a more cowardly love, but I myself feel
strong. I believe that it is easier to pray for people from a distance than to see them suffer right next to you.

Should you get one of those telegrams, then please pass the
news on to our friends in Amsterdam and also to Mejuffrouw
J. C. J. C. van Nooten, Noorderbergersingel 7, Deventer, and to

Mevrouw M. Gans, Roodenburgerstraat 60, Leiden. If it is at all possible I shall write again. If they are still here and I am not allowed to write, then I shall wire, "Send handkerchiefs." All right? Alas, one more sad bit of news: your Aunt Hermine is no longer here. I am so sorry, Milli my dear, that I have nothing but gloomy news.

Good-bye.
Love,
*Etty*

Maria, hello,

Ten thousand have passed through this place, the clothed and
the naked, the old and the young, the sick and the healthy—and
I am left to live and work and stay cheerful. It will be my
parents' turn to leave soon, if by some miracle not this week,
then certainly one of the next. And I must learn to accept this as
well. Mischa insists on going along with them, and it seems to
me that he probably should; if he has to watch our parents leave
this place, it will totally unhinge him. I shan't go, I just can't. It
is easier to pray for someone from a distance than to see him
suffer by your side. It is not fear of Poland that keeps me from
going along with my parents, but fear of seeing them suffer.
And that, too, is cowardice.

This is something people refuse to admit to themselves: at a
given point you can no longer *do,* but can only *be* and accept.
And although that is something I learned a long time ago, I also
know that one can only accept for oneself and not for others.
And that's what is so desperately difficult for me here. Mother
and Mischa still want to "do," to turn the whole world upside
down, but I know we can't do anything about it. I have never
been able to "do" anything; I can only let things take their
course and if need be, suffer. This is where my strength lies, and
it is great strength indeed. But for myself, not for others.

Mother and Father have definitely been turned down for
Barneveld; we heard the news yesterday. They were also told to
be ready to leave here on next Tuesday's transport. Mischa
wanted to rush straight to the commandant and call him a
murderer. We'll have to watch him carefully. Outwardly, Father
appears very calm. But he would have gone to pieces in a matter
of days in these vast barracks if I hadn't been able to have him
taken to the hospital—which he is gradually coming to find just

as intolerable. He is really at his wits' end, though he tries not to show it. My prayers, too, aren't going quite right. I know: you can pray God to give people the strength to bear whatever comes. But I keep repeating the same prayer: "Lord, make it as short as possible." And as a result I am paralyzed. I would like to pack their cases with the best things I can lay my hands on, but I know perfectly well that they will be stripped of everything; about that we have been left in no doubt. So why bother?

I have a good friend here.[54] Last week he was told to keep himself in readiness for transport. When I went to see him, he stood straight as an arrow, face calm, rucksack packed beside his bed. We didn't mention his leaving, but he did read me various things he had written, and we talked a little philosophy. We didn't make things hard for each other with grief about having to say good-bye. We laughed and said we would see each other soon. We were both able to bear our lot. And that's what is so desperate about this place: most people are not able to bear their lot, and they load it onto the shoulders of others. And that burden is more likely to break one than one's own.

Yes, I feel perfectly able to bear my lot, but not that of my parents. This is the last letter I'll be allowed to write for a while. This afternoon our identity cards were taken away, and we became official camp inmates. So you'll have to have a little patience waiting for news of me.

Perhaps I will be able to smuggle a letter out now and then. Have received your two letters.

'Bye, Maria—dear friend,
*Etty*

First thing in the morning, before six o'clock, I walk across to Father's barracks, fetch his thermos bottle, then take it to the boiler house: four hot-water taps along the outside wall; a long row of people with bowls, buckets, and coffeepots; a gentleman with a professorial appearance who controls the traffic. I wait my turn—that little packet of tea from Swiep always in my left-hand coat pocket—burn my fingers at the tap, and the tea has drawn by the time I've walked back. Then to Mother in the hospital (with bronchitis and some exhaustion), fetch her thermos flask, and begin the same pilgrimage. Then to Mischa (who lies three bunks up under a sloping beam in the big barracks, like a prince in disguise) to see if he needs anything.

All the parcels come to me. I try to act fairly as the family rations-distribution center. I walk about with little tin boxes from one person to the other and get real pleasure out of doing it. I simply have no words for the way our friends, including Father's colleagues, are caring for us; sometimes it weighs almost too heavily on my mind. Father is an imperturbable gypsy—just occasionally a decline, during which he would like to step into the freight train and be rid of the whole mess—but he always pulls himself out of it again. He passes his days here with half a dozen little Bibles—Greek, French, Russian, etc.—and keeps surprising me with particularly apposite texts. He is modest in his demands, and lives mainly on bread. On the day before the transport that he was firmly convinced he would be joining, he was as cool as a cucumber, read Homer with his sick boys, and gossiped with former student friends who have turned into gray-haired rabbis.

I learned in good time from an unforgettable friend[55]—for whose death I still give thanks every day—the great lesson from

Matthew 24: "Take therefore no thought for the morrow: for the morrow shall take thought for the things of itself. Sufficient unto the day is the evil thereof." This is the only attitude that allows you to carry on at Westerbork.

And so every night, with sure peace of mind, I lay down my many earthly cares at the feet of God Himself. They are often trivial cares—for instance, how I am going to finish the family wash. The big worries are worries no longer; they have all merged into a fate to which one has been joined. The Puttkammer story has filled me with shame.[56] It shows you just what mad antics people in need will get up to.

But I'm sure there are limits. And a money business like that is certainly not for us. Don't in heaven's name worry your head about it any longer. What tens and tens of thousands before us have borne, we can also bear. For us, I think, it is no longer a question of living, but of how one is equipped for one's extinction.

Dearest Christine,

Your choice collection of goggles is already in place protecting our eyes from the dust, and the other good things of life have also arrived safely. The little sponge cakes were unsurpassed. I am putting some of them by in a tin so I can gladden my father's heart with a couple each day. It's wonderful to be able to bring him something really delicious from time to time. Please tell Hansje Lansen when you have a chance that Father isn't able to write back to her. She sent a moving letter which was very much appreciated; do please tell her. Have a good time in Groningen.

　More later.

'Bye,<br>
*Etty*

Maria, dear friend,

This morning there was a rainbow over the camp, and the sun
shone in the mud puddles. When I went into the hospital barracks, some of the women called out, "Have you got good news?
You look so cheerful." I considered saying something about Victor
Emmanuel, about a popular government, and about peace being
on the way.[57] I couldn't fob them off with the rainbow, could
I?—even though that was the only reason for my cheerfulness.

"It's going to come to an end soon, it's all going to come
tumbling down," chanted a little old wrinkled professor opposite
me at the wooden table. People's spirits are high. Italian sounds
blossom between the iron bunks and the rags. There must be a
modicum of truth in the reports repeated in conversations here as
if through distorting mirrors. An "Aryan" with bullet wounds
was brought into the camp and put in a separate corner of one of
the hospital barracks. Not long after, a police car with detectives
came driving down our muddy little paths, the polo-shirted
commandant bicycling in front to show the way. They say that the
man with the bullet wounds was interrogated nonstop for hours.
But otherwise he was treated with great respect, they say. The
commandant fetched from his own house a little cushion for the
man. They say that he is a Dutch resistance fighter. They also say
that he is the mayor of Beilen. They say that several more Aryans
have been brought into the camp, all with bullet wounds. They
say that there is great unrest in Drenthe. A few evenings ago a fire
blazed against the gray sky over our steppe; I stood watching it for
a long time in the rain. The next morning a Jew in green overalls
mounted guard in front of the barracks opposite the orphanage,
where the children play on a small piece of sandy ground surrounded by barbed wire. Green Overalls was guarding twenty
non-Jews: men, women, children, picked up in the middle of the

night from their beds in Drenthe as hostages because of the fire. (Privately, resentment was expressed by some inmates that we should have to keep watch over non-Jews in a Jewish camp.) But that very same day, the twenty all vanished again.

Yesterday we had a general come to visit us. We were driven from our beds at the crack of dawn. A fever of spring-cleaning burst out in the camp; for a few hours I wandered homeless through the mud. The patients in the hospital had to keep to their beds, the food appeared to be somewhat better than usual, the patients in the large barracks had to have stars sewn on their pajamas, and no one was allowed to wear a loose star. A fat toad in a green uniform—surely the general—shuffled about between the barracks. They say that he came because there is so much unrest in Drenthe. Spirits here are very high. For a few weeks now no transports have left, and it looks as if no more will be leaving.[58] So they say. This place will be turned into a labor camp with a concentration camp as an annex. The people in the punishment barracks, whose number is growing every day, will have to have their heads shaved and wear prison uniform. They don't know what to do with the old people and the children; no ruling has been made about them yet. The commandant has decided that they will be allowed to stay on. So they say. My father is lying sick in a shed with 130 people. "The Lower Depths,"[59] he chuckles. He chuckles a great deal. Little Bibles in various languages and French novels are strewn all over his untidy blankets. His suit, his winter coat, all his worldly goods, are lying crumpled in a heap behind his pillow. The men's beds have been put right next to each other. The "brothers"—the male nurses—walk quickly past; God forbid you should ask them anything. "You have to be as fit as a fiddle to survive in this hospital," says Father, "if you're sick you haven't a hope." For a few days he was really ill, with a temperature of about 104°F and diarrhea. I toast bread for him at Anne-Marie's and keep running to the boilerhouse to fetch hot water for tea. I barter rye bread for rusks and other easily digestible things; I'm doing a roaring trade in rye bread. Yesterday a kind lady brought him a royal gift: a roll of toilet paper. She is the wife of a leading rabbi who works here in the charity department. Father thanked her with extreme courtesy. I often slip in to see him; it always means a minor battle with the doorkeeper, who is a stickler for the rules. Father once forgot himself to the point of calling him a *Feldwebel*.[60] Almost bursting into tears, the man said in a strong German accent, "But look, mister, I've been living in Holland for the past ten years." "And I for three hundred," Father answered tersely. But next day he wanted to make it up: he said, "I didn't mean to insult you or any *Feldwebel*." Anyway, that doorkeeper takes up too much of my cunning and energy. We chuckle together a lot, Father and I; you can't really call it laughing. He has a primitive sense of humor, which becomes more profound and sparkling as the grotesque process of his reduction to poverty assumes ever more wretched dimensions.

They still do not realize, my God, that apart from You, everything here is quicksand. That just slipped out.

I'm sitting in one of the big barracks at a wooden table, three bunks behind my back, three bunks in front of me. The barracks is like some colorful, sultry back street in the Orient. People shuffle along the narrow pathways between bunks. A little old woman asks, "Can you tell me where So-and-So lives?" "At number so-and-so," says Mechanicus, who is sitting next to me and writing, a sort of tramp's trilby hat on his head against the flies. Every bunk here has a number, and someone lives at every number. Though it resembles an Eastern bazaar, when I walk between the beds and look out of the open window I see gray Dutch rain clouds, potato fields, and far in the distance, two Dutch trees. Opposite me sits Jo Spier's seventy-year-old father, eternally youthful; he draws rust-brown barracks in a sketchbook.[61] Beside him somebody mutters prayers over a book with Hebrew letters.

A raw wind blows through the barracks, several windowpanes are broken, yet the air is stale and foul-smelling. Like an agile monkey, Mechanicus has just clambered up onto his third-tier bunk and triumphantly reappears with a tin of pea soup. A small space has become free on the stove in the washhouse. It is half past twelve; I am invited to stay on in this Eastern back street on the Drenthe heath to eat pea soup. I have a good life, indeed!

*Sunday morning, eight o'clock, 8 August*

I've had a wash at the tap in our tiny kitchen and crept back into bed. A huge pan of endives is bubbling away on the little hot-plate; the ten of us in our small barracks have a few hours of cooking time first thing this morning. My roommates are domestic women whose lives revolve around that one small hot-plate. With comical results, sometimes; mostly enough to make you weep. I am hardly ever at home. We have three books in our little house: *Quicksilver* by Cissy van Marxveldt, *The Divorce* by Henri van Booven, and *Conversations with Sri Krishna*. People almost come to blows for browsing rights to Cissy van Marxveldt. When I last took out the Bible, one of my roommates said smugly, "I've hidden my own Bible away somewhere safe!" The rain beats against our small windows, it is cold, it looks as if summer is definitely over. From my bunk I can see gulls in the distance moving across the flat gray sky. They are like free thoughts in an open mind.

Last night I went with Mechanicus to see Paul's mother. She found a louse, so for the past few days she has been in the quarantine barracks. Not only did she have the louse; at the same time she had an inoculation and a back tooth pulled. And now she must sit on a narrow little bench and peel potatoes every day for hours. "Slave labor," she says. She is in a bad way. The quarantine barracks looks like a house of correction, without a single object that provides home comfort. The three of us talked about the many parentless children, some of them already like little old men and women, who are herded together outside in the rain every morning, while the barracks are cleaned. We talked about the soul-destroying work of picking peas and beans, about the danger of letting go and becoming demoralized, about all the dreary and grotesque details of camp life. "You can never describe things like that, you can only suffer them," said Mechanicus grimly. He is leaning with his elbows on the wooden table; he has fleas, holey socks, and cold shivers. He remarks with good-natured self-mockery, "This evening I feel just like a very small boy afraid of the wolf." Later I saw him back to his own barracks and took his holey socks home with me. Paul's mother went with us part of the way through the night, a large woolen shawl around her shoulders, her gray hair loose in the wind. Do you still remember that musical afternoon when Paul played the flute in the bay window and his mother sat with such stately dignity in the middle of the room?

Many feel that their love of mankind languishes at Westerbork because it receives no nourishment—meaning that people here don't give you much occasion to love them. "The mass is a hideous monster; individuals are pitiful," someone said. But I keep discovering that there is no causal connection between people's behavior and the love you feel for them. Love for one's fellow man is like an elemental glow that sustains you. The fellow man himself has hardly anything to do with it. Oh Maria, it's a little bit bare of love here, and I myself feel so inexpressibly rich; I cannot explain it.

In your reply, please don't let it slip that you received this letter outside my writing day—there is strict censorship on incoming mail at the moment. Love to you all.

*Etty*

Dear Christine,

Best, warmest greetings from us all. I thought I would send this letter, meant for a girlfriend, to you first. Much that is in it might easily have been written to you, and this way you'll have more news of us. And when you've read the enclosed pages, will you please forward them to Sister Maria Tuinzing, c/o Heer Wegerif, 6 Gabriel Metsustraat? One Sunday morning she brought you a cup of coffee when you were sitting by my bed, and we spoke about the *Stundenbuch,* do you remember?[62] That *Stundenbuch* now lies under my pillow, together with my small Bible. And yes, the words from Isaiah are magnificent and comforting and time and again give one the secret inner peace that passes all understanding. And what was magnificent as well— and now I am taking a huge jump down to earth—was the little tin of crabmeat and the toast and all the other precious things. We suspect that you gave us not only the best but the last things from your own supplies, and the feeling that arouses in us can't be expressed in words. The parcels from your mother were so sweet, too. And the apples were wonderful—I can't mention everything or I shall run out of paper. We got a very nice letter from Kraak with lots of music in it. We hope you've had a good rest and are going back to work refreshed. Father is a little better, though he's still not allowed to eat much. He is patient enough, the good man, and yet you know, I hope for him (and for so many, many others, too) that things won't go on for much longer—

I must bother you again with some mundane requests; I feel awful, but there's no help for it. What we need urgently for Father is rusks and things like that. He hasn't eaten for days and must be helped back to his usual form slowly; the camp bread is terrible. And we have no sugar—we finished what we had, and we don't get any sugar at all here. Is it still possible to get hold of some, down a dark alleyway? At the moment we have no butter either, but it's possible that some will arrive any day from Deventer; you can never tell. That half pound of yours from Amsterdam came exactly when it was needed. Well, the truth is out again: long live material things. We shall all of us bear up, on both sides of the barbed wire, won't we? Things are going well, they say. The rest is in the enclosed letter. Thanks for your goodness and love, dear child. Love to Hansje Lansen.

'Bye,
*Etty*

*11 August 1943*

Later on, when I no longer have to sleep on an iron bunk in a camp surrounded by barbed wire, I shall have a little lamp above my bed so that I can have light around me at night whenever I want. When I lie drowsing, thoughts and little stories often whirl through my brain, as random and transparent as soap bubbles, and I would so like to be able to capture them on paper.

In the mornings when I wake up, I lie cocooned in these stories; it is a rich awakening, you know. But then I get twinges of pain; the ideas and images simply demand to be written down, but there is nowhere for me to sit in peace. Sometimes I walk around for hours looking for a quiet little corner. Once a stray cat came in during the night. We put a hatbox for it on the WC, and it had kittens inside. I sometimes feel like a stray cat without a hatbox.

Tonight Jopie's son was born. His name is Benjamin, and he sleeps in a drawer. They have now put some sort of madman beside my father.

You know, if you don't have the inner strength while you're here to understand that all outer appearances are a passing show, as nothing beside the great splendor (I can't think of a better word right now) inside us—then things can look very black here indeed. Completely wretched, in fact, as they must look to those pathetic people who have lost their last towel; who struggle with boxes, trays of food, cups, moldy bread, and dirty laundry, on, under, and around their bunks; who are miserable when other people shout at them or are unkind, but who shout at others themselves without a thought. Or to those poor abandoned children whose parents have been sent on transport, and who are ignored by the other mothers—who have worries enough with their own brood, what with the diarrhea and all the other complaints, big and small, when nothing was ever wrong with them in the past. You should see these poor mothers sitting beside the cots of their wailing young in blank and brute despair.

I have visited ten different places in order to fill this one sheet of paper: my makeshift little table in our workshop; a wheelbarrow opposite the laundry where Anne-Marie works (standing for hours in the heat surrounded by children whose thoughtless screaming she finds very difficult to cope with right now; yesterday I dried her tears but didn't tell her that I was writing it all down—these scribblings to you are meant for Swiep as well); a lecture given last night in the orphanage by a long-winded professor of sociology; a windy bit of "dune" under the open sky this morning—each time I add another few words—and now I am sitting in the partitioned-off hospital canteen, which I have only just discovered, a place to which I shall be able to withdraw now and then for a little while.

Tomorrow morning Jopie leaves for Amsterdam. For the first time in the months I have been here, I feel a small stab in my disciplined heart. Why am I being left behind? But still—everyone's time will come. Most people here are much worse off than they need be because they write off their longing for friends and family as so many losses in their lives, when they should count the fact that their heart is able to long so hard and to love so much among their greatest blessings. Well, dear Lord, I thought I had found a quiet little spot, but it is suddenly full of kitchen staff with clattering pans of stew and hospital staff settling down around the trestle tables to eat. It is past noon, and I am off to look for somewhere else.

Had a stab at philosophy late at night, with eyes that kept closing with fatigue. People sometimes say, "You must try to make the best of things." I find this such a feeble thing to say. Everywhere things are both very good and very bad at the same time. The two are in balance, everywhere and always. I never have the feeling that I have got to make the best of things; everything *is* fine just as it is. Every situation, however miserable, is complete in itself and contains the good as well as the bad. All I really wanted to say is this: "making the best of things" is a nauseating expression, and so is "seeing the good in everything." I should like to explain why in greater detail, but if you only knew how tired I feel—I could sleep for fourteen days at a stretch. Now I'm going to take this to Jopie. Tomorrow morning I'll go with him to the police station, and then he is off to Amsterdam, and I back to the barracks.

Well, my children, good-bye!
*Etty*

Christine,

Today you really were a guardian angel, never have I watched so desperately for a parcel as this week. And now one has come at last, and what a parcel! I took the rusks and rolls straight to Father. The poor soul is thin as a rake after all the fasting; he has an abscess on his eye and a bullying doorkeeper. It's rather sad, but one mustn't dwell on it too much. And yet he is considered the miracle of the barracks: the only person there who can read with concentration—Hebrew, French, Dutch, whatever you like, he goes on reading. No one can understand how any man can do it in such surroundings. You won't mind too much, will you, if I mix things up a bit? I am on night duty again—have to attend to people now and then, and I'm giddy with fatigue. I hope you have heard from me twice: a piece from my letter to Amsterdam and a note enclosing a letter to Sister Tuinzing. I think you must have got the last one, because I'm almost sure that your lavish parcel was a direct response. I am so glad that I can get a short message through, thanks to some brave people. It looks as if our official letters are being held back for the time being. We aren't receiving incoming mail anymore either, it would seem. But keep on writing, please; sooner or later it will get through to us again.

I'm curious to know whether the Jewish Council in Deventer is still functioning. I have heard nothing from them recently. The Gelder family is here. You know that packets can be sent by letter post from the provinces up to a maximum weight of two kilos—best not registered, since the registered parcels are waylaid. There's always a new rule here. Should they forbid all contact with the provinces, then it would probably be best for you to get in touch with Mevrouw M. Kuyper, 61 Reynier Vinkeleskade, Amsterdam, who looks after all sorts of luggage for us via the Amsterdam Jewish Council. We are causing you a lot of trouble, aren't we? Oh Christine, I mustn't even think about it, this week I really saw what a misery it all is. I was so touched to get the tea, and the butter was a gift straight from heaven. We had run out of it for a few days; that's not such a dramatic event in itself—after the war began, I often ran out of butter for a few days in Amsterdam—but everything is so much worse here, particularly since people are so debilitated by illnesses and minor complaints and the bad climate. Physically Father isn't all that well at the moment, and by way of a change, Mother is beginning to suffer with bladder trouble.

Will you think badly of me if I make more requests? Could you get some little Antifones at a chemist's? They're the things you put in your ears to block out noise. In Mother's barracks it is very noisy at night, with a lot of small children who are sick— really there's nowhere here that isn't noisy—and now she wants to try sleeping with earplugs.

And again: do you know a product called Reformite? It's something like Marmite, and you spread it on bread. It has helped to keep Mother's appetite up. There is a peculiar kind of disease here: for days on end a person feels not the slightest need for food. It's a mad place, this. And now one more thing: it appears that there may still be some of our lard left at Brian's. If you could send us a small chunk now and then, I could probably fry some potatoes on a hotplate belonging to some friends. And that's enough requests; they're making me feel ill.

Now I'm going to send you something nice, too, something I've just read about Paula Modersohn-Becker: "A deeply unexpectant attitude toward life was in her blood, something that was, in fact, a genuine expression of a supreme expectation: disregard of all things external thanks to an instinctive perception of one's own riches, and a secret, not entirely explicable, inner happiness."

Father wants to write to you on his writing day, but it may

not be sent through. Oh well, the bonds that exist between people can't be broken by small setbacks. Start your new course in good heart, and think of us now and then.

We send you our love.

*Etty*

Darling Tide,

I thought at first I would give my writing a miss today, because I'm so terribly tired, and also because I thought I had nothing to say just now. But of course I have a great deal to write about. I shall allow my thoughts free rein; you are bound to pick them up anyway. This afternoon I was resting on my bunk and suddenly I just had to write these few words in my diary, and I now send them to you:

"You have made me so rich, oh God, please let me share out Your beauty with open hands. My life has become an uninterrupted dialogue with You, oh God, one great dialogue. Sometimes when I stand in some corner of the camp, my feet planted on Your earth, my eyes raised toward Your heaven, tears sometimes run down my face, tears of deep emotion and gratitude. At night, too, when I lie in my bed and rest in You, oh God, tears of gratitude run down my face, and that is my prayer. I have been terribly tired for several days, but that too will pass. Things come and go in a deeper rhythm, and people must be taught to listen; it is the most important thing we have to learn in this life. I am not challenging You, oh God, my life is one great dialogue with You. I may never become the great artist I would really like to be, but I am already secure in You, God. Sometimes I try my hand at turning out small profundities and uncertain short stories, but I always end up with just one single word: God. And that says everything, and there is no need for anything more. And all my creative powers are translated into inner dialogues with You. The beat of my heart has grown deeper, more active, and yet more peaceful, and it is as if I were all the time storing up inner riches."

Inexplicably, Jul has been floating above this heath of late.[63] He teaches me something new every day. There are many miracles in a human life. My own is one long sequence of inner miracles, and it's good to be able to say so again to somebody. Your photograph is in Rilke's *Stundenbuch,* next to Jul's photograph. They lie under my pillow together with my small Bible. Your letter with the quotations has also arrived. Keep writing, please, and fare you well, my dear.

*Etty*

[Fragment to Father Han and others[64]]

Now, that is something I can't say to the young mothers with their babies, women who will probably be riding straight to hell in a bare freight train. They would reply, "It's easy for you to talk, you haven't got any children," but that really has nothing to do with it.

There is a passage in the Bible from which I always draw new strength. I think it goes something like: "He that loveth me, let him forsake his father and mother." Last night I had to struggle again not to be overwhelmed by pity for my parents, since it would paralyze me if I gave in to it. I know that we must not lose ourselves so completely in grief and concern for our families that we have little thought or love left for our neighbors. More and more I tend toward the idea that love for everyone who may cross your path, love for everyone made in God's image, must rise above love for blood relatives. Please don't misunderstand me. It may seem unnatural—And I see that it is still far too difficult for me to write about, though so simple to live—

This evening Mechanicus and I will visit Anne-Marie and her long-standing host, the barracks leader, who has a little room of his own. We shall be sitting in what passes in Westerbork for a large apartment, with a big, low window that stands open; and the heath outside the window is as vast and rolling as the sea. It's where I wrote my letters to you last year. Anne-Marie will no doubt make the coffee, and our host will talk about camp life in the early days (he has already been here five years), and Philip will write short stories about it all. I shall delve into my little tins to see if there is anything good to eat with some coffee; and who knows, little Etty, perhaps Anne-Marie will have made another pudding, like that unforgettable almond pudding she served up last time. It was hot today; it will be a lovely summer evening in front of that open window and the heath. Later on, Philip and I will leave and find Jopie. A peaceful trio, we shall then go for a walk around the great gray Bedouin tent that rises up from a broad stretch of sand. They used to put people with lice in it; now it houses stolen Jewish household goods that will ultimately adorn the commandant's house or go to Germany as "gift parcels." A different sunset is staged every night in the sky behind the tent. There are many landscapes in this camp on the Drenthe heath. I believe the world is beautiful all over, even the places that geography books describe as barren and dull. Most books are no good, really; we shall have to rewrite them all—

I wrote my fortnightly letter to Tide; we are only allowed to write on one side of the page now—

My children, how did you manage to come by something as princely as that half-pound of butter? I got the fright of my life, it was colossal. Please forgive this materialistic ending. It is half past six. Now I must go and pick up the family's bit of food.

My fondest, fondest love to you all.

*Etty*

[Postcard to Christine van Nooten, 19 August]

Many thanks for
multifarious parcel!

*Etty*

*Sunday morning, 22 August 1943*

A pampered nine-month-old baby, a little girl, lies in the maternity ward here. Something very sweet, blue-eyed, and beautiful. She arrived here a few months ago with a "criminal record," for the police had found her abandoned in a clinic. No one knows who or where her parents are. The baby has been in the maternity ward here for so long that the nurses have become very fond of her, and treat her like a little plaything. But what I wanted to tell you is this: when she first came, the baby was not allowed out. All the others were put out in the fresh air in prams, but this one had to stay inside, for after all, she had a criminal record. I checked this with three different nurses, because I found it so hard to believe, even though the strangest things happen here all the time, and they all confirmed the story.

I met a slightly built, undernourished twelve-year-old girl in the hospital barracks. In the same chatty and confiding manner in which another child might talk about her sums at school, she said to me, "I was sent here from the punishment block; I am a criminal case."

A little boy of three and a half who broke a windowpane with a stick got a hiding from his father and began to howl noisily, crying, "Ooooh, now I'll be sent to 51 (= the prison), and then I'll have to go on the transport all by myself."

What children here say to each other is appalling. I heard one little boy say to another, "You know, the 120,000 stamp isn't really any good; it's much better to be half-Aryan and half-Portuguese."[65] And this is what Anne-Marie heard one mother say to her children on the heath: "If you don't eat your pudding up straightaway, then Mummy won't be with you on the transport!"

This morning the woman who has the bunk above my

mother dropped a bottle of water. Most of it landed on Mother's bed. In this place something like that is like a natural disaster of scarcely imaginable proportions. The nearest thing in the outside world would be a flooded house.

I am getting quite fond of this hospital canteen. It is just like a Wild West log cabin. A low, rough-hewn wooden hut, rough-hewn tables and benches, small rattling windows, nothing else. I look out on a barren strip of sand with unkempt grass, bounded by a high bank of sand thrown up from a ditch. A deserted railway track curves along in front. During the week, half-naked sunburned men push trolleys about out there. From here the view of the heath is quite unlike anything you can see from any other spot in this hole of a place. Beyond the barbed wire is an area of billowy, low shrubs: they look like young spruce. This pitilessly barren landscape, the rough cabin, the sand, the small, stinking ditch—it's all reminiscent of a gold-mining camp somewhere in the Klondike. Opposite me across the rough wooden table, Mechanicus is chewing at his fountain pen. We look at each other now and then over our little scraps of scribbled-on paper. He records everything that happens here most faithfully, almost officially. "It's too much," he says suddenly. "I know I can write, but here I am face to face with an abyss—or a mountain. It's too much."

The place is beginning to get crowded again as people with threadbare hand-me-downs and the right stamps sit down to eat turnips out of enamel bowls.

*Later*

Elly dear, your letter made me very happy and said a great deal to me.

Jopie brought a vivid reminder of you all back with him. It was doubly welcome because hardly any mail has been allowed through recently. As far as letters are concerned, we are just about cut off—one of the worst vexations of all. But we mustn't let it depress us; we must try to remain inwardly strong.

Anne-Marie was deliriously happy with Swiep's scribbles.

To my regret, the rye bread from Leonie ended up in the wrong stomachs. Our bread position, so to speak, was favorable when it arrived, so I hastily distributed it among people whose situation was less favorable. The next day I could hardly ask for perishable goods like that back again; but next time, at least, I'll know who it's for.

So touching, the grapes and pears. Parcels always leave me at a loss; I never can say much. I am, as always, overjoyed with the Sanovite. I save it mainly for Father and Mother, to make a change from the camp bread, which quickly goes moldy. Thank you for the loan of your flashlight, Father Han; it's extremely useful in the dark, what with all the puddles and barbed wire.

Jopie told me a breathtaking story about Hans. Each one of us still lives under his own star, it appears. Jopie also said that he kept coming across me in all sorts of nooks and crannies in the old house—that I was with you still.

*24 August 1943*

There was a moment when I felt in all seriousness that after this night, it would be a sin ever to laugh again. But then I reminded myself that some of those who had gone away had been laughing, even if only a handful of them this time . . . There will be some who will laugh now and then in Poland, too, though not many from this transport, I think.

When I think of the faces of that squad of armed, green-uniformed guards—my God, those faces! I looked at them, each in turn, from behind the safety of a window, and I have never been so frightened of anything in my life. I sank to my knees with the words that preside over human life: And God made man after His likeness. That passage spent a difficult morning with me.

I have told you often enough that no words and images are adequate to describe nights like these. But still I must try to convey something of it to you. One always has the feeling here of being the ears and eyes of a piece of Jewish history, but there is also the need sometimes to be a still, small voice. We must keep one another in touch with everything that happens in the various outposts of this world, each one contributing his own little piece of stone to the great mosaic that will take shape once the war is over.

After a night in the hospital barracks, I took an early-morning walk past the punishment barracks. And prisoners were being moved out. The deportees, mainly men, stood with their packs behind the barbed wire. So many of them looked tough and ready for anything. An old acquaintance—I didn't recognize him straightaway; a shaven head often changes people completely—called out to me with a smile, "If they don't manage to do me in, I'll be back."

But the babies, those tiny piercing screams of the babies, dragged from their cots in the middle of the night . . . I have to put it all down quickly, in a muddle, because if I leave it until later I probably won't be able to go on believing that it really happened. It is like a vision, and drifts further and further away. The babies were easily the worst.

And then there was that paralyzed young girl, who didn't want to take her dinner plate along and found it so hard to die. Or the terrified young boy: he had thought he was safe, that was his mistake, and when he realized he was going to have to go anyway, he panicked and ran off. His fellow Jews had to hunt him down. If they didn't find him, scores of others would be put on the transport in his place. He was caught soon enough, hiding in a tent, but "notwithstanding" . . . "notwithstanding," all those others had to go on transport anyway, as a deterrent, they said. And so, many good friends were dragged away by that boy. Fifty victims for one moment of insanity. Or rather: he didn't drag them away—our commandant did, someone of whom it is sometimes said that he is a gentleman. Even so, will the boy be able to live with himself, once it dawns on him exactly what he's been the cause of? And how will all the other Jews on board the train react to him? That boy is going to have a very hard time. The episode might have been overlooked, perhaps, if there hadn't been so much unnerving activity over our heads that night. The commandant must have been affected by that, too. "*Donnerwetter,* some flying tonight!" I heard a guard say as he looked up at the stars.

People still harbor such childish hopes that the transport won't get through. Many of us were able from here to watch the bombardment of a nearby town, probably Emden. So why shouldn't it be possible for the railway line to be hit, too, and for the train to be stopped from leaving? It's never been known to happen yet: But people keep hoping it will, with each new transport and with never-flagging hope . . .

The evening before, I had walked through the camp. People were grouped together between the barracks under a gray, cloudy sky. "Look, that's just how people behave after a disaster, standing about on street corners discussing what's happened," my companion said to me. "But that's what makes it so impossible to understand," I burst out. "This time, it's *before* the disaster!"

Whenever misfortune strikes, people have a natural instinct to lend a helping hand and to save what can be saved. Tonight I shall be helping to dress babies and to calm mothers—and that is all I can hope to do. I could almost curse myself for that. For we all know that we are yielding up our sick and defenseless brothers and sisters to hunger, heat, cold, exposure, and destruction, and yet we dress them and escort them to the bare cattle cars—and if they can't walk, we carry them on stretchers. What is going on, what mysteries are these, in what sort of fatal mechanism have we become enmeshed? The answer cannot simply be that we are all cowards. We're not that bad. We stand before a much deeper question . . .

In the afternoon I did a round of the hospital barracks one more time, going from bed to bed. Which beds would be empty the next day? The transport lists are never published until the very last moment, but some of us know well in advance that our names will be down. A young girl called me. She was sitting bolt upright in her bed, eyes wide open. This girl has thin wrists and a peaky little face. She is partly paralyzed, and has just been learning to walk again, between two nurses, one step at a time. "Have you heard? I have to go." We look at each other for a long moment. It is as if her face has disappeared; she is all eyes. Then she says in a level, gray little voice, "Such a pity, isn't it? That everything you have learned in life goes for nothing." And, "How hard it is to die." Suddenly the unnatural rigidity of her expression gives way, and she sobs, "Oh, and the worst of it all is having to leave Holland!" And, "Oh, why wasn't I allowed to die before . . ." Later, during the night, I saw her again, for the last time.

There was a little woman in the washhouse, a basket of dripping clothes on her arm. She grabbed hold of me; she looked deranged. A flood of words poured over me: "That isn't right, how can that be right? I've got to go, and I won't even be able to get my washing dry by tomorrow. And my child is sick, he's feverish, can't you fix things so that I don't have to go? And I don't have enough things for the child, the rompers they sent me are too small, I need the bigger size, oh, it's enough to drive you mad. And you're not even allowed to take a blanket along, we're going to freeze to death, you didn't think of that, did you? There's a cousin of mine here, he came here the same time I did, but he doesn't have to go, he's got the right papers. Couldn't you help me to get some, too? Just say I don't have to go, do you think they'll leave the children with their mothers, that's right, you come back again tonight, you'll help me then, won't you, what do you think, would my cousin's papers . . . ?"

If I were to say that I was in hell that night, what would I really be telling you? I caught myself saying it aloud in the night, aloud to myself and quite soberly, "So that's what hell is like." You really can't tell who is going and who isn't this time. Almost everyone is up, the sick help each other to get dressed. There are some who have no clothes at all, whose luggage has been lost or hasn't arrived yet. Ladies from the "Welfare" walk about doling out clothes, which may fit or not, it doesn't matter so long as you've covered yourself with something. Some old women look a ridiculous sight. Small bottles of milk are being prepared to take along with the babies, whose pitiful screams punctuate all the frantic activity in the barracks. A young mother says to me almost apologetically, "My baby doesn't usually cry; it's almost as if he can tell what's happening." She picks up the child, a lovely baby about eight months old, from a makeshift crib and smiles at it. "If you don't behave yourself, Mummy won't take you along with her!" She tells me about some friends. "When those men in green came to fetch them in Amsterdam, their children cried terribly. Then their father said, 'If you don't behave yourselves, you won't be allowed to go in that green car, this green gentleman won't take you.' And that helped—the children calmed down." She winks at me bravely, a trim, dark little woman with a lively, olive-skinned face. She is dressed in long gray trousers and a green woolen sweater. "I may be smiling," she says, "but I feel pretty awful." The little woman with the wet washing is on the point of hysterics. "Can't you hide my child for me? Go on, please, won't you hide him, he's got a high fever, how can I possibly take him along?" She points to a little bundle of misery with blond curls and a burning, bright-red little face. The child tosses about in his rough wooden cot. The nurse wants the mother to put on an extra woolen sweater, tries to pull it over her dress. She refuses. "I'm not going to take anything along, what use would it be? . . . my child." And she sobs, "They take the sick children away and you never get them back."

Then a woman comes up to her, a stout working-class woman with a kindly snub-nosed face, draws the desperate mother down with her on the edge of one of the iron bunks, and talks to her almost crooningly. "There now, you're just an ordinary Jew, aren't you? So you'll just have to go, won't you . . . ?"

A few beds farther along I suddenly catch sight of the ash-gray, freckled face of a colleague. She is squatting beside the bed of a dying woman who has swallowed some poison and who happens to be her mother . . .

"God Almighty, what are You doing to us?" The words just escape me. Over there is that affectionate little woman from Rotterdam. She is in her ninth month. Two nurses try to get her dressed. She just stands there, her swollen body leaning against her child's cot. Drops of sweat run down her face. She stares into the distance, a distance into which I cannot follow her, and says in a toneless, worn-out voice, "Two months ago I volunteered to go with my husband to Poland. And then I wasn't allowed to, because I always have such difficult pregnancies. And now I do have to go . . . just because someone tried to run away to-night." The wailing of the babies grows louder still, filling every nook and cranny of the barracks, now bathed in ghostly light. It is almost too much to bear. A name occurs to me: Herod.

On the stretcher on the way to the train, her labor pains begin, and we are allowed to carry the woman to the hospital instead of to the freight train—which, this night, seems a rare act of humanity . . .

I pass the bed of the paralyzed girl. The others have helped to dress her. I never saw such great big eyes in such a little face. "I can't take it all in," she whispers to me. A few steps away stands my little hunchbacked Russian woman; I told you about her before. She stands there as if spun in a web of sorrow. The paralyzed girl is a friend of hers. Later she said sadly to me, "She doesn't even have a plate, I wanted to give her mine, but she wouldn't take it. She said, 'I'll be dead in ten days anyway, and then those horrible Germans will get it.' "

She stands there in front of me, a green silk kimono wrapped around her small, misshapen figure. She has the very wise, bright eyes of a child. She looks at me for a long time in silence, searchingly, and then says, "I would like, oh, I really would like, to be able to swim away in my tears." And, "I long so desper-ately for my dear mother." (Her mother died a few months ago from cancer, in the washroom near the WC. At least she was left alone there for a moment, left to die in peace.) She asks me with her strange accent in the voice of a child that begs for forgive-ness, "Surely God will be able to understand my doubts in a world like this, won't He?" Then she turns away from me, in an almost loving gesture of infinite sadness, and throughout the night I see the misshapen, green, silk-clad figure moving between the beds, doing small services for those about to depart. She herself doesn't have to go, not this time, anyway . . .

I'm sitting here squeezing tomato juice for the babies. A young woman sits beside me. She appears ready and eager to leave, and is beautifully turned out. It is something like a cry of liberation when she exclaims, arms flung wide, "I'm embarking on a wonderful journey; I might find my husband." A woman opposite cuts her short bitterly. "I'm going as well, but I certainly don't think it's wonderful." I remembered admitting the young woman beside me. She has been here only a few days, and she came from the punishment block. She seems so level-headed and independent, with a touch of defiance about her mouth. She has been ready to leave since the afternoon, dressed in a long pair of trousers and a woolen sweater and cardigan. Next to her on the floor stands a heavy rucksack and a blanket roll. She is trying to force down a few sandwiches. They are moldy. "I'll probably get quite a lot of moldy bread to eat," she laughs. "In prison I didn't eat anything at all for days." A bit of her history in her own words: "My time wasn't far off when they threw me into prison. And the taunts and the insults! I made the mistake of saying that I couldn't stand, so they made me stand for hours, but I managed it without making a sound." She looks defiant. "My husband was in the prison as well. I won't tell you what they did to him! But my God, he was tough! They sent him through last month. I was in my third day of labor and couldn't go with him. But how brave he was!" She is almost radiant.

"Perhaps I shall find him again." She laughs defiantly. "They may drag us through the dirt, but we'll come through all right in the end!" She looks at the crying babies all around and says, "I'll have good work to do on the train, I still have lots of milk."

"What, you here as well?" I suddenly call out in dismay. A woman turns and comes up between the tumbled beds of the poor wailing babies, her hands groping around her for support.

She is dressed in a long, black, old-fashioned dress. She has a noble brow and white, wavy hair piled up high. Her husband died here a few weeks ago. She is well over eighty, but looks less than sixty. I always admired her for the aristocratic way in which she reclined on her shabby bunk. She answers in a hoarse voice, "Yes, I'm here as well. They wouldn't let me share my husband's grave."

"Ah, there she goes again!" It is the tough little ghetto woman, who is racked with hunger the whole time because she never gets any parcels. She has seven children here. She trips pluckily and busily about on her little short legs. "All I know is, I've got seven children and they need a proper mother, you can be sure of that!"

With nimble gestures she is busy stuffing a jute bag full of her belongings.

"I'm not leaving anything behind; my husband was sent through here a year ago, and my two oldest boys have been through as well." She beams. "My children are real treasures!" She bustles about, she packs, she's busy, she has a kind word for everyone who goes by. A plain, dumpy ghetto woman with greasy black hair and little short legs. She has a shabby, short-sleeved dress on, which I can imagine her wearing when she used to stand behind the washtub, back in Jodenbreestraat. And now she is off to Poland in the same old dress, a three-days' journey with seven children. "That's right, seven children, and they need a proper mother, believe me!"

You can tell that the young woman over there is used to luxury and that she must have been very beautiful. She is a recent arrival. She had gone into hiding to save her baby. Now she is here, through treachery, like so many others. Her husband is in the punishment barracks. She looks quite pitiful now. Her bleached hair has black roots with a greenish tinge. She has put on many different sets of underwear and other clothing all on top of one another—you can't carry everything by hand, after all, particularly if you have a little child to carry as well. Now she looks lumpy and ridiculous. Her face is blotchy. She stares at everyone with a veiled, tentative gaze, like some defenseless and abandoned young animal.

What will this young woman, already in a state of collapse, look like after three days in an overcrowded freight car with men, women, children, and babies all thrown together, bags and baggage, a bucket in the middle their only convenience?

Presumably they will be sent on to another transit camp, and then on again from there.

We are being hunted to death all through Europe . . .

I wander in a daze through other barracks. I walk past scenes that loom up before my eyes in crystal-clear detail, and at the same time seem like blurred age-old visions. I see a dying old man being carried away, reciting the Sh'ma to himself[67] . . .

Slowly but surely six o'clock in the morning has arrived. The train is due to depart at eleven, and they are starting to load it with people and luggage. Paths to the train have been staked out by men of the Ordedienst, the Camp Service Corps.[68] Anyone not involved with the transport has to keep to barracks. I slip into one just across from the siding. "There's always been a splendid view from here," I hear a cynical voice say. The camp has been cut in two halves since yesterday by the train: a depressing series of bare, unpainted freight cars in the front, and a proper coach for the guards at the back. Some of the cars have paper mattresses on the floor. These are for the sick. There is more and more movement now along the asphalt path beside the train.

Men from the "Flying Column" in brown overalls are bringing the luggage up on wheelbarrows. Among them I spot two of the commandant's court jesters: the first is a comedian and a songwriter. Some time ago his name was down, irrevocably, for transport, but for several nights in a row he sang his lungs out for a delighted audience, including the commandant and his retinue. He sang *"Ich kann es nicht verstehen, dass die Rosen blühen"* ("I know not why the roses bloom") and other topical songs. The commandant, a great lover of art, thought it all quite splendid. The singer got his exemption. He was even allocated a house, where he now lives behind red-checked curtains with his peroxide-blonde wife, who spends all her days at a mangle in the boiling-hot laundry. Now here he is, dressed in khaki overalls, pushing a wheelbarrow piled high with the luggage of his fellow Jews. He looks like death warmed over. And over there is another court jester: the commandant's favorite pianist. Legend has it that he is so accomplished that he can play Beethoven's Ninth as a jazz number, which is certainly saying something . . .

Suddenly there are a lot of green-uniformed men swarming over the asphalt. I can't imagine where they have sprung from. Knapsacks and guns over their shoulders. I study their faces. I try to look at them without prejudice.

I can see a father, ready to depart, blessing his wife and child and being himself blessed in turn by an old rabbi with a snow-white beard and the profile of a fiery prophet. I can see . . . ah, I can't begin to describe it all . . .

On earlier transports, some of the guards were simple, kindly types with puzzled expressions, who walked about the camp smoking their pipes and speaking in some incomprehensible dialect. One would have found their company not too objectionable on the journey. Now I am transfixed with terror. Oafish, jeering faces, in which one seeks in vain for even the slightest trace of human warmth. At what fronts did they learn their business? In what punishment camps were they trained? For after all, this is a punishment, isn't it? A few young women are already sitting in a freight car. They hold their babies on their laps, their legs dangling outside—they are determined to enjoy the fresh air as long as possible. Sick people are carried past on stretchers. I almost find myself laughing; the disparity between the guards and the guarded is too absurd. My companion at the window shudders. Months ago he was brought here from Amersfoort, in bits and pieces. "Oh, yes, that's what those fellows were like," he says. "That's what they looked like."

A couple of young children stand with their noses pressed to the windowpane. I listen in to their earnest conversation. "Why do those nasty, horrid men wear green; why don't they wear black? Bad people wear black, don't they?" "Look over there, that man is really sick!" A shock of gray hair above a rumpled blanket on a stretcher. "Look, there's another sick one . . ."

And, pointing at the green uniforms, "Look at them, now they're laughing!" "Look, look, one of them's already drunk!"

More and more people are filling up the spaces in the freight cars. A tall, lonely figure paces the asphalt, a briefcase under his arm. He is the head of the so-called Antragstelle, the camp Appeals Department. He strives right up to the last moment to get people out of the commandant's clutches. Horse trading here always continues until the train has actually pulled out. It's even been known for him to manage to free people from the moving train. The man with the briefcase has the brow of a scholar, and tired, very tired shoulders. A bent little old woman, with a black, old-fashioned hat on her gray, wispy hair, bars his way, gesticulating and brandishing a bundle of papers under his nose. He listens to her for a while, then shakes his head and turns away, his shoulders sagging just a little bit more. This time it won't be possible to get many people off the train in the nick of time. The commandant is annoyed. A young Jew has had the effrontery to run away. One can't really call it a serious attempt to escape—he absconded from the hospital in a moment of panic, a thin jacket over his blue pajamas, and in a clumsy, childish way took refuge in a tent, where he was picked up quickly enough after a search of the camp. But if you are a Jew you may not run away, may not allow yourself to be stricken with panic. The commandant is remorseless. As a reprisal, and without warning, scores of others are being sent on the transport with the boy, including quite a few who had thought they were firmly at anchor here. This system happens to believe in collective punishment. And all those planes overhead couldn't have helped to improve the commandant's mood, though that is a subject on which he prefers to keep his own counsel.

The cars are now what you might call full. But that's what you think. God Almighty, does all this lot have to get in as well? A large new group has turned up. The children are still standing with their noses glued to the windowpane; they don't miss a thing. "Look over there, a lot of people are getting off, it must be too hot in the train." Suddenly one of them calls out, "Look, the commandant!"

He appears at the end of the asphalt path, like a famous star making his entrance during a grand finale. This near-legendary figure is said to be quite charming and so well disposed toward the Jews. For the commandant of a camp for Jews, he has some strange ideas. Recently he decided that we needed more variety in our diet, and we were promptly served marrowfat peas—just once—instead of cabbage. He could also be said to be our artistic patron here, and is a regular at all our cabaret nights. On one occasion he came three times in succession to see the same performance and roared with laughter at the same old jokes each time. Under his auspices a male choir has been formed that sang *"Bei mir bist du schön"* on his personal orders. It sounded very moving here on the heath, it must be said. Now and then he even invites some of the artistes to his house and talks and drinks with them into the early hours. One night not so long ago he escorted an actress back home, and when he took his leave of her he offered her his hand; just imagine, his hand! They also say that he specially loves children. Children must be looked after. In the hospital they even get a tomato each day. And yet many of them seem to die all the same . . . I could go on quite a bit longer about "our" commandant. Perhaps he sees himself as a prince dispensing largesse to his many humble subjects. God knows how he sees himself. A voice behind me says, "Once upon a time we had a commandant who used to kick people off to Poland. This one sees them off with a smile."

He now walks along the train with military precision, a relatively young man who has "arrived" early in his career, if one may call it that. He is absolute master over the life and death of Dutch and German Jews here on this remote heath in Drenthe Province. A year ago he probably had not the slightest idea that it so much as existed. I didn't know about it myself, to tell the truth. He walks along the train, his gray, immaculately brushed hair just showing beneath his flat, light green cap. That gray hair, which makes such a romantic contrast with his fairly young face, sends many of the silly young girls here into raptures—although they dare not, of course, express their feelings openly. On this cruel morning his face is almost iron-gray. It is a face that I am quite unable to read. Sometimes it seems to me to be like a long thin scar in which grimness mingles with joylessness and hypocrisy. And there is something else about him, halfway between a dapper hairdresser's assistant and a stage-door Johnny. But the grimness and the rigidly forced bearing predominate. With military step he walks along the line of freight cars, bulging now with people. He is inspecting his troops: the sick, infants in arms, young mothers, and shaven-headed men. A few more ailing people are being brought up on stretchers. He makes an impatient gesture; they're taking too long about it. Behind him walks his Jewish secretary, smartly dressed in fawn riding breeches and brown sports jacket. He has the sporty demeanor yet vacuous expression of the English whisky drinker. Suddenly they are joined by a handsome brown gundog, where from, heaven knows. With studied gestures the fawn secretary plays with it, like something from a picture in an English society paper. The green squad stare at him goggle-eyed. They probably think—though *think* is a big word—that some of the Jews here look quite different from what their propaganda sheets have led them to believe. A few Jewish big shots from the camp now also walk along the train. "Trying to air their importance," mutters someone behind me. "Transport Boulevard," I say. "Could one ever hope to convey to the outside world what has happened here today?" I ask my companion. The outside world probably thinks of us as a gray, uniform, suffering mass of Jews, and knows nothing of the gulfs and abysses and subtle differences that exist between us. They could never hope to understand.

The commandant has now been joined by the *Oberdienstleiter*, the head of the Camp Service Corps. The *Oberdienstleiter* is a German Jew of massive build, and the commandant looks slight and insignificant by his side. Black top boots, black cap, black army coat with yellow star. He has a cruel mouth and a powerful neck. A few years ago he was still a digger in the outworkers' corps. When the story of his meteoric rise is written up later, it will be an important historical account of the mentality of our age. The light green commandant with his military bearing, the fawn, impassive secretary, the black bully-boy figure of the *Oberdienstleiter,* parade past the train. People fall back around them, but all eyes are on them.

My God, are the doors really being shut now? Yes, they are. Shut on the herded, densely packed mass of people inside. Through small openings at the top we can see heads and hands, hands that will wave to us later when the train leaves. The commandant takes a bicycle and rides once again along the entire length of the train. Then he makes a brief gesture, like royalty in an operetta. A little orderly comes flying up and deferentially relieves him of the bicycle. The train gives a piercing whistle. And 1,020 Jews leave Holland.

This time the quota was really quite small, all considered: a mere thousand Jews, the extra twenty being reserves. For it is always possible—indeed, quite certain this time—that a few will die or be crushed to death on the way. So many sick people and not a single nurse . . .

The tide of helpers gradually recedes; people go back to their sleeping quarters. So many exhausted, pale, and suffering faces. One more piece of our camp has been amputated. Next week yet another piece will follow. This is what has been happening now for over a year, week in, week out. We are left with just a few thousand. A hundred thousand Dutch members of our race are toiling away under an unknown sky or lie rotting in some unknown soil. We know nothing of their fate. It is only a short while, perhaps, before we find out, each one of us in his own time. For we are all marked down to share that fate, of that I have not a moment's doubt. But I must go now and lie down and sleep for a little while. I am a bit tired and dizzy. Then later I have to go to the laundry to track down the facecloth that got lost. But first I must sleep. As for the future, I am firmly resolved to return to you after my wanderings. In the meantime, my love once again, you dear people.

Christine,

My dear, considerate friend, I am sending you one of the two postcards we are allowed. The family is still together so far. Father and Mother are now housed in a large barracks again, so life has become much more difficult. You cannot imagine what such a barracks is like. Father is childishly happy if he is not actually trampled underfoot. He sits on his wooden bench and, while small children crawl all over his back, reads about King Solomon and about love. Me you know about. Mischa is stamping tickets in the bathhouse, with a musical score lying open under the bath tickets. Mother looks after her awkward menfolk and will thank heaven if they are allowed to remain. If. None of the Adelaars is left here now. Will you tell Simon that he doesn't have to send things to the Frank family anymore? And will you thank him for the careful packing and dispatch of so many good things? We voice our wishes and you fulfill them. Please give our warm regards to kind Hansje Lansen. We only wish we could thank everyone personally for everything; it would be so very nice if we could.

It won't be long, perhaps, before you hear something from Maria Tuinzing again. The griddle cakes were lovely and fresh! And to continue on this theme: it's a very good thing that the bulk of the bread and butter arrives at the end of the week here, or at the very latest on Monday, so that we are prepared for any eventuality each time a transport is assembled. The greatest recent family drama: Father's only pair of shoes were missing (to avoid the word *stolen*) one bad night, and now he walks about in a borrowed pair that's too big. It's really pitiful, but never mind, we'll get over that, too. We could get over everything here, actually, if only we were allowed to remain in this small country. Oh well. It's gradually becoming quite empty here. And are you taking classes of eager young students again? Father still reads Sallust and Homer with a bright boy who digs ditches in the daytime. Luckily Father has been exempted from picking beans and similar edifying labor; physically he's in no state for that sort of work. There isn't much to tell you this time, my friend. It's an oppressive, gray day. I am sitting on an upturned bed on a patch of grass behind the hospital barracks. Your sister sent us a dream of a Groningen cake. The response to Father's longing for rusks has been touching. The need is no longer so urgent; rye bread would be as welcome again—and perhaps easier? My God, what a lot of trouble we are. Sometime I will write you nothing but lyrical outpourings with never a word on the subject of food, which in fact I find odious. How glorious the Psalms are. Do you think that there is a spare blanket anywhere in Deventer? At the end of a card full of nonsense I send you my love, dearest friend, until the next time. We all send you our love. And best wishes too, please, to Father's colleagues.

*Your Etty*

E. Hillesum, Bar. 41, Westerbork

My little Maria,

I sent the first half of this letter to Father Han; I hope they both
arrive at the same time. The first part is just some journalism, not
for you, really. Hello, dear child, how are things? I am longing
for a few words. Letters are beginning to get through again. If
they are registered, we get them without fail. Please be sure to tell
Swiep: he can pass it on to people who know Anne-Marie, who is
under a lot of strain because she hasn't heard from any of her
friends for some time. Hans's scribble made me happy. Took the
note for Reb straight to his parents, since I am not allowed to visit
him myself. At the moment he is in the big barracks with my
papa, who is back from the hospital again. Spirits go up and
down, but humor keeps breaking through. For the old people
here, though, it's a macabre business. We have managed to get
through another Tuesday. If there is a transport next Tuesday,
the chances of keeping them here will be slight. One is consumed
worst of all by this tension—tension for others, of course.

When I went into our little office this morning, it was in a
terrible mess; it had been requisitioned as a dressing room for the
revue. The revue is taking over the whole camp. There are no
overalls for people on outside duty, but the revue has an "overall
ballet"—so day and night, people sewed overalls with little
puffed sleeves for the dancers. Wood from the synagogue in
Assen has been sawed up to make a stage. One of the carpenters
exclaimed, "What would God say if He knew what His synagogue was being used for?" Marvelous, isn't it: God's synagogue
in Assen. Oh, Maria, Maria—Before the last transport, the people
who were due to leave worked all day for the revue. Everything
here has an indescribably clownish madness and sadness.

I am fine, doing my Russian again every day for an hour,
reading the Psalms, and talking with hundred-year-old women

who attach great importance to telling me their entire life stories. Really I live here just as I used to with you in Amsterdam: in a community, but also very much for myself. This is possible even when one lives with other people, on them, under them, over them, in the middle of them.

Do you know what I would still love to have here? The blue woolen dressing gown that I got from Hesje and my blue felt hat, which is the most comfortable thing I have for my head. It might be good if I had my blue knitted dress as well; it's fairly cold here sometimes, and in case I should suddenly be put on transport—you never know what will happen. Please don't think me too much of a nuisance—

I would like to make another arrangement with you: each Tuesday I'll send the Nethes a short telegram, "Food for four persons" (nothing to do with hunger); if Father and Mother have gone, then, "Food for two persons." Many of us here will never get over the fact that we allowed our old and our sick to go first. This is a deliberate policy based on the "self-preservation instinct." Father asked a male nurse from the last transport, "How can people who are near death in the hospital be forced to go? Surely that's against all medical ethics." And the nurse answered solemnly, "The hospital gives up the corpses in order to hang on to the living." He wasn't trying to be facetious, he was perfectly serious.

Do you see Tide to talk to, sometimes? Tell her about the registered letters, too. I am writing everything in a jumble again and not making much sense. People here often feel strangely tired, and I happen to be so myself this morning. But the letter has to be sent off in a little while, so I'm scribbling away. Please would you be kind enough to mail on or hand on the enclosed letters from Mechanicus? It's thanks to him that I'm able to get this off. Jopie's whole family is now in the hospital; the littlest boy is being kept alive with great difficulty.

How terribly young we were only a year ago on this heath,

Maria! Now we've grown a little older. We hardly realize it ourselves: we have become marked by suffering for a whole lifetime. And yet life in its unfathomable depths is so wonderfully good, Maria—I have to come back to that time and again. And if we just care enough, God is in safe hands with us despite everything, Maria.

I myself fail to measure up in every way, of course. I can't cope with the many people who want to involve me in their affairs; I am often much too tired. Please give Käthe a cheerful look from me—and press your cheek to Father Han's for me, too? And do you still get on well together? And please will you give my love to my dear desk, the best place on earth? And to Swiep and Wiep and Hesje and Frans and the others? I can see you in front of me, my dear, and I don't have to say any more.

*Etty*

I have just heard from Hilde Cramer that registered letters aren't coming in anymore either, so save yourselves the bother. But now and then a small postcard or something still manages to filter through.

And how is Ernst? This morning one of my colleagues said, referring to all sorts of awful practices here: "Each moment of your life that your courage fails is a lost moment." And now I am going to the hairdresser. And it's possible that next we shall have to move from our little house into one of the big barracks; five minutes is all the warning you get for anything. This morning I spoke to Liesl Levie; she suffers from dizziness all the time, and says, *"Ich schwindle mich durch."*[69] Werner's mother has been sent through.

'Bye, my dear,
*Etty*

Christine,

Opening the Bible at random I find this: "The Lord is my high tower." I am sitting on my rucksack in the middle of a full freight car. Father, Mother, and Mischa are a few cars away. In the end, the departure came without warning. On sudden special orders from The Hague. We left the camp singing, Father and Mother firmly and calmly, Mischa, too. We shall be traveling for three days. Thank you for all your kindness and care. Friends left behind will still be writing to Amsterdam; perhaps you will hear something from them. Or from my last letter from camp.

> Good-bye for now from the four of us.
> *Etty*

[This card, thrown out of the train by Etty on 7 September, was found by farmers outside Westerbork camp and posted by them.]

*Dear Mr. Wegerif, Hans, Maria, Tide, and everyone else I don't know quite so well,*

*It is not going to be easy for me to tell you this. It all happened so suddenly, so unexpectedly. Strange that it should have felt so unexpected and sudden, since we have all been ready and waiting for such a long time. And when the time came she, too, was ready and waiting. And, alas, she, too, has gone.*

*The news from The Hague came quite late on Monday: Mischa's exemption has been turned down, and he and all his family would be put on transport on 7 September. Why? Well, that is the kind of question no one can answer. To start with, we all hoped and believed it would never happen. And then we were certain that the notice would be deferred for her at least, particularly since it was agreed only today that the former staff of the Jewish Council, sixty in all, would be allowed to stay on for a while. It became clear quite quickly that while nothing much could be done for Mischa and the old people, Etty might stand a very good chance.*

*So we concentrated on the rapid packing of bags for three people. Oh, they took it all very well, they had known for such a long time it was bound to happen one day, and anyway the parents, all the parents of people with red stamps without exception, are due to leave next week. And Mischa had already decided to go along, to forfeit all his privileges to be with his parents. And now it was happening one week earlier, a bit suddenly, but . . . it was only a difference in time. However, for Etty it was a complete surprise—she had decided that she was not going to travel with her parents and would have much preferred to go through these experiences without the pressure of family ties. For her it was a slap in the face, which did in fact literally strike her down. Within the hour, however, she had recovered and adapted herself to the new situation with admirable speed. We went together to barrack 62 and were kept busy for hours with the picking out, parceling up, hunting out, and sorting of all kind of articles of clothing and food.*

*Etty's father hid his nervousness behind a string of humorous remarks, which never failed to make Mischa cross—he thought the old man wasn't taking things seriously enough. Mischa could not understand why the deferment that had seemed so certain had suddenly been canceled and continually asked me to intercede with all sorts of more or less important "connections." He simply did not realize that German orders cannot be changed by anyone here and that all such efforts are bound to be futile. He remained quite composed, however, and took things tolerably well. Having to leave all his music behind was what upset him most. I managed to squeeze four scores into his bag, and the rest (including the food parcel that had just arrived) now fills a suitcase that will have to be sent back to Amsterdam at the first possible opportunity.*

*Mother H., bustling as ever, saw to everything and displayed an admirable peace of mind.*

*During earlier transport nights, the family had often been kept awake by all the noise and excitement such preparations invariably produce in a large barracks. This time they were all fast asleep when Etty and I went in at three o'clock to see if any more packing had to be done. Before that we had gone once more to find out what chance there was of Etty still getting an exemption. It was then that it was finally brought home to us that her chances, too, were nil. While she herself had been occupied with looking after her parents and her brother, Etty's girlfriends had expertly packed everything for her, down to the smallest detail.*

*Even when the leaders of the Jewish Council declared that nothing could be done for her, we still rushed off a letter to the first Dienstleiter (duty officer) asking him to intervene.*

*We felt that something might still be able to be done even on the train but only if everything was ready for departure, so her parents and Mischa went to the train first. Then I trundled a well-packed rucksack and a small hamper with a bowl and mug dangling from it* to the train. And there she stepped onto the platform she herself had described only a fortnight before in her own unforgettable way. Talking gaily, smiling, a kind word for everyone she met on the way, full of sparkling humor, perhaps just a touch of sadness, but every inch the Etty you all know so well. "I have my diaries, my little Bible, my Russian grammar, and Tolstoy with me and God knows what else." One of the camp leaders came to take his leave of her and told her that he had used every argument he knew to plead her case but in vain. Etty thanked him very much. I only wish I could describe for you exactly how it happened and with what grace she and her family left!

So here I sit now, a little sad, certainly, but not sad for something that has been lost, since a friendship like ours is never lost, it is and it endures.

That is what I wrote down, too, on a slip of paper that I pushed into her hand at the last moment. Then I lost sight of her for a bit and wandered around the platform. Tried again to find someone who could still do something for her but in vain. I saw Mother, Father H., and Mischa board wagon no. 1. Etty finished up in wagon no. 12, having first stopped to look for a friend in wagon no. 14 who was pulled out again at the last moment. Then a shrill whistle, and the thousand "transport cases" were moving out. Another flourish from Mischa, who waved through a crack in wagon no. 1, a cheerful "bye" from Etty in no. 12, and they were gone.

She is gone. We stand bereft, but not with empty hands. We shall find each other soon.

It was a hard day for all of us. For Kormann, for Mech, and for all who had been in such close contact with her for so long. Being with a dear person in spirit is not the same as having her near you, in person. You feel quite drained at first. But life goes on even while I write this and while she herself moves closer and closer to the East, where she once wanted to travel so much. I think she really quite preferred to share the experiences they have prepared for us all. And we shall see her back again. On that we (her special friends here) are all agreed. After her departure I spoke to a little Russian woman and various other protégés of hers. And the way they felt about her leaving speaks volumes for the love and devotion she had given to them all.

Please forgive this inadequate scribble. You, who have been so spoiled with much better accounts, much better put. I know that many questions must remain, and one above all: Couldn't it have been avoided? To that I can answer unequivocally: No! That's the way it obviously had to be. If the opportunity arises, I shall try to send you some of Etty's books. I would have liked to send her typewriter to Maria, she told me just this week that's what she wanted me to do. But I don't know if it will be possible.

I shall send you news from time to time. I enclose a few letters for Etty opened by the censor. Please give them back to the senders.

Be strong. We shall all be back one day, and people like Etty are able to hold their own in the most difficult situations. My thoughts are often with you.

Jopie Vleeschhouwer

Etty Hillesum died in Auschwitz on 30 November 1943.

# Notes

*An Interrupted Life: The Diaries, 1941–1943*

1. Etty had felt for some time that her life needed to be sorted out and given a clear direction. In February 1941 she consulted Julius Spier, who appears as S. in these diaries.
2. Adri Holm (1910–1970). She is said to have had a major influence on Spier's religious beliefs and his understanding of Christianity.
3. This young girl was Liesl Levie, who would become Etty's close friend.
4. Albert Verwey (1865–1937), the Dutch poet.
5. Etty's fellow residents at 6 Gabriël Metsustraat, in the order she lists them, are Käthe; Maria Tuinzing (1906–1970); the owner of the house, Han Wegerif (1879–1946); Bernard Meylink (1911–1952), and Han's son, Hans Wegerif (1919–1983).
6. It was still possible to send letters outside Holland. Mail traveled via Switzerland and Spain.
7. Frans van Steenhoven, painter and economist. Reijnders is a café on the Leidseplein.
8. Willem Adriaan Bonger was a well-known sociologist and criminologist. Ter Braak, Du Perron, and Marsman were the most important antifascist writers in Holland. Pos and Van den Bergh, professors at the University of Amsterdam, were both active anti-Nazis.
9. A women's magazine.
10. In spring 1941 the Germans conducted the first roundup of Dutch

Jews. The general strike that was called in response was met with waves of reprisals, including arrests and deportations. Another roundup occurred on June 11, shortly before this diary entry.

11. Leonie Denney-Snatager, Etty's good friend, now lives in Washington, D.C.
12. Etty was visiting her parents' home.
13. This was where Spier lived.
14. Etty's brother.
15. Annie Romein was the wife and collaborator of Jan Romein (1893–1962), a Dutch historian. Carry van Bruggen (1881–1932) was a Dutch novelist.
16. Hertha Levie was the woman Spier intended to marry. She lives in the United States.
17. Henny Tideman (1907–1989), whom Etty generally calls Tide.
18. Swiep van Wermeskerken (1907–1992), to whom Etty taught Russian.
19. Gera Bongers married and lived in South Africa for many years. She now lives in Berlin. (She has no connection with Professor Bonger.)
20. Aleida Schot was a Slavic scholar.
21. Jaap Hillesum, Etty's brother.
22. Max Geiger, a pianist from Bern, Switzerland.
23. Spier's daughter, Ruth Busse-Spier, lives in Berlin.
24. A cousin of Han Wegerif.
25. A student friend of Etty.
26. Cultura was a bookshop that specialized in selling Communist literature.
27. Veluwe is a heavily wooded part of Holland.
28. The Austrian composer (1860–1903).
29. The Nuremberg Laws were gradually extended to the Netherlands; parks and gardens were henceforth forbidden to Jews, in order to "protect the health and pleasure of Aryans."
30. Evaristos Glassner, a friend of Mischa. He became an organist and piano teacher in Amsterdam after the war. He died in 1988.
31. Lippmann, Rosenthal & Co. were the bankers appointed by the Germans to liquidate all Jewish assets.
32. At the time, the blackout regulations were not severe.
33. Werner and Liesl Levie, both originally from Berlin, emigrated to Amsterdam in 1939. Etty met them through Spier, and they became her close friends. Werner, an opera director and a committed Zionist, had helped various artists and musicians to emigrate to Palestine.

34. Amsterdam's Jewish district, of which little remains, was located on the eastern edge of the historic city center. During the winter of 1941–1942, the Germans planned to turn it into a ghetto for Dutch Jews, surrounding it with barbed wire and starting the transfers that created the overcrowding that Etty mentions. The project was never completed.

35. The laws prohibiting Jews from buying fruit, certain fresh vegetables, and fish—except in stores "reserved for Jews" (where produce was rarely fresh)—and from riding bicycles or trains or visiting non-Jewish homes were imposed in May 1942 and completed the application of the Nuremberg Laws to the Netherlands.

36. Jews were forbidden to leave the city and sometimes the quarter where they lived.

37. Liesl and Werner Levie's two daughters.

38. Because of the law prohibiting Jews from entering the houses of non-Jews. Etty constantly flouted this regulation and was also guilty of *Rassenschande* ("intimate relations with non-Jews"), a "crime" punishable by immediate deportation.

39. Dicky de Jonge, a woman of twenty-one, lived with the Nethe family in the same house as Spier. She was the youngest of the Spier group.

40. Etty is referring to her expectation that, because she lives in a house owned by a non-Jewish family, she'll either be transferred to the Jewish quarter or deported.

41. Mien Kuyper (1898–1957), pianist and patron of the arts, held concerts and recitals in her house in Amsterdam, at which Mischa Hillesum often played, especially after Jewish artists were forbidden to perform in public. It was probably at one of these evenings that Etty first met Julius Spier.

42. The name is indecipherable in the handwritten diary.

43. Leo de Wolff, the son of Sam de Wolff, an influential economist and politician, was deported to Bergen-Belsen, where he died.

44. This undated fragment entry, apparently written in the summer of 1942, as Etty was preparing to leave Amsterdam, was recorded on a loose sheet and inserted into her notebooks on 22 July 1942. This was probably the day Etty volunteered at the Jewish Council to go to Westerbork.

45. Etty's pass was subsequently extended because of her illness.

46. Jopie Vleeschhouwer, a close friend from Westerbork, was in Amsterdam when Spier died. He returned to Westerbork the same day.

47. Klaas Smelik, Sr. (1897–1986), a Communist and an author, first met Etty in Deventer in 1934. They remained friends, and he and his daughter Johanna ("Jopie") Smelik repeatedly tried to persuade Etty to go into hiding and offered her various places to stay. She always refused.

48. The headquarters of the so-called Central Office for Jewish Emigration.

49. Johanna Smelik. Not to be confused with Jopie Vleeschhouwer. (Jopie is a nickname given to both sexes.)

50. Maria Tuinzing, her close friend at Han Wegerif's house.

## Letters from Westerbork

1. Joseph and Hedwig Mahler were German Jews who fled to Holland in 1935. Both were printers and members of a Jewish resistance group in Holland, and both were killed by the Nazis. Eichwald is unidentified.

2. "My dear people" were Etty's former housemates at Han Wegerif's house. Her letters were often passed around the larger circle of friends.

3. Joseph Isodoor Vleeschhouwer, known as Jopie, was a close friend of Etty's; his long letter describing the Hillesum family's last day in Westerbork is reprinted at the end of this volume. He too was deported; he died on 23 April 1945 at Treubitz, after the Germans evacuated Bergen-Belsen. His wife, Cato Cahen, also died at Treubitz.

4. Werner Sterzenbach managed to escape from Westerbork at the end of 1943 and joined the Resistance. Several times he begged Etty Hillesum to follow him, but she refused. Sterzenbach and his wife, Alice Sterzenbach-David, survived the war and are living in Germany.

5. Max Witmondt, who had previously held an important position with an insurance company in Amsterdam, was married to a Christian woman—a union that, though illegal, saved him from deportation. Imprisoned first in Amersfoort, a camp for political prisoners, he was subsequently moved to Westerbork. Etty often served as messenger between him and his wife.

6. Ellecom was the site of a training center for the Dutch SS. Approximately 150 Jews were used to build new sports fields. Their work completed, they were sent to Westerbork.

7. Paul Cronheim (1892–1875), member of the Jewish Council, was a well-known musician and Wagner specialist.

8. Eduard Spier (1902–1980), was one of the leaders of the Jewish Council in Westerbork. Deported to Theresienstadt, he survived the war.

9. This is one of the two letters that were illegally published by the Dutch Resistance in 1943. The two women to whom it was sent were the sisters of the Dr. K. mentioned in the first paragraph—probably Dr. Herbert Kruskal, who survived the war and now lives in Israel. Dr. K. asked Etty to send his sisters her impressions of Westerbork; she used his request as an opportunity to detail life in the camp. These letters, published under the false title *Three Letters by the Painter J. B. van der Pluym (1843–1912),* were the only writings of Etty Hillesum to be published prior to 1981.

10. Westerbork was built in 1939 by the Dutch Ministry of Justice to house refugees from Germany. Its earliest inmates included Jews who had been incarcerated in Buchenwald and Dachau. As of 1 July 1942, it came under the jurisdiction of the German authorities.

11. The SS *St. Louis,* carrying nearly a thousand Jews to Cuba, made its unfortunate voyage in 1939. The ship was finally allowed to dock in Antwerp. Belgium accepted two hundred passengers; the rest were divided among England, France, and the Netherlands.

12. Limburg was a predominantly Roman Catholic province. The reference here is to a public gesture of support for the departing Jews.

13. A group of nuns and priests of Jewish origin. After a protest against the persecution of the Jews by Archbishop Johannes de Jong on 1 August 1942, the Nazis held a roundup among the cloistered Jewish Catholics. They captured about three hundred nuns and priests. On 2 August, sixty-three Jewish Catholics came to Westerbork; Etty describes them in this letter and in her diary. One of the nuns described Edith Stein, a well-known mystic writer and philosopher, with whom Etty has often been compared. Stein was killed in Auschwitz on 9 August 1942.

14. The roundups on the 2 and 3 of October 1942 brought more than twelve thousand people to Westerbork.

15. The Herengracht is a fashionable street in Amsterdam; its *bocht* (curve) is the most exclusive stretch.

16. Max ("Osias") Kormann survived the war and rejoined his family in America in 1946. He died in 1962. His son, Professor Gerd Korman, has kindly provided this note:

During the Weimar Republic, Max O. Kormann, the son of a Hasidic family from Narol in Galicia, became an active Zionist and in 1927 married Rosa Laufer, a German-born daughter of Jews who migrated from Galicia to the Rhineland at the turn of the century. The couple took their place among Weimar's many westernized Zionist families who still remained loyal to rabbinic Judaism. When they settled in Hamburg, they joined the orthodox congregation of Joseph Carlebach. Here the rebel from Narol, now a traveling shoe salesman, cultivated his interest in Freud and, perhaps influenced by Rabbi Carlebach, became a devotee of Maimonides. Although Max spoke Yiddish and Hebrew, the language of the home was German. By the time Hitler became Chancellor of the Republic, there were two sons, who were being reared as modern religious Zionists.

The sons called him Pappi. To everyone else he was Max—to everyone, that is, except officials, who insisted on using the name represented by his middle initial. From the moment he illegally crossed the Polish frontier, his papers identified him as Osias Kormann, the name he had taken from an older brother who had fallen during the war. Polish, German, and Dutch authorities insisted on Osias, a name without meaning to those who loved him and among whom he lived and worked. It was the name used by the Hamburg policeman who awoke Max and his family on the morning of 28 October 1938, to inform him that he must leave Germany in twenty-four hours. And by other officials—the German who authorized his deportation to Poland; the clerks who approved his one-month return to Hamburg; the shipping-line employees who, while he was separated from his family, helped him embark on the SS *St. Louis* for its vain journey to Cuba and, when Cuba refused to accept the Jewish passengers, back to Europe; the Dutch officials who accepted the ship's refugees for internment in Holland; the Westerbork authorities who in 1939 turned him into a founding inmate, and then into a minor official of a new kind of prison; and the German occupiers who assumed direct command over Westerbork in 1942, the year Etty Hillesum arrived as a representative of Amsterdam's Jewish Council.

She dared to call him Osias, and he accepted this use of the name as a term of endearment. Thus they gave new meaning to a name that had been only official. Together they marked a friendship in a Holocaust that had cut him off, apparently forever, from the ties that bound him to a devoted family desperately waiting in America, now also at war. Before she returned to Westerbork for the last time in 1943, Etty could not have seen him very often. After her initial stays in Westerbork she returned to Amsterdam for several months. There my father, who could obtain permission to leave the camp, visited her, perhaps only once for a few hours, while she was entertaining some friends. During this winter and the spring of 1943, most of her letters to him, and some of his to her, were written, sustaining the moment when their souls had suddenly touched between the barracks and the barbed wire.

17. Rosenberg was Kormann's barracksmate and close friend. Unfortunately, nothing more could be found out about him, but he was liberated by the Canadians in April 1945.
18. *V* stands for Verzorging ("Care"), an organization providing material and food for the camp inhabitants.
19. Osias Kormann gave lessons on Jewish history and rituals at the Westerbork camp school.
20. The Zentralstelle für Jüdische Auswanderung (Central Office for Jewish Emigration) was set up by the Germans.
21. Het Leven is Amsterdam's red-light district.
22. At Vught, there was a concentration camp for Jews as well as non-Jews. For the Jewish prisoners, it was both a work camp and a transit camp, since all were transferred to Westerbork sooner or later, and from there, to Poland. On 6 and 7 June 1943, two transport convoys arrived, carrying 1,288 women and 1,266 children. These are the transports to which Etty refers. As of 8 June all the new arrivals were sent to Sobibor, where they were exterminated.
23. NIZ: the Nederlands-Israëlitisch Ziekenhuis, or Netherlands-Israelite Hospital.
24. Etty's father, Dr. Louis Hillesum, a classicist, had been headmaster of the Stedelijk Gymnasium in Deventer.
25. The man is probably Herman Boasson (1908–1981), one of Etty's friends in the Westerbork hospital, a scholarly man with whom she often had discussions. Finally deported to Auschwitz, he managed to survive by securing a position with the camp orchestra.

26. The green police, or *grüne Polizei,* were the special German police forces, mostly used to round up Jews.

27. Etty's friend Milli Ortmann, wife of the renowned painter Theo Ortmann and member of Amsterdam's intellectual and artistic circle. Jewish herself, she managed to escape persecution thanks to false papers. After Theo's death in 1942, she married a non-Jewish man to avoid deportation.

28. There was a camp in a castle in Barneveld for a supposed elite of "cultural Jews." Most of those known to have been interned there survived the war. Mischa—the older of Etty's two brothers, a musical prodigy and one of Holland's best pianists—was an obvious candidate for the "Barneveld option." Milli Ortmann, through the influence of Willem Mengelberg, the Dutch conductor, secured permission for Mischa to go to Barneveld, but he refused unless his parents could accompany him.

29. Christine van Nooten taught Latin and Greek at the Stedelijk Gymnasium in Deventer and was Etty's teacher. A very close friend of the Hillesums, she did much to sustain them during their time in Westerbork. She contributed a number of Etty's letters to this volume.

30. As a journalist in Paris, Anne-Marie van den Bergh-Riess had worked with the Russian writer Ilya Ehrenburg, whom Etty admired. In 1933 she moved to Amsterdam, where she married and divorced Herman van den Bergh, a well-known Dutch poet. Arrested at the end of June 1943, she was sent to Westerbork and ultimately to Bergen-Belsen, where she was freed by the Russians. Etty refers to the goggles Anne-Marie wore to protect her eyes from the sand and dust omnipresent in Westerbork.

31. Swiep van Wermeskerken, mutual friend of Etty and Anne-Marie.

32. Sam de Wolff (1878–1960), father of Leo de Wolff, was an economist and politician. A leading socialist and one of the pioneers of Zionism in the Netherlands, he was able to leave for Palestine in 1944.

33. The Hollandsche Schouwburg was the assembly point for the deportation of Jews from Amsterdam.

34. Jaap Hillesum, Etty's younger brother, was a doctor working at the Hollandsche Schouwburg. He was not transferred to Westerbork until September 1943, after Etty, Mischa, and their parents had already been deported.

35. Philip Mechanicus (1889–1944), one of the most renowned Dutch journalists of the time, arrived in Westerbork in November 1942 and

managed to stay there until March 1944, when he was deported to Bergen-Belsen. In October 1944 he was sent to Auschwitz, where he died. His diary of the events in Westerbork, the most complete portrait of life in the camp, was published after the war as *In Depôt*. He was very close to the Hillesum family, particularly to Etty.

36. Friedrich Weinreb, born in 1910, was a well-known economist and Old Testament scholar. His actions during the war gave rise to one of the most complex legal cases in Dutch history. In the hope of avoiding deportation, he pretended to put himself in the service of the Germans. In fact, he was probably manipulated by them and, intentionally or not, may have caused the death of several Jews. Condemned for treason in 1948, he was pardoned shortly thereafter. The ambiguity of his case has never been fully resolved.

37. Renate Laqueur was the daughter of professor Ernst Laqueur, a chemist who had helped the German army develop poison gas in World War I and had therefore enjoyed some degree of special protection. He was the companion of Maria Tuinzing, Etty's friend. Renate Laqueur was eventually deported to Bergen-Belsen along with her husband, Paul Goldschmidt.

38. Julius Simon, born in 1906, was the main contact for the Jews from Deventer who were brought to Westerbork. Simon organized the food parcels and distributed as many as two hundred a week for an extended period. He escaped to Switzerland in 1943.

39. Klaas and Johanna Smelik.

40. NSB: the initials of the Dutch Nazi party, which apparently provided supplementary manpower for a number of German police actions.

41. The Levies, Etty's close friends, had arrived in Westerbork on 20 June 1943 and were transferred to Bergen-Belsen in 1944. Werner died of typhus in the last days of the war; Liesl and her children survived and emigrated to Israel.

42. This list was usually assembled in the forty-eight hours preceding the departure of each transport and could be modified up to the very last moment.

43. Although Mechanicus's departure was delayed, he was eventually sent to his death in Auschwitz.

44. Leo Krijn was Julius Spier's brother-in-law. His wife and son had in fact already died at Auschwitz. Krijn and his brother would die a week apart in Sobibor.

45. Wiep Poestra, the fiancée of Herman Boasson.

46. Grete Wendelsgelst was Milli Ortmann's sister. Like Milli, she frequently interceded for the Hillesums.

47. Lars Söderblom (1866–1931), Swedish theologian, was awarded the Nobel Peace Prize in 1930.

48. *Dienstleiters,* or section leaders, who were Jewish.

49. Max Ehrlich, Clara (Chaya) Goldstein, and Willy Rosen were famous cabaret entertainers before the war. Ehrlich and Rosen died at Auschwitz; Goldstein owed her survival to her marriage to a German cameraman.

50. Professor David Cohen was copresident with Abraham Asscher of the Jewish Council.

51. Gera Bongers was one of Julius Spier's students.

52. Mevrouw Nethe had been Julius Spier's landlady at 27 Courbetstraat in Amsterdam. "Jim" was the nickname of Simon van Gelder, who had lived in hiding at the Nethe's house, and then at Mien Kuyper's.

53. Dr. Johannes Brouwer, a scholar of Spanish literature and member of the Dutch Resistance, was shot on 1 July 1943.

54. Philip Mechanicus; see notes 35 and 43 above.

55. The friend was Julius Spier. The lesson Etty learned from him is not found in Matthew 24 but at Matthew 6:34, which Etty quotes from the Dutch Authorized Version.

56. E. A. P. Puttkammer, German functionary of a Dutch bank, served during the war as an intermediary between the Nazis and wealthy Jews who wanted to emigrate. A high sum in foreign currency would buy a spot on "Puttkammer's list," which the German authorities would then consider. Needless to say, none of the Jews thus tricked emigrated. Etty's parents had tried unsuccessfully to get themselves included on the list through the intervention of Christine van Nooten.

57. On 25 July 1943, King Victor Emmanuel II accepted Mussolini's resignation, bringing fascism to an end in Italy.

58. In reality, the hiatus was fairly brief; the trains only stopped running for a short time, from 20 July to 24 August 1943. It was their destination that changed, from Sobibor to Auschwitz.

59. Maxim Gorky's play *The Lower Depths* is set in a crowded Moscow flophouse.

60. *Feldwebel* is a German rank equivalent to sergeant.

61. Joseph ("Jo") Spier, a Dutch illustrator, was deported to Theresienstadt and emigrated to the United States in 1951.

62. *Stundenbuch (The Book of Hours)*, by the German poet Rainer Maria Rilke, Etty's favorite author.

63. "Jul" is Julius Spier.

64. The first part of this letter is lost, which explains its abrupt beginning. It probably consisted of four pages (on two sheets), since the first page here bears the number 3. But the other side is not numbered, so this page may have been preceded by two sheets, or four pages.

65. The stamps that protected against deportation—temporarily—were numbered. Stamps bearing the number 120,000 were reserved for those who could pay considerable sums (approximately 20,000 to 40,000 florins in precious stones or currency). The 1,300 Dutch Jews in possession of that number were supposed to be exchanged for German prisoners. In reality, they were deported to Bergen-Belsen.

As for the Portuguese Jews, who formed one of the oldest settlements in the Netherlands, they were originally meant to be not deported but "repatriated" to their "country of origin," that is, Spain or Portugal, which they had left about four hundred years before. In 1943 they were instead transferred to Westerbork, then to Theresienstadt in spring 1944, and from there to Auschwitz, where almost all died.

66. This is the second of the two letters (along with the one dated 18 December 1942) published illegally by the Resistance in 1943.

67. Sh'ma: "Hear, O Israel: the Lord our God, the Lord is one." This is a line of prayer said when death is approaching.

68. The Service Corps, made up of Jews, was started in March 1942. It was their job to maintain order during the departure of transports. They were held personally accountable for all escapes and at times showed themselves to be as zealous as their persecutors.

69. In German, *"Ich schwindle mich durch"* is a pun meaning both "I'm dizzy" and "I'll wangle my way through."